Norfolk
in the
Second World War

Norfolk children queue up to see Santa Claus at an American airbase, 1944.

Norfolk

in the

Second World War

Frank Meeres

Phillimore

2006

Published by
PHILLIMORE & CO. LTD
Shopwyke Manor Barn, Chichester, West Sussex, England
www.phillimore.co.uk

ISBN 1-86077-389-3
ISBN 13 978-1-86077-389-1

Printed and bound in Great Britain by
THE CROMWELL PRESS
Trowbridge, Wiltshire

Contents

List of Illustrations

Acknowledgements

Thanks are due to Hannah Verge, Victoria Horth and Irene McLaughlin for help in preparing the text and illustrations.

Many of the illustrations are from documents held by the Norfolk Record Office: I am grateful for permission to use these images. Several are from the archive collections of the United States Army Air Force Memorial Library held at the Record Office: their consent to the publication of these images is very much appreciated.

Photographs 20, 49, 50 and 69 are from the Wymondham Heritage Society; photographs 22, 48 and 111 are from the Fakenham Local History Society; photographs 2, 42-5 and 110 are from a private family collection: I am extremely grateful for permission to use these pictures in this book. All other images are from the author's collections.

References to Norfolk Record Office images are given below: those with the prefix MC 371 or MC 376 are from the USAAF collections.

Frontispiece, MC 376/350; 1. MC 2333/1/3, 3. MOT 111; 4-5. MC 2043/40; 6. MC 2279/2/18; 7. Y/ED 854; 8. MC 2279/2/17; 9. MC 2146/2; 10. MC 2146/11; 11. MC 2146/19; 13. MC 2169/3/7; 14. MC 2169/3/5; 18. MC 2153/1; 21. MC 2333/1/3; 23. MC 371/908/104; 24-8. MC 371/910; 29-30. MC 376/108; 31. MC 371/27; 32. MC 376/336; 33. MC 376/336; 34. MC 371/815; 35. MC 371/814; 36. MC 371/435; 37. MC 371/814; 38. MC 695/12/5; 39. MC 695/12/4; 40. MC 695/12/53/1; 41. MC 695/12/54/2; 46. KHC 114; 47. MC 2279/2/9; 51-5. MC 631/1; 56. C/ED 4/21; 57. PD 78/152; 58-60. DC 15/3/4; 63. Y/ED 854; 64. D/ED 9/225; 65. D/ED 9/343; 66. MC 2333/1/3; 67. MC 2043/40; 68. PD 82/44; 70. MC 2333/1/4; 73-4. BR 266 UNCAT; 76. MC 371/908/40; 80-2. PD 523/156; 84. MC 376/29; 91. MC 198/77; 92. MS 10605/76; 93. MC 198/77; 94. MC 630/31; 96. MC 376/29; 102-3. MC 371/912; 104. MC 371/910; 106. BR 221/173; 108. Y/ED 854; 112. MC 2169/6/3; 113. MC 371/910.

1 *German 'Invasion Map' published in the British press to 'show' that Germany had a long-term plan for conquest of Europe.*

One

Men at Arms

By the late 1930s, war with Germany was expected and the nation was preparing for the worst. In May 1939, Parliament passed the Military Training Act: all men aged between 20 and 29 were to be called up for six months of military training. For most this meant the army, but men were allowed to try for the Navy or the Royal Air Force if they wanted to, although they might of course be rejected as unsuitable.

On the day that war broke out, 3 September 1939, a further Act was passed by Parliament, the National Services (Armed Forces) Act. All men between the ages of 18 and 41 were now liable to be called up. Of course, they could not all be called up at once as there were not the facilities for training so many men at the same time. Instead they were summoned in blocks, with the youngest being called up first: men between 20 and 22 in December 1939, between 19 and 27 in January 1940, and up to the age of 37 in May 1940. In 1942, the Act was amended and men up to the age of 46 could be called up. In addition, there was, of course, a stream of young men reaching the age of 18 and thus coming into the system.

The Army

Naturally, many local men chose to go into the Norfolk Regiment. Percy Burrows has described what it was like to be called into the forces at the start of the war:

> I was called up into the second lot of 'the Militia' on 15 Sept 1939. Had war not been declared on 9 Sept [*sic*] I would have had, under this scheme, 6 months training and then returned to civilian life. As it was, I was in the army for 6½ years. My calling up papers declared that I must register at Catterick Camp in Yorkshire by 10 am. I remember I arrived about 12 hours late, was given a tin mug of tea and a mess tin of soup before being returned to the station and put on a train to Prestatyn in N Wales. Not a very impressive start. On arrival we were herded into the major half of the Holiday Camp. People still ending their holiday were in the remainder. We were allowed to use all the facilities but not allowed to leave camp. We were in charge of a L/Corp, but there was no uniforms for about a week. Then it all started and we knew we were in the ----- Army. Uniforms, heavy boots, medicals, dentist, inoculations and above all, endless square bashing.[1]

The Hamond family of Westacre were also caught up in preparations for war. Anthony Hamond did his training in Wales in 1940-1. His brother Bob, already in the Norfolk Regiment, wrote to him:

2 *Russell Beckett and friends in the Norfolk Regiment, ready for war: Beckett is in the centre. Both his friends were to die in Japanese prisoner of war camps.*

I hope that all is well on the Welsh Front – the Atlantic Front particularly. I picture you on some tactics exercise struggling with a sodden map, trying desperately to impart some feeling into your fingers and also to prevent the rain and spray from entering the neck of an inadequate mack or groundsheet in large quantities. And anyway you will have left the pencil somewhere and no one knows what the scheme is about, least of all those supervising. How well I know the feeling of frigid despair and hopelessness that pervades such gatherings, particularly on the Welsh Front.[2]

Frederick Jude was another man to be summoned to play his part in war, but not with the Norfolks. He recalled his period of training:

Today I am requested to report at the training centre at Exeter for enlistment into the 9th Essex Infantry Division as a private soldier. Leaving Uxbridge by train … on the platform I had seen a group of rough looking chaps with no collars or ties and I hoped they were not bound for Exeter. I had heard their conversation which included expletive adjectives all beginning with f---, which with our upbringing in Norfolk, would have been excluded as undesirable and completely unfit to be included in any sort of society.

They were, of course, but Jude's attitude soon changed:

A week has gone and firstly I must retract my first opinion of the no collar/tie chaps. They are very fussy about their personal hygiene and for spit and polish treatment to their boots they are unbeatable, certainly I can't match them. They enjoy sprucing themselves up for things like Church parade as they did on Sunday at the Exeter Cathedral … So what's wrong with that I admitted to myself! These Londoners are very witty and are good company, one has to get used to their expletives and the cockney accent: they are generous and honest.[3]

France 1939-40

The Norfolk Regiment had a most distinguished war, winning more Victoria Crosses – five – than any other regiment. In September 1939, the 1st Battalion was in Delhi: it was brought back to England around Africa, avoiding the dangers of the Mediterranean. The 2nd Battalion went to France as part of the British Expeditionary Force. Private Pete Reynolds with the BEF in France wrote to his cousin, also Peter Reynolds, in Dersingham, in February 1940: 'just a few lines from Somewhere in France to let you know I'm still alive and kicking and have not forgotten you. The weather here now is so much better thank goodness, it's been a very severe winter, but now it's gradually thawing out and we are considerably better for getting about. We're in what were vacant houses in a very nice village, quite a large one incidentally.'[4]

In May 1940, the Germans advanced into France. The battalion came under heavy attack. Company Sergeant Major Gristock won a Victoria Cross for his bravery while defending on the line of the river Escaut near Tournai on 21 May. Although wounded in both legs, he was able to kill a German machine gun crew: he later died of his wounds.

Signaller Albert Pooley was among a group of one hundred men of the 2nd Norfolk Regiment who were taken prisoner at Le Paradis on 27 May:

> We turned off the dusty French road through a gateway and into a meadow beside the buildings of a farm. I saw, with one of the nastiest feelings I've ever had in my life, two heavy machine guns inside the meadow. They were manned and pointing at the head of our column. I felt as though an icy hand gripped my stomach. The guns began to spit fire and even as the front men began to fall I said fiercely, 'This can't be. They can't do this to us!' For a few seconds the cries and shrieks of our stricken men drowned the cracking of the guns. Men fell like grass before a scythe. The invisible blade came nearer and then swept through me. I felt a terrific searing pain in my left leg and wrist and pitched forward in a red world of tearing agony. My scream of pain mingled with the cries of my mates but as I fell forward into a heap of dying men the thought stabbed my brain, 'If I ever get out of here the swine who did this will pay for it'.

Pooley was one of two men who were able to crawl away from the site of the massacre: the other was Signaller William O'Callaghan. He fulfilled his vow: thanks to his efforts the German commander who ordered the massacre, Fritz Knoechlein, was tried by a British Military Court in Hamburg after the war. He was sentenced to death and hanged.[5]

Polens Friedensheeresstärke: 299041 Mann
Englands Friedensheeresstärke: 186100 Mann (ferner: Territorial-Armee von 180227 Mann)
Deutschlands Friedensheer: 100000 Mann
Frankreichs Friedensheeresstärke: 650700 Mann
Italiens Friedensheeresstärke: 638300 Mann (Armee und Miliz)

3 *The faces of the various armies, as portrayed in a German newspaper.*

4   *Norfolk Regiment training camp at Falmer in the South Downs.*

5   *Men of the Norfolk Regiment at Falmer in the summer of 1939.*

The remainder of the 2nd Battalion was forced onto the beach at Dunkirk – just 139 officers and men were evacuated out of a force originally 1,000 strong. The 7th Battalion was even harder hit. It retreated to a beach at St Valery-en-Caux to await rescue. No ships came and eventually the men had to surrender. Just 17 got back to England: they commandeered a fishing boat and used shovels for oars as they crossed the Channel.

D.H. Chisholm recalled his experiences on the beach at Dunkirk:

> At high tide there were bodies being washed ashore so I gave a hand to drag them above the high tide mark … A rumour went round that we should make our way to the East Mole at dusk, so I thought I'd give it a try. It was dark when I got to the Mole and we were marshalled by a group of sailors into single file and then told to

6   *German paratroopers landing on Crete, 20 May 1941: just seven days later, the British withdrew from the island leaving 12,000 men behind to become prisoners.*

move along, there seemed to be hundreds of French soldiers just standing there watching, it was very eerie. Once on the mole we realised why we were in single file, great holes had been blown in the concrete and these had been bridged by planks about two feet wide and we could hear the waves about twenty feet below. When we got on a solid piece of mole we were told 'wait, make way for the wounded'. Some were on foot, others on stretchers, when they passed we moved on again. Finally some more sailors helped us on to a slide made from planks and we slid down quite a distance and landed on the deck of a ship, we were told to spread ourselves round the ship. I got my back against a rail of some sort and sat down. I woke up to the fact that we were moving so dozed off again. I vaguely remember hearing a machine gun on the ship firing, and thought that everything must be under control, so went back to sleep.[6]

Norfolk men were involved in the rescue as well. The Yarmouth lifeboat, the *Louise Stephens*, crossed the Channel and brought off 49 soldiers. Frank Patrick of Reedham was a crew member on the Thames estuary steamer the *Crested Eagle*.

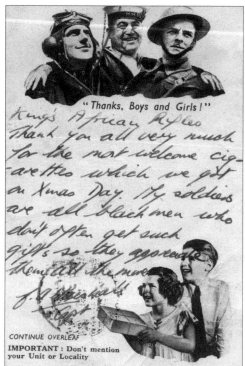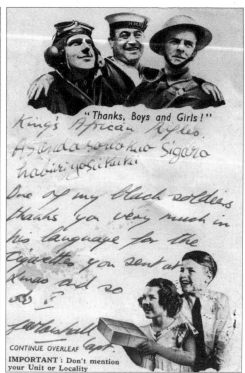

7   *'Thank-you' letters from soldiers for gifts of cigarettes from the children of Greenacre School, Yarmouth.*

The ship moored alongside the East Mole, casting off at 6pm loaded with soldiers including many wounded. After going about two miles the ship was dive-bombed and caught fire: there were about one thousand men on board and over 600 died. Patrick, a non-swimmer was one of the last to leave the burning boat, grabbing a float: he was rescued by a minesweeper. [7]

Singapore

Japan entered the war in December 1941. Reinforcements were sent to Singapore at the urgent request of the Australians, who saw their own country at risk if the city fell. Whether or not Churchill really thought there was a serious chance of saving Singapore may never be known. There was no chance. The 5th and 6th battalions of the Norfolk Regiment arrived on 13 January 1942, and attempted to halt the Japanese but were forced back into Singapore. The 4th arrived on 29 January to help defend the city but after 17 days of fighting was forced to surrender on 15 February.

   Russell Beckett was there with the 6th Norfolks. He recalled his final piece of action:

> Morning came and the Battalion was lined up and 120 of us picked to try and break through the Jap lines to release a Battalion that had been cut off. It was hopeless from the start, we climbed on to our lorries, open trucks, and moved off and it was not very long before we came under fire, we broke through the first road block only to come under fire from at least 2 Batts of Japs. Three of us from our truck survived

that hail of bullets, we then came to a complete block on the narrow jungle road. The driver got out only to be cut down at once. I said sod this and got out of the truck pretty fast, climbed down under the truck as did the other two. We fired back into a Jap machine gun nest that had taken so many of our troops, then as we were outnumbered we slid backwards into a monsoon ditch, and returned fire from there.

Our ammunition truck blew up after being hit by Jap mortar fire and it was hopeless to get one's head above ground, with red hot steel falling from the ammunition truck. We could not get out of the monsoon ditch, could only wait for darkness to come to allow us to get out and back into the jungle.

During all this the red hot metal was falling from the truck into the ditch, and extraordinary under these conditions to see the funny side, one of our three, an older man, ducked his head to avoid the dropping steel, put his face in the ditch and his false teeth flew out, he was reaching about in the mud to try and find them, we laughed in spite of it all.[8]

Beckett was just one of many Norfolk men unfortunate enough to become a prisoner of the Japanese. Reggie Burton was another. A captain in the 1st Battalion, Royal Norfolk Regiment, he recalled his last moments in the defence of Singapore. He and his men were in an old quarry behind Adam Road:

There were warning cries along the quarry as a solitary aircraft was sighted. Flying very low it came towards us. I could see the pilot's goggled face and I even saw him signalling by flash lamp to the Jap guns. A Bofors gun opened up on him. He was so low I fired a few shots with a rifle, but he swept past safely. His work was done only too well. The most tremendous bombardment struck us. It was like a sudden blast. The ground rocked and loose earth and stones went up in great pillars all around us. We dived into our painfully inadequate slit trenches and tried to claw into the earth. Above the explosions I could hear the screams of wounded men. There was a blinding flash and the slit trench fell in on me. I was sinking into a black pit. Then there was darkness.[9]

When Burton came to, the British had surrendered: he was a prisoner.

The Middle East and Africa

Other fighting men found themselves in the Middle East and Africa. Stanley Farrer commented:

We were not supposed to know where we were going, but as the only fighting taking place was in the Middle East, it did not take a genius to work out that that was where we were heading. Whilst in camp, we had all been issued with tropical kit including pith helmets which we were told, next to our rifle, was the most important piece of our equipment. Later, when we reached Port Tefik we were told to get rid of them, we had enormous fun throwing them into the sea. There were 11,000 troops on the ship and 11,000 pith helmets floating on the surface of the Red Sea.

His journey had been hellish. He went up to Scotland by train and boarded the *California* at Greenock:

During the night the floor of C deck became covered in vomit. The smell was beyond belief, my worst nightmare. I knew that if I were to stay there it would kill me, so taking a chance of being shot, I took my blanket and lifejacket, the lifejacket was good for 24 hours only, but it made a super pillow. Waiting for the right moment, I slipped up onto the deck and to fresh air. It was worth the risk. I found a place beside what I thought was a wall and settled down for the night … Before first light, I had to slip back to C deck. Passing A and B decks I knew that there was no way I could face that awful smell, whatever the cost, and eating greasy food with six inches of vomit around one's feet would make anybody's stomach turn. I am sure that little was eaten that morning, or if it was, it soon reappeared.[10]

For Robert Nunn in the Royal Air Force, however, the same journey provided a very different experience:

We were issued with saltwater soap and given directions where to find the ablutions and loos, which were called the 'heads' on board ship. There were about 50/60 of us in this group. There was a very strong smell of jute when we first arrived, which came from brand new hammocks … About 6 o'clock in the morning we were woken by an Irishman with the words:

Wakey, Wakey, Rise and Shine.
You're travelling on the Cunard Line.
How many loaves do you want for breakfast?

He then proceeded to toss fresh loaves onto each table as required. He told us 'take a tray to the galley and state how many at your table'. I went to the Galley and was dished out with about three dozen fried eggs, umpteen slices of bacon stood on edge at the other end of the tray and a pound of fresh butter in the centre. I wasn't quite sure whether it was for our table of 16 men or for everybody. We had never eaten like this before and I thought it must be a 'one-off', but that is how we fed all voyage.[11]

For many of these men it was their first experience of a hot country. There was no shortage of practical advice. Walter Viner, also in the RAF preserved his *Health Hints For Warm Climates* offering 24 pages of wise advice. The advice was summed up in 14 bullet points to remember:

1. To wear proper clothing and to change frequently.
2. To avoid undue fatigue, excesses and chills.
3. To be cleanly in all habits.
4. To drink and bathe in officially approved waters only.
5. To refrain from taking alcohol until after sundown, then only in moderation.
6. To eat freshly cooked foods and only fruits with thick skins.
7. To avoid bazaars, crowded places and native quarters where disease is rampant.
8. To take anti-malaria drugs daily and always sleep under a mosquito net when in malarious areas.
9. To wage constant war on flies, fleas, mosquitoes, sandflies, lice, bugs and rats.
10. To have the available protective inoculations against disease yearly or in season.
11. That a very high proportion of native women have venereal disease.
12. To refrain from concealing disease and so spreading it to others.
13. To keep the mind occupied with work and interesting hobbies.
14. To keep the bowels open daily and the skin active.

A cartoon on the same page of the booklet was even more succinct, 'Beware of sparkling waters, sparkling wines and sparkling eyes'.

There were many other practical tips on offer:

> DON'T buy soft drinks from hawkers. They are made up of water from the
> Sweetwater Canal, which is dilute sewage.
> DON'T get married to any local inhabitants if you can help it. You won't be allowed
> to stay on in this country even if you want to.[12]

Bill Carr of Ditchingham Hall commanded tanks at Sidi Rezegh in North Africa. In
August 1941, he wrote home to his mother:

> It is useless for me to write a long goodbye letter. We will be quite all right, I feel it
> inside me, but I hate leaving you for such a long time ... No one could have possibly
> had a happier time than we did up to the war ... now that all the old ideas of a good
> time are finished with, I was glad I enjoyed them up to the hilt, but am even more
> prepared to work day and night to rebuild our country for Annabel after the war.[13]

Carr fought with distinction and was awarded the DSO for his part in the battle.
His friend Sandy Cameron wrote back to Bill's wife Nenella after the award:

> I can hardly say how proud we are that our first Colonel should have made a name
> for himself in such a short time and I only wish his connection with us had not been
> severed. No doubt it will not be long before he has a 'knife and fork' on his shoulder
> and then maybe we will be under him once more.[14]

A less educated man, Private Freddie Pratt, wrote more concisely to his parents in
Gorleston: 'The weather here is a lot better than it was a few days ago as we had some
bad sandstorms, but it is getting quite warm again & as usual when the sun comes so
do the flys [sic] ... I go pictures nearly every night as it passes the nights away.'[15]

Italy

The story of the men who fought in Italy is often forgotten, but theirs was a life-
and-death struggle against a skilled and determined German resistance. Many Norfolk
men were among the British soldiers who moved from North Africa into Italy and
slowly fought their way northwards. Farrer landed at Anzio:

> After leaving the beach head we drove inland for about two miles and took cover in
> a wood. As a matter of habit, most of us had dug slit trenches – an infantryman's
> home. As it was fairly quiet at that time, very little shelling, a few did not bother to
> dig themselves in and made rude remarks about those of us that did. 'Windy Sid' was
> the usual greeting, windy meaning scared. However, no sooner had we completed the
> task and settled down – all hell broke loose. Shells simply rained upon us and those
> without slit trenches suddenly found that they had a huge desire to join us in ours,
> and jumped in on top of us. During the next few hours screams from the wounded
> and a good deal of swearing from those that were nearly hit could be heard all over
> the woods.[16]

Sergeant Horatio Taylor of the Royal Corps of Signallers was moved by the plight of
the Italian civilians, writing: 'Sometimes I wish that some of the complacent people
at home could be with the armies after the front line troops have passed through and
see the destruction and wickedness that has been wrought upon defenceless citizens.
It's one thing to be bombed from the air, it's another thing to have not only bombing

but actual ground fighting in and around one's home, loved ones taken away, and all one's worldly possessions wantonly destroyed.'[17]

Jude was also in the Italian campaign. His diary records:

I imagine the Gothic Line has proved to be more formidable than our command had expected; as we advance we pass through pile upon pile of debris that only a few days ago would have been a fine village or town, nothing is left, absolutely nothing. The German defence is so inclusive that every house, Church, Monastery or cowshed capable of housing their enemy is obliterated. The Italians who lived in these villages or towns who saved their lives by escaping to the caves in the hills are now returning and what a sad sight to see them rummaging beneath these piles of rubble endeavouring to find a lost mother, father, sister, child or sweetheart. We see lots of dead Germans and British soldiers referred to by the tommies as 'stiffies', a term which would have disgusted the worst of us in peace time but these are not times of peace. Their lifeless bodies have been there for possibly four days, the stench of death, that unforgettable odour is everywhere, and to see these women folk turning over the rubble with their bare hands seems so inhuman to say the least. It can't be their constitution is better than mine, it's utter tearful desperation which drives them to do this.[18]

Europe 1944-5

The 1st Norfolk Battalion landed in France on D-Day, 6 June 1944. The day was unforgettable for Alan Colman:

I shall always remember my first view of the beach, which was almost silver in colour but in the semi-darkness looked as though snow had just fallen and there were little red lights winking everywhere. I thought that our few lorries were the only party on the beach but when the dawn broke, I could see that the road along the beach was packed with hundreds of lorries. Joining the queue, we drove off the beach and through the shell-wrecked village of Graye-sur-Mere and took the road to Banville. It started to rain at 0700 hours and continued raining all day. Quite soon, I saw my first grave. Well, three graves to be precise, newly dug, with the three neat white crosses, standing in a row and there were bunches of flowers on the graves, probably laid there by the villagers. I went cold at the sight and Sergeant Williams who was sitting beside me and I both remarked about being 'right in it now'!

Frank Howes followed some days later. His task was to construct airfields immediately behind the front line: 'The Landing Craft (Tank) … was hit on the ramp and began to sink. No 2876 Squadron boat took off all the airmen not already dead and then carried on towards the beach but had to slow down, to bury at sea, one of the 2817 Squadron R.A.F. Regiment.'[19]

The Germans defended desperately as they were slowly forced back. On 6 August, Sidney Bates saved a desperate situation for his company near Sourdeval: he advanced with a light machine gun and though wounded continued to fire until finally succumbing to a fatal shot. He was awarded the VC for his valour. Two days later Captain David Jameson of the 7th Battalion also won a VC for his bravery, which included climbing onto an enemy tank to disable it. Jameson was the only VC winner in the regiment to survive the war. He died in 2001 and is buried in Burnham Norton churchyard.

Losses were so great that, after two months in France, the 7th Battalion was disbanded, with some of its men being absorbed into the 1st Battalion. The latter continued in the vanguard of the advance and eventually became a part of the allied armies occupying a defeated Germany.

Ken Wilby still recalls his experience as the men advanced to Lingen in April 1944:

> Something that's always been on my mind – I can't remember where it was, but I know it was in a bake-house. There was a young German in the bakery and he kept throwing grenades through a hole in the wall, like a ventilator. I looked around and I could see only one position where he could escape and that was through a narrow road on the left hand side. Once again I trained my Bren gun on the position I thought he would come out and truly enough he did exactly the thing I predicted, anyhow I shot him, he was only a few yards away and I could tell he was only a young boy, about fifteen … I put another burst into him. The point I'm trying to get at is if I hadn't put that second burst into him, would he still be alive today?
>
> That's the reason that sometimes I think about it, would he still be alive today if I hadn't fired a second time? He was only a young lad of fifteen. I have that on my mind still.[20]

Some Norfolk men were present at the liberation of Bergen-Belsen Concentration camp on 14 April 1945. They saw for themselves the horrors of the Nazi regime: although the SS had been burying the dead as fast as they could, there were 23,000 unburied bodies lying around when the British Army entered the camp. It was too late for over 2,000 of the 29,000 people still alive: they died before they could be looked after. Because of the dreadful disease in the camp, the liberation was not itself without risk: Wilfred Wiseman of Narborough contracted a fatal illness while helping clear the camp.[21]

By the beginning of May 1945, the end was at last in sight. Geoff Sneezum of the Devons wrote back to his parents on 5 May 1945:

> Well it is all over now, but to clear up the mess. Some mess too. For two days now I have been handing German prisoners along, and trying to stop a solid square mile of jammed civilians from stampeding. I don't suppose you will understand the above sentence. Nor will you realise how scared they all are of the Russians, both soldiers and civilians … I felt we were just a tiny party moving east. We reached our final objective just ahead of schedule – to my complete surprise. And awaited the link-up – which was preceded by Russian shells.
>
> We all 'stood-to' during the hours of darkness ready for anything, and waking each other up as we kept dozing off on our feet. Three hours after dawn I was asleep when a Russian private soldier was brought to me. He was absolutely dripping with sweat, having arrived on a bicycle. I thought at first that he was drunk but he was not. Only intoxicated with the sight of British troops. During the day other Russian troops arrive, and proceed to loot all the German vehicles scattered around. And to fire off the thousands of German weapons, in all directions, but mainly up into the air.[22]

The Far East

In 1944, the Japanese controlled Burma. Their army crossed into India and met the British at Kohima. This was a key moment in the war in Asia: if Kohima fell, the way into India lay open. The 2nd Battalion of the Norfolks helped halt the Japanese advance. John Randle won a VC in the battle. On 4 May, he took command when his company commander was hit. Although badly wounded he continued until the company had captured their objective, and then went out to bring in the wounded. Two days later he charged a Japanese machine gun post single-handed, armed only with rifle and bayonet. He silenced the machine gun with a grenade and then flung his own body across the slit. A captured Japanese gun from Kohima, a 70 mm howitzer, is now on display at the entrance to the Norfolk Regimental Museum.

Private Dick Fiddament was blunt about the horrors of this campaign:

> The smell, oh the wind changed, the vile smell. Once you've smelled death in all its ugly form, you can never forget it. I can sit quietly now and I can smell it. You can lose a pal, or you see one of the enemy and within a very short time they bloat and blow up. You can hear them explode. You can hear the gasses coming from them.

One of his comrades who died was Private Crampion: 'We went forward to where he lay. He was six foot two at the very least and all you could see was maggots. He was completely obliterated it was just a mass of maggots. By that time we had seen practically every horror that man could inflict on man, none the less the thought of maggots was repugnant – they're horrible hideous creatures That's how he lay.' [23]

After Kohima, the tide in the Far East turned. Fierce fighting continued for three months, with the Japanese being driven back to Mandalay. Lt George Knowland won a VC near Kangaw in Burma on 31 January 1945. He manned a bren gun single handed after its crew had all been wounded. He stood on the top of a trench, firing from his hips, then using a mortar and finally a tommy gun seized from a casualty before succumbing to his many wounds. The Japanese subsequently withdrew to Rangoon, where they surrendered in May 1945.

The Japanese defended their conquests with incredible tenacity, courage and stubbornness, preferring to die rather than to yield. It took a new weapon to finish the war, and one that marked a new era of warfare. At 8.15 am on 6 August 1945, the first atomic bomb fell on Hiroshima: more than 130,000 people were killed. A second nuclear bomb followed at Nagasaki three days later, killing 35,000 more. On 15 August the Japanese surrendered: the war was over at last.

The Navy and Merchant Navy

For Norfolk men in the Navy and Merchant Navy there was no phoney war: battle commenced at once. Albert Flogdell of Methwold was in the Marines; he was just one of 833 men killed on 14 October 1939 when the *Royal Oak* was sunk by a German torpedo. They also became prisoners of war before the army first entered into battle: Petty Officer Albert Webster of Norwich was one of several members of the crew of the submarine *Starfish* to be captured: the submarine had sunk in the Heligoland Bight in the early months of the war.[24]

In January 1940, there was fierce fighting off Great Yarmouth. The local press told the story:

> The latest outburst of Nazi frightfulness at sea has brought the war much closer to East Anglia. German aircraft started the week with a series of indefensible attacks

8 *Mine exploding in Alexandria harbour, Egypt. Photograph taken by Leslie Berry of Norwich, who joined the Royal Navy in 1940.*

upon merchant shipping along the whole length of the East Coast, and one machine distinguished itself by committing an attack that was particularly revolting. As has happened before, the target for its bombs and machine guns was an unprotected lightship, this time the East Dudgeon, and all but one of the crew of eight have perished. [25]

In fact, all eight men on board the lightship took to a small boat. They reached the shore but seven of the men died trying to come on land on the Lincolnshire coast. The one survivor was James Sanders of Yarmouth.

Shipping was also attacked by enemy planes. The Latvian steamer *Tautmila* was hit by ten bombs on 29 January: seven of her crew were killed. Sixteen people took to the boats and reached the coast, 12 landing at Great Yarmouth. The *Tautmila* drifted ashore off Walcott: eventually she was refloated. Mines laid off Cromer in February caused the loss of six vessels.[26]

Another example of a ship on which several Norfolk men died was the *Princess Victoria*. She was a former ferry with space for 1,500 passengers and 88 cars. Converted into a minelayer, she was sunk by an enemy mine in May 1940. The Commanding Officer, two officers and 31 ratings died, but 85 survivors were brought ashore. One said: 'There was a terrific bang. We were unable to launch any boats, and all the crew were pitched into the water. I clung to a raft for about half an hour before being picked up.' Several of her crew lie in North Norfolk churchyards: Commander Louis Lambert and AB Denis Self at Sheringham, Thomas Davidson, Jack Mitchell and Thomas Rickett at Cley, and Leading Signalman Henry Evans at Warham.[27]

The area of sea off Great Yarmouth was nicknamed 'E-Boat Alley' as so many German boats waited there to attack convoys. The first attack was in September 1940 and led to flotillas of coastal defence craft being based at Yarmouth. On the night of 6/7 August 1941, six ships from a convoy ran aground on Happisburgh Sands. All the lifeboats along the coast were called out and 119 men were rescued. The rescuers included Henry Blogg of Cromer, displaying his bravery in war as he had done many times before in peace.

Appalling losses of ships led to the adoption of a new defensive policy from 1942, based on defending an imaginary line 30 miles off the coast, known as the 'Z Line'. This led to a decline in losses and made it harder for the Germans to lay mines in the waters between the line and the English coast. By 1944, the tide of war had turned and the main task in the North Seas was the rescue of Allied pilots who had been forced to ditch in the water. By 1944, Air Sea Rescue launches were based at Wells and Cromer. Rescue planes were often equipped with small lifeboats which could be dropped to help save the lives of men drifting in the icy water.[28]

Ships with local names were naturally adopted by Norfolk communities, including the cruiser HMS *Norfolk*, adopted by the city of Norwich. The ship took part in several key episodes of the naval war. In May 1940, she and HMS *Suffolk* were on patrol in the Atlantic looking for the German battleship *Bismarck*. *Norfolk* was the first to spot her and came under fire. Four days later she engaged the *Bismarck* alongside

9 *The scuttling of the* Graf Spee, *1939. This and the following two photographs are from the collection of William Nicholls, who served in the war in both the Merchant and Royal Navy.*

10   *War in the Pacific: a British convoy escort carrier passing the Golden Gate Bridge, California.*

the battleships *King George V* and *Rodney*. In October and November 1942, she was escorting convoys to Russia. On Boxing Day 1943, she helped attack the battleship *Scharnhorst* and was damaged by enemy fire. After the war had ended she carried King Haakon of Norway back to Oslo from his enforced exile in Britain. Another local adoption was of the *Gorleston*. This was one of the ships lent to Britain by the United States under the Lease-Lend Agreement. She escorted convoys to Gibraltar and West Africa. In August 1944, she was transferred to the Indian Ocean and she was in the Far East when the war finally ended in August 1945.[29]

The men of the Merchant Navy were risking life and limb to bring essential supplies back from abroad. John Turner of Titchwell recorded in his diary that he went to 'a good talk tonight by an RNVR officer about the gallantry of the little merchant ships. "Small and frail vessels". He was on a collier. The skipper who had been on the bridge for forty-eight hours said on reaching port, "I hope the English housewives enjoy this coal. We've had a devil of a job getting it here". They had been bombed practically all the way across the North Sea.'[30]

John Waine of Acle was just one of many Norfolk men who travelled the world in the Merchant Navy. He was in the Pacific in October 1944:

> It was at this time I was Deck Officer supervising the coming alongside of the American cruiser Phoenix when the terrifying noise of a diving aircraft was heard. Seconds later a huge explosion threw me to the deck. A lone Kamikaze had hit the ship about thirty feet from where I had been standing. As I gathered myself to my feet, my first impression was that of the cruiser frantically cutting away her mooring ropes and departing at full speed away from us. I grabbed my lifejacket and came-to to see that the lower deck was in a shambles but I could see no sign of fire – our greatest danger.

Waine was lucky: one man had been killed in the attack, but the ship was able to make it to Brisbane –1,000 miles away – for repairs. [31]

11   *War in the Artic: the deck of a convoy escort carrier in snow.*

The War in the Air

Norfolk's position, so close to occupied Europe, meant that the county had a key role to play in the war. The possibility of invasion was a very real risk, especially in the summer of 1940, and the county was one of the places where the enemy might choose to land. It suffered from more than its share of bombing raids because of its proximity to enemy airfields. This worked in reverse as well – East Anglia came to have an enormous number of air bases from which the Allies sought to bomb the Germans into surrender. Several of these bases were run by the Royal Air Force. These included Coltishall, Horsham St Faiths, Bircham Newton and Methwold. Others were American bases: these are discussed in chapter three.

In the early years of the war, Norfolk's main role was as a fighter base. The fighter squadrons of Norfolk formed part of No. 12 group and were called south to help against the enemy offensive in the Battle of Britain. After the battle, the Germans began bombing Britain and the fighters were used to defend the country against them. Later, British fighters began to operate against enemy shipping and airfields in occupied France.

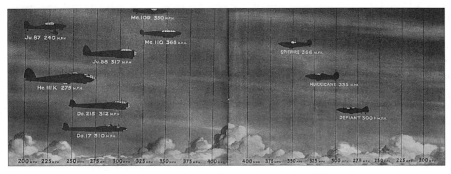

12   *Aeroplane speeds – a comparison. The Defiant was produced in Wolverhampton by the Norwich engineering firm Boulton and Paul.*

13   *Walter Viner fully kitted out while training for the RAF at Evanton, Scotland.*

The story of the base at Bircham Newton has been recorded by Peter B. Gunn. This airfield was not a new one: in fact it had been established towards the end of the First World War. These airfields were obvious targets for German attack. One ploy was to set up dummy airfields, either with buildings and dummy aeroplanes, or simply with landing lights in fields, to fool night raiders into dropping their bombs in the wrong place. There were 32 decoy airfields in Norfolk, including that on Mousehold Heath near Norwich, and others at Coxford, Sedgeford, Gateley and Terrington St Clement. They served their purpose well: Coxford collected a total of 60 bombs in 1940, compared with 29 on the 'real' airfield at Bircham Newton.[32]

Flying was a dangerous activity: at least 355 men flying from Bircham Newton alone were killed, and a further eight became prisoners of war. The first deaths occurred on 5 September, just two days after the declaration of war. A plane with a crew of four was shot down: three men were killed and the fourth became a prisoner of war. As the Germans conquered in Europe, the casualties inevitably increased. On 27 June 1940, four planes from Bircham Newton were shot down on the Dutch coast: they were looking for possible German invasion barges. Thirteen men were on board the four planes: 12 were killed outright and the 13th, Sergeant Aubrey Lancaster, became a prisoner of war in Germany. The enemy suffered casualties too, of course: 20 German aircraft were brought down over Norfolk during the war, and 141 German bodies were washed ashore on its coastline.

Coltishall was used as a rest and re-grouping station for exhausted men and machines from the south during the early part of the war. It was from here that Wing Commander Douglas Bader led 242 (Canadian) Squadron and a wing of no 12 Group to the assistance of the hard-pressed no 11 Group on the fateful day of 15 September 1940. With him, and leading no 74 Squadron, was Squadron Leader 'Sailor' Malan. By the evening of that day, 56 of the enemy had fallen for the loss of under 40 RAF fighters.

Horsham St Faiths was completed just before the outbreak of hostilities and was a front line operational station throughout the war. The first two squadrons arrived in August 1939. These squadrons, equipped with Spitfires, remained until April 1940, when they were replaced by Blenheims of Bomber Command. It was these Blenheims that, on 7 July 1941, took part in a low level daylight raid on Bremen, and it was for this daring display that the Wing Leader, Wing Commander Edwards, was awarded the Victoria Cross.[33]

To be an airman was regarded as a privilege despite the danger. Many did not pass the strict tests. Elliot Philipp was one. He had qualified as a doctor before joining the Royal Air Force. However, he never got his 'wings'. He did a stint at the Air Ministry in London and tested new officers for colour-blindness. He tested six candidates and found that all of them were colour blind! The eye specialist gently pointed out that perhaps it was Philipp himself who was colour blind. This turned out to be the case and Philipp became a medical officer at RAF Marham.[34]

Between the dangerous missions, there was time for relaxation. F/Lt Peter Hobbs was based at Downham Market airfield. There were dances twice a week in the local Town Hall, with a few outings further afield. Hobbs recalled:

> We made occasional jaunts to King's Lynn, generally to the Duke's Head with its cockroaches, which you could race across the dining room tables between courses:

14   *Viner in relaxed mood while serving in Egypt.*

or perhaps the Ouse Booze, provided one remembered which way to turn on leaving, otherwise one was liable to fall in the river! The Ouse Booze was the airmen's name for the Yacht Club.[35]

Norfolk also played a vital role as a bomber base. Bombers covered the retreat to Dunkirk and attacked enemy shipping. They were joined by American bombers a few months after America joined the war in December 1941. From 1942 until the end of the war, East Anglia became in effect a huge aircraft carrier for bombing raids on Germany and the occupied countries. From 1941 to the middle of 1942, Bircham Newton became primarily a base for shipping strikes: targets ranged from barges and flak ships to 10,000-ton motor vessels. During this period Hudsons attacked and fired oil tanks, warehouses and harbour installations. In 1942, Mosquito squadrons arrived at Horsham and from here took part in the first daylight raid on Berlin.

At Home

Not all soldiers could be heroes, of course. There are plenty of cases in the criminal records for Norfolk of men from the armed forces who deserted from the army, or stole – often under the influence of drink – or even occasionally committed murder. Here we consider just a few examples. Reginald Cain was charged at Methwold in November 1943 with being a deserter from HMS *Dundonald*, and was remanded to await a military escort. At Easter 1941 Muriel Steward was charged with assisting an absentee from the army to conceal himself: she was found not guilty. In contrast, Robert Perry was charged in 1944 with unlawfully wearing the badges of an officer in the RAF, and of making false statements: he did not turn up in court. At a later hearing he was found guilty of the first charge only and bound over in the sum of £10.[36]

On 2 January 1942, at King's Lynn, six soldiers were found guilty of being absent without leave from their regiments. They were all young, between 18 and 21, and – in view of the date – had probably been at home over Christmas. They were handed over to army escorts. There are a good many similar cases in the register: in November 1942 two soldiers, Gunner George Russell and Private Ernest Fretwell, responded to arrest by trashing their cells in Lynn police station: they were fined five shillings each and ordered to pay for the damage.[37]

William McCulloch, a soldier, was charged in September 1942 with breaking into the shop of Eric Loveday in St Gregory's, Norwich, and stealing money and goods. He also broke into a dwelling house in St Giles and stole ten shillings. He admitted the offences, saying that he was fed up and in want of money, and that he had been an absentee from his regiment since 26 July 1942. He clearly thought this might tell against him as he wrote to the court from prison:

> When I absented myself I didn't just lead a useless life, for 6 weeks out of the 7 weeks I was absent, I worked on Farm's harvesting. (This has been verified by the Police.) Then when the Harvest was done I did the foolish thing

He was bound over for two years and ordered to rejoin his regiment immediately.

A group of three soldiers were convicted for theft at the same court. Arthur Armon, Walter Yaxley and George Johnson broke into Alexander Carr's shop in Golden Ball Street on 25 September 1942 and stole a wireless set, bicycle parts, torches and batteries. Johnson wrote a letter of mitigation from prison while awaiting trial:

> I am very sorry that I have to take this privelege [*sic*] of writing this letter to you as regards to the predicament I am unfortunately placed in. I am hoping to God that you will give it your utmost consideration solely for the sake of my wife and newly born child and also myself. First of all sir I am a soldier and also a fully qualified parachutist. I have never before been in any kind of trouble with the law so its obvious why I am worried. I was sent up to Britannia Barracks from the parachute battalion a few weeks ago. It was during my stay at the above mentioned barracks that unfortunately I became friendly with 2 other soldiers named Yaxley and Armon. I have never before in my life been to Norwich sir so naturally I was very grateful to be shown around by someone. I was absolutely ignorant of their characters sir or otherwise I would not have been in the horrible ghastly mess that I find myself in at present. Since I have been in this trouble sir I have been informed from different sources that the above mentioned soldiers have criminal records. I have cursed the day I met them ever since ... The whole episode was the result of a very drunken evening.

Armon received six months' prison, Yaxley three months. Johnson was bound over for two years and ordered to return to his regiment at once.[38]

Cases of murder involving soldiers also came before Norfolk courts. Drummer James Hanson shot Provost-Sergeant William Anderson in a military camp at Ormesby. They were in a room together, with Hanson sitting on a bed cleaning a gun. A shot was heard and people ran into the hut. Hanson said, 'I did it: he is not going to call me a bastard.' Hanson clearly felt he had been victimised by Anderson but claimed he only meant to frighten him: he was sentenced to ten years in prison.

Another soldier charged with the death of another was 20-year-old Private Reginald Barlow, accused of manslaughter after the death of Private John Mitchell. Mitchell died outside the Wellesley Street Drill Hall in Lynn, where a dance was being held. There was a fight between men from two different regiments, between whom there had long been bad feeling, and Mitchell fell to the ground. Barlow was found not guilty.[39]

Essential Workers

Some people were not called up because of poor health. Others were not called up because the job they were already doing was thought to be vital to the welfare of their country in wartime. These included jobs in engineering and manufacturing, and also on farms – in fact the *Schedule of Reserved Occupations* issued in 1939 is 107 pages long!

It is often forgotten how many men 'did their bit' while not becoming members of the armed forces. These men were doing key jobs at home. Mrs Heading in Norwich wrote to her soldier son, John, about a family friend:

> Reg started work at Coventry on July 31st [1940]. I am afraid he hasn't settled to it very comfortable so far, it's such long hours, 7.30 am till 12, 1-5.30, 6-7.30. Saturday and Sundays he leaves off at 5 o/c instead of 7.30.
> It is the Fitting Dept that Reg is in at Rootes Ltd Aircraft Factory, he said after the first day he could hardly walk downstairs for stiffness because the job was standing & stooping all the time & he has got blisters on his fingers so I expect you can guess what it's like, no doubt you are experiencing something similar. What we would like to do to that Hitler![40]

In some cases, industries were moved to what were thought to be safer areas of the country. Grout's of Yarmouth made parachute silks: the Ministry of Aircraft Production ordered them to move inland in case of air raids. The looms were moved to Leigh in Lancashire and other departments to Leekbrook near Leek in Staffordshire. They left Yarmouth in September 1940. The factory in Yarmouth continued to make parachute and bandage cloths, which were sent to Leek by lorry each week. Although some of the men at Leek were involved in fire watching there was never an air attack, in sharp contrast to Yarmouth, which, as we shall see, suffered many air raids.[41]

Such a large number of miners had joined up that there was a shortage of men to work in the mines: mining work was offered to men as an alternative to military service. However, there were not enough volunteers so some men were given no choice but to go into mining rather than into the forces. Both volunteers and conscripts were known as the Bevin Boys. Geoffrey Rose of Fakenham was one: he was ordered to report at Doncaster for training and recalled his first day in a mine:

> After getting into the cage we just seemed to fall freely for 500 yards before the brakes were applied, giving the impression that we were returning again to the surface. We were accompanied by an instructor and walked along the 5 ft-high tunnel towards the coal face. On the way we passed a sealed tunnel upon which was painted a white cross. One of the boys enquired why and was told that was the site of an explosion in 1931 when ninety-two men, with their ponies and equipment, were lost. This did not help our morale.[42]

An acquaintance of the Newstead family was also a Bevin Boy:

> Mum to John: Did Joy tell you that Jack Wilde has to go to the coal mines! Poor lad! Whatever will such work do to his hands, his lot is worse than yours I think, because he has had a taste of university life, & then to leave that for coal mining.[43]

The Conscientious Objector

A small number of men had a *conscientious objection* to being called up: they refused to fight, and, in some cases, to assist the war effort in any way at all. This was less controversial an issue in the Second World War than it had been a generation earlier. This was partly because the Germany of Adolf Hitler, with its aggressive foreign policy and gross mistreatment of groups of its own citizens, was much more clearly an evil than the Germany of 1914 had been. It was also because a more tolerant and flexible attitude was adopted.

There were just 11 tribunals for the whole country – that for East Anglia was based at Cambridge. Whereas there was always a military man on the Tribunal in the First World War, there was none in 1939-45. Conscientious Objectors could normally find some form of occupation depending on the exact nature of their beliefs. If they were already in a job deemed of national importance, they could stay where they were. Others might join the Royal Army Medical Corps or the Non Combatant Corps, where they would not have to use weapons. Others worked on the Home Front as Wardens or Fire Fighters. Only a very small number of men were so set against the war as to refuse any of these options: these were the ones who were sent to prison. One such man was David Burrow of Sprowston. He refused to attend the medical examination preceding call-up and was imprisoned for six months. He was a man of strict principle. In November 1942, he refused to register for fire-watching: he was already doing voluntary fire-watching but had a 'a conscientious objection extending to all conscriptive measures directly connected with the war effort'. He was fined £25, which he refused to pay: he was therefore sentenced to a further two months in prison.

Some, but not all, conscientious objectors had religious grounds for their refusal to enlist: very often they were Jehovah's Witnesses. In July 1942, two of these, William Filby of Wymondham and Ronald Atkinson, came before the courts in Norwich. At first the magistrate ordered that the police would forcibly take them to the Medical Board, and that they could stay in prison for up to seven days while waiting for this. He must have been convinced that they would never conform: on the following day he fined them £5 and sentenced them to three months' imprisonment.

The conscientious objector could sit out the war, or he could be more assertive in his protests, risking further clashes with the law. One such man was Jack Ebbage of South Walsham. He accepted the option of agricultural work rather than military service but then wrote to a young man working with him, offering to help the latter evade military service. He was fined £3.

The conscientious objector ran the risk of losing his job, especially if he was a teacher, and might therefore 'corrupt' the children in his charge. One such teacher was Herbert Storey of Chalk Hill, Norwich. He had refused to go for medical examination, but eventually found a role that would suit his conscience. He did voluntary work for the Friends' War Victims Relief Committee at Petersfield in Hampshire, where he was given food and accommodation and a few shillings pocket money.[44]

Two

Women at War

Women in uniform were a common sight in the Second World War. They did not actually take up arms and fight, but they could play many supporting roles, which men would otherwise have to do. Each force had its own women's arm. The largest was that of the Army, the *Auxiliary Territorial Service*. Many people had rather a low regard for this service at first, seeing it as undisciplined, and its members sometimes drunk and liable to immorality. After the first two directors were removed, its image greatly improved: however, the khaki uniform was thought unflattering by many women! Some women preferred to join the *Women's Royal Navy Service* (WRNS, generally known as Wrens). Their advertising poster ran 'Join the Wrens and free a man for the Fleet'. The blue uniform was much more attractive than that of the ATS. The third service was that of the *Women's Auxiliary Air Service* (WAAF). The blue-grey uniform worn by the WAAFs was often preferred to that of the ATS, but both were unflattering compared with that of the Wrens. Many women volunteered for these services. Strictly speaking they were recruited as civilians, until the ATS and WAAF were given full military status in April 1941. The Wrens never received military status but, from 1941, they were in practice treated in the same way as male naval personnel.

In March 1941, all women between 19 and 40 had to register at Employment Exchanges: they could then be directed into 'essential work'. In December 1941 a new National Service Act was passed. All unmarried women between 20 and 31 were to be called up. They would have to choose between the Armed Forces, Civil Defence, the Land Army or specified essential work. The age limit was soon lowered to nineteen. For the first time ever in Britain, the compulsion to serve had been extended to women. The *Eastern Daily Press* saw it as an opportunity that they would welcome:

THE CALL TO WOMEN

The recent announcement by the Ministry of Labour and National Service of the choice placed before the young women now being registered for national service makes it clear that they are being placed on an equal footing with their brothers in the matter of responsible service for their country. We believe that they and the nation at large welcome a firmness of action which will allow none to shirk what thousands have already undertaken.

'Conscription' may be a slightly exaggerated term to apply to the action being taken by the Ministry. There is, in fact, no power to conscript women into the auxiliary Services, but women in the 'under thirty' classes, who will all be registered before the end of the year, are given the choice either of entering one of these uniformed

Services, or of going into a war factory. Women already engaged in essential work or in certain reserve occupations are exempted, as also are married women with household responsibilities. But apart from these there is an immense labour force which has got to be available to the nation if our war potential is to reach the maximum.

Side by side with the drafting of the younger women into the new war factories and the Forces there is issued a call to the older woman to take over the jobs their younger sisters were doing. The nation looks to its women for help in this hour of greatest need. It will not look in vain. Other generations of women would have envied them the responsibility, which is also a proud privilege.[1]

As this was the first time that women had been called up, this was the first time that the issue of Conscientious Objection had been faced by women. As with men, the great majority who did object to directly helping the war effort could find a place somewhere without offending their conscience: the traditional role of nursing was the obvious choice. There were a very small number of women who refused service in any form, and these would be fined: if they refused even to pay the fines, then the last resort for the authorities was imprisonment.

Two Norwich women were among the first to be prosecuted under the National Service Act. Edith Briers, aged 30, said that her life was dedicated to full-time missionary work as a Christian missionary: she was a Jehovah's Witness. Maud Davison, 22, also had religious scruples and was involved in 'healing work' with her mother. They were directed to munitions work, which they refused, and then told to do domestic work in the Norfolk and Norwich Hospital: on refusing to do such work, they were sent to prison for a month.

Another female 'CO', Alice Lake, was working for the Salvation Army as a domestic servant in Reepham and hoping to become an officer of the Army. The Ministry of Labour offered her a choice of 'land work, munitions work or serving with the Forces'. She came before the East Anglian Board at Cambridge in May 1942 and claimed exemption: if she became an officer in the Salvation Army, she 'would give her life to the work'. The Board granted her unconditional exemption.

The definition of 'essential work' could be a matter of dispute in itself. Edith Bennett, a music teacher in Cromer, was told that music was not essential in wartime, and that she must work in munitions. This angered the local vicar, G.A. Barclay: 'To leave Cromer without a music instructor is a blow for the duration. Mrs Bennett can better serve the war effort in that capacity than filling shells. Music is an important part of a child's education and one of the amenities of our civilisation which should be kept up in wartime.'[2]

The ATS

Dorothy Calvert of Caister on Sea joined the ATS and was sent to a training camp in Northampton. She recalled her first day:

> When we had marched past quite a lot of soldiers and ATS, who stared at us as if we were a set of freaks, we were told to halt, which we did beautifully, falling over each other as we did so. But did I need to ask; the smell of stale cooked cabbages came out to greet us, so we were about to experience what every rookie dreaded, we were about to be given a cook house (Army for the use of) meal. I shall never forget it; my

15   *ATS outside Britannia Barracks, Norwich.*

stomach turns over at the thought of it, even now. On the plates we were holding out in nerveless hands, they put firstly a dollop of grey cement type potato, quickly followed by something that looked like pond scum, which was actually cabbage; next to follow was something I took to be batter pudding, which to put it mildly looked as if our fat Sgt had sat on it, as it looked more like a pancake; next came what had to be a slice of meat which, to be fair, would have done fine service as the sole of some poor squaddie's boot; then the final touch, a grey gluey liquid was poured over the lot. Hypnotised, I walked to the table, as the other girls did, to poke, prod and examine, but only to eat if desperate.[3]

Jessie Dunlop also joined the ATS:

I was working in the box office of a local theatre when the tribunal, which decided what war work one did, informed me that my job was not considered necessary, and that I should either go into a factory making munitions or else join one of the forces. It was 1942 and I was 22 years old.

I chose the forces but was seconded into the ATS, and in June I was sent to the King's Own Yorkshire Light Infantry barracks in Pontefract, Yorkshire.

We lived in Nissen huts, about 40 of us in each hut, with a sergeant in charge. There were medicals and haircuts for most of us, and we were issued with uniforms, which were supposed to be fitted! Endless drill and marching filled most days.

After three weeks we were all gathered together in the drill hall with a Senior Commandant in front of us. She proceeded to tell us what jobs were available and how many were needed of each kind: 200 cooks, 300 clerks, 100 drivers etc. Just two of us sat still whilst all the others were signed up for whatever they chose.

The two wanted to go into *cipher*, that is, breaking of the enemy's coded messages. After training at a Low Grade Cipher school in London, Jessie was sent to Horstead Hall: 'At first there were only two other girls beside myself, both telephonists, and me in charge of cipher. We were put into a huge Nissen hut with twelve beds and an iron stove, which burned coal, with a few chairs round it. There were other Nissen huts in the grounds, which were used for the male soldiers, mostly older men back from overseas duty. The mess was in the main house, as were all the offices, but there was a Nissen hut that housed the NAAFI, and in the evening anyone who was off duty gathered there.'

Cigarettes, sweets and odds and ends were on sale: 'I soon found myself running this because there wasn't much to do in the way of messages. Sometimes I manned the teleprinter or the telephone switchboard.'[4]

Gladys Cresswell of Acle was another Norfolk girl who served in the ATS. She worked at various battery operating rooms in England and then came back to Norfolk to be near her sick parents, working at Redcliffe House in Brundall. Later, in autumn 1944, she transferred to the Royal Army Pay Corps: 'I found myself working in the Non-effective Dead section and had to help deal with the affairs of service men who had died

16   *Grave of Eva Gill of the ATS, Rosary Cemetery, Norwich. Eva died on 20 April 1944.*

or been killed. At first I found it rather grim but soon got hardened to coping with Pay Books covered in white blotting paper to conceal the bullet holes. The work became a job just like any other'.[5]

Rachel Dhonau in Sheringham saw both sides of the ATS. She recorded in her diary: 'After tea one of the ATS came to see my mother. She was enormously fat, rather dirty and very untidy. The WAAFs about here are quite different – all very smart.' However, another entry says: 'Mr J was talking about the *Grand Hotel* today now occupied by ATS. He says he has never seen it so clean – not even in peacetime.'[6]

The ATS did not serve abroad and did not receive training in the use of arms. However, their lives were not without danger and some died for their country. Two ATS girls, Beatrice Perkins and Alice Johnson, were killed in Cromer in the early hours of the morning of Christmas Eve 1941. A group of girls were heading home in the back of an army lorry when it appears to have hit a building in the High Street. Apparently the two were travelling on the side-board of the lorry, a practice that was forbidden. The coroner recorded a verdict of accidental death, but said that the girls should have been better supervised.[7]

Joan Burton of Stanfield died on Remembrance Day 1941 while serving in the ATS: she is buried at nearby Mileham. At just 17 years of age, she is the youngest of the ATS burials to be found in any Norfolk churchyard.

On 11 May 1943, 26 ATS girls were killed in a bombing raid on Great Yarmouth: their place of death is given as Wellesley Recreation Ground, where the bodies were laid after having been pulled out of the wrecked building. These girls came from all over Britain. The youngest was a local girl, 18-year-old Lilian Grimmer, but others came from as far away as the Shetlands. Their effects were returned to their commanding officer after being duly listed. They make moving reading. May Johnson had a gold ring and wrist watch and nothing else. The others usually had their pay books and a small sum of money, in most cases just a few shillings in cash. The list of Isobel James's possessions is typical:

> Pay book; gold ring; fountain pen; comb; purse containing charms and 9/11 in cash; necklace; brooch; nail file; powder puff; cigarette case; keys; handkerchief; letter; envelope of cards etc.[8]

The Wrens

Wrens did not go to sea, although some people have the mistaken impression that a wren ancestor did serve on a ship from a misreading of their service record or related papers. This is because navy training centres on land are also given the title of HMS: that at Yarmouth was HMS *Midge*.

Ena Howes served in the Wrens. In February 1942, she was based at HMS *Ganges* in Shotley. On one occasion, she recalled: 'The German battleships *Scharnhorst* and *Gneisenau* were sighted going up the Channel, and I had to ring all the cinemas in Ipswich, so that they could put a 'recall signal' on the screen. This brought all the sailors on shore leave back to their ships immediately.' She served later at HMS *Raven*, a Royal Naval Air Station at Eastleigh – now Southampton Airport. After flying had finished for the day the Wrens would go onto the airfield and pick the mushrooms that grew there!

In the summer of 1944, Ena was in charge of the telephone exchange while stationed at Fort Southwick, the headquarters for the D-Day landings. However, day-to-day activities had to continue even during the war. In Ena's case this led to her missing an important development: 'Just before D-Day, all personnel were called to a conference, to be told that D-Day was about to take place … Unfortunately, I was in town having my hair permed at the time.'

On D-Day itself, Ena listened to a conversation between General Bradley, Commander of the 1st U.S. Army group and Supreme Allied Commander, General Eisenhower: 'I went down to the switchboard room, to watch and listen to the messages coming in. Sergeant Wally Riseborough was there and had a 'scrambler' and so we both listened to the messages. There were so many but the voice I remember was General Eisenhower's. "How's it going, Brad?… Yeah. O.K. Brad" he drawled.' Her shift over, Ena walked through the tree-lined drive at Southwick where red squirrels were at play: never was the contrast between peace and war more striking.

In August 1944, Ena became one of the first Wrens to go abroad: she was one of a group of officers who volunteered for service in newly liberated Paris. It was not a very romantic experience:

> It was bitterly cold and we had little chance of getting warm, and so, duffle-coats and men's thick woollen 'long johns' were issued: the long johns to be worn under our bell bottoms when on night duty, because it was so cold. They were lilac and grey in colour and were made for the sailors on the Arctic convoys, going up to Murmansk in Russia. No one wore them, but they came in very useful later in the war. Some

17   *Poster for the Wrens.*

18   *Ena Howes in Wren uniform outside Buckingham Palace.*

people simply took out the crotch and they had a ready made pullover. For my part, I pulled them out and got several balls of very thick wool, with which I knitted cot blankets for my first child, because cot blankets were 'on coupons', if they were available at all.

After the war, Ena was awarded the British Empire Medal at Buckingham Palace by King George VI.[9]

As women came of age during the war, they had to consider what form of service to take up. Marjorie Hayward explained her decision to join the Wrens in November 1944 in letters to John Heading: 'Like you I shall soon be away from home for I've volunteered for the Wrens. On Friday I went to London for my medical, which I passed Grade 1. The War Officer, who interviewed me, said they would fit me into some clerical job and that I would be called up in two or three weeks. I am looking forward to it in some ways as it should be quite a change from the Women's Land

Army. Probably I shall get moved about a good bit & thus see various parts of the country.' In another letter, she explained her decision in more detail:

> I volunteered for the WRNS, because otherwise I would have been sent to a munitions factory as soon as I was nineteen. I could have gone into the ATS, but I preferred the WRNS. It is now a month since I entered the Wrens and so far I love it. I hope you like the Army better than you did when you wrote. At present I am at Chatham waiting to be drafted to my permanent post. While I am here I am a messenger, but I am going to be a fleet mail Clerk. Previously I was in London. We are going to dinner & tea on board a ship here tomorrow – it should be fun! Then we are giving a dance in the evening for some of the soldiers, sailors & marines around here.[10]

David Jefferson described the work of the Wrens in a port like Great Yarmouth:

> A team of Wrens would board the boats as they returned to base, to service the armament, engines, radio and radar, while ashore there would be Wrens in the torpedo and shipwright workshops, and operating the tractors which moved the boats in and out of the boat sheds.[11]

Olive Swift (later Partridge) volunteered for the Wrens when she reached the age of 19 in 1941. She trained at HMS *Midge* in Yarmouth and recalled the dangers of service there:

> We were regularly shot at by low-flying German planes as we marched down to the base at work. We ran for cover, they weren't very good shots, nobody was hit. I must say, though, the bombing was devastating, a lot of the service quarters were razed to the ground, including our own. I was sleeping in a top bunk, but found myself blasted from my bed, lying on the floor at the far end of the room, amongst a lot of rubble and glass. It was fortunate for me that I was not in my bed, as a large section of wall and a window fell on it.
>
> There were seven of us in the cabin, and I can truthfully say that nobody panicked, we had great faith in our Naval friends, they dug us out alright, and if they hadn't got a spade, they dug with their hands. Fire broke out, and being short of fire engines, we formed a chain and passed buckets of water along from a standpipe. When the losses were made known, we found many of our friends were injured, or in shock, and had to be sent home. Worst of all, seven wrens and our officer were killed, but wartime is no time for brooding and we survivors attended a memorial service for our dead comrades, and went back to work.[12]

The WAAFs

The Women's Auxiliary Air Service also had its attractions for many – and also had its risks. Mary Beckett was brought up in Thetford, attending the Grammar School there. In 1941, she was conscripted, serving her training time at Innsworth Camp in Gloucestershire:

> The thing that hit me most was lack of privacy. Everything was communal. We fed together in the cookhouse. Thirty girls slept in a bare, drafty Nissen hut. Our bedding was made up of three solid square mattresses, termed 'biscuits', a hard pillow; and three grey blankets. If you were tough enough and tired enough to fall asleep, in spite of the unquestioned discomfort, you were rudely awakened at 6.00 by the blaring tannoy. The ablutions offered a nice little row of wash basins. There was a good supply of water but not from the taps. We had to wade out through murky water to reach the basins. Being kitted out, lectures and drill occupied the time between sleep and meals.

Beckett was stationed in Happisburgh:

Christmas 1943 was a strange but happy occasion. Of course, it is a family time, but this wartime Christmas my beloved C Watch room-mates were my family. None of us could afford to buy expensive gifts but the little parcels daintily packed and labelled with loving messages that covered each bed on Christmas morning were joyfully received … Three of us went to church, but alas, it was not a very inspiring service. A super dinner was served by the officers and NCOs. The rest of the day was not exactly a rave-up, but we enjoyed ourselves.[13]

Mary Pettit (later Blood) was in the WAAF at Coltishall. She recalled the danger:

Squadrons changed about every six weeks or so to give those on active service a rest. Early in 1942 we got the first Polish and Czech squadrons at Coltishall and, of course, many different aircraft types. The Czech pilots had mainly Beaufighters. One night we were getting ready for bed when we heard a crash. Going out, a fighter had crashed in front of the WAAF Officers' Mess. There was nothing anybody could do, as live ammunition was shooting in all directions. We went to bed more than shaken at the sight. About the same time, another pilot, this one Polish, crashed nearby. Within a week we had two military funerals and had to parade for them … The Beaufighters had an unfortunate reputation. If you were unlucky enough to crash, then it was a considerable problem to escape from the aircraft such were the cockpit arrangements. That reputation gave then the name 'flying coffins'.[14]

Irene Storer (later Forsdyke) described her work at RAF Downham Market:

A normal day began with our arrival at the Instrument Section where we read the barometer and noted down the reading. Next, we went to the flight sergeant in charge to see if he had any reports from the pilots of instruments having faulty readings, or other snags. These had to be dealt with first in case they turned out to be long jobs. For instance, if an oil pressure gauge had to be changed it could take most of the day. Our next job was the worst of all. We had to read the 'Board'. The Board contained a list of all the aircraft in alphabetical order, with those required for the coming night's operation indicated. On this board were one or two gaps sometimes, where an aircraft had been rubbed out, leaving a chalk smear. These were the ones which had not returned the previous night. We thought of the faces of the men who had flown in those aircraft, and had to pull ourselves together and get on with our work. Having read the Board we set off to the aircraft with our tools, where we checked and set everything necessary.[15]

Two aspects of women's work in war were recalled by Peggy Taylor. She was a WAAF, serving at the radar station at Stoke Holy Cross between 1942 and 1944. She arrived there immediately after a Blenheim had crashed on the site, with loss of life. She wrote: 'My early work was with the standby equipment we were forced to use, until the mast was rebuilt, mostly by Irish crews who defied the laws of gravity. I remember the medical orderly, a girl named Paddy, who had the courage to climb to the first platform to extricate one of the unfortunate young airmen.'[16]

The Women's Land Army

A non-military alternative for women was to join the Women's Land Army, and free up men to join the fighting forces. Despite the experiences of the First World

19   *Women's Land Army poster.*

War, Norfolk farmers were often reluctant to take on women. An *Eastern Daily Press* editorial warned that this would be their loss in the long term:

> If the farmers of Norfolk refuse to accept for training members of the Women's Land Army they must not expect much sympathy when they are faced with a labour shortage. These volunteers for farm work are anxious to prove their usefulness and

20 *Women's Land Army girls, Browick, near Wymondham.*

when encouraged they are invariably quick to learn. The farmer may feel that their needs will not be regarded now that the labour resources of the county are to be mobilised in every field essential to the winning of the war. Even if this is the case it will be some time before they get the men they want, and in the meantime they are doing themselves a dis-service in neglecting the opportunities that the Women's Land Army is extending. The girls will be trained, but not in Norfolk, and when they are experienced they will be employed elsewhere.[17]

Land Girls were trained for a month and then received 32 shillings for a 48-hour week. In October 1941, the *Eastern Daily Press* talked to girls from London who were working on a farm of 1,000 acres staffed by 13 men and seven land girls. Ethel Mole, formerly a worker in a London clothing factory, had become an expert on the tractor after just six weeks: 'During harvest she cut up to 24 acres of corn a day and now she is ploughing up grassland and cutting straight furrows.' Her sister, Irene Ive, handled the horses and helped in the stacking: 'She handles the fork as well as any man', was the tribute of the farm steward. Rosie Mills, an 18-year-old Londoner, also worked on stacking. The newspaper concluded: 'Dairy work is something at which the Land Girls generally excel, while another type of work at which they are particularly successful is calf rearing. In some parts of the county, Land Girls have learned highly specialised jobs including thatching. On some farms the girls worked the full harvest.[18]

There were other opportunities to work on the land, such as in forestry and market gardening. The latter might appeal to older women:

Volunteers for the Women's Land Army who have been unable to pass the stiff medical tests necessary before they can be admitted will find another gate to the land open to them. The demand for trained women gardeners for estates both large and small is growing every day as more and more men are called up for the Services. Girls as young as 16 can be trained for the work under a special 'apprenticeship scheme'. The age limit goes up to 40, thus giving the older woman a chance. The training deals entirely with food production in private gardens, a very valuable piece of war work.[19]

Joan Snelling enrolled in the WLA at their head office in Castle Street, Norwich in 1941:

I was given my uniform: corduroy breeches, cotton dungarees, two aertex shirts, three pairs of long socks, a green jumper, shoes and a cowboy type hat. Wellingtons were in short supply and were reserved for dairy workers. I was lucky as my brother's rubber boots were available. They were a size too large but I stuffed them with clean dry hay and kept warm and dry.[20]

Christina Ward recalled that she was sent to Norfolk from her home in Yorkshire to work as a Land Army girl:

We had to milk the cows on the farm, then deliver the milk, then go back to the farm to muck out. We worked seven days a week and had one weekend off every two months. We earned 12/6 per week. We were out in all weather, even when there was ice on the vegetables. Then I went into general farming, harvesting sugar beet. One girl chopped off her finger when she was working.
      We stayed in the hostel and were then sent out in a group to whichever farm needed workers. We got up at 4 am to collect the cows. I worked with one other girl and a farm man, and then a milk man.[21]

According to information in the Norfolk Regimental Museum, there were over 1,650 land girls in Norfolk by 1944. This, however, represented only about a quarter of the number of women actually working on the land: many, including wives and daughters of farmers, did so without the formality of joining the Land Army.

For women, as for men, there was the possibility of working in an 'essential' industry such as the making of munitions – at its peak, in 1943, there were no fewer than 3.5 million people, both women and men, working in munitions. Naturally these industries were concentrated in the Midlands and the North West, traditional areas of industry and also further away from the disruptions of air raids and possible invasion. Thus the experiences of Norfolk women do not feature this kind of work as heavily as those from other parts of Britain.

For other women, there was the traditional role of nursing. As the *Eastern Daily Press* said in 1942: 'I suppose thousands of women would rather wear nurses' uniforms than the blue or khaki of the Services, feeling their abilities more in line with those of Florence Nightingale and Edith Cavell than those of the girls serving splendidly on gun sites'. Those not qualified as nurses could still serve by doing domestic work in hospitals – some 60,000 women were doing this in 1942, although a large number were women with families working part time. Full-time workers were counted as being in an essential occupation and were not transferred to other forms of work.[22]

Nursing in wartime can be summed up in the experiences of two former pupils of the Blyth School in Norwich, Margaret Moore and Mary Huntly, as described by

21   *Ann Turner and other girls working on the land at Stanhoe in north-west Norfolk.*

them in the school magazine. Margaret became a nurse in London before the war and found herself caught up in wartime conditions:

> On 7 September 1940, we were sent from Edmonton, where our hospital is situated, to an Emergency Hospital, and it was there that we had our first experience of air raid casualties. It was a time that I shall never forget, and I shall have an everlasting admiration for the homeless, injured people whom we nursed in this hospital. We day nurses were due off duty at 8 pm, but many of us worked until 2 am, helping the night nurses. The most serious cases were rushed to the theatre, and others were dealt with in the ward.

Like many nurses she volunteered to work overseas, in her case travelling to the Far East. She described her experiences as a nurse in Bombay during the monsoon season: 'Both the staff and the patients had an extremely wet time, and very often we plodded from tent to tent up to our knees in water and mud.'

Mary Huntly was with the British Army in France in 1940. The German offensive began in May:

> Air raid sirens wailed continuously; convoys of wounded were rushed in for treatment and through to Boulogne; troop trains and munition wagons were passing through by day and night; and refugees fled through in their thousands.
>
> On 21 May, we were ordered to pack hand cases ready to leave for England, as apparently we were being wedged in by the advancing enemy from the north, east and south. All our officers and men left the camp that day after destroying all the tents, equipment, and our personal property, but they worked among the wounded in Boulogne until it was captured.

Later she worked in North Africa, helping the wounded and sick men of the Eighth Army.[23]

22   *Women's Voluntary Service van, Fakenham.*

These were all full-time opportunities. Many, especially married women, wanted to help defend their country, but not in a full-time capacity. As early as 1938, Lady Reading founded the Women's Voluntary Service for Civil Defence (the last part of the title was soon dropped, the word 'Royal' was to be added later). It began with just five members: there were well over 300,000 by the time that war broke out, and a million by 1941. Apart from 200 full-time officials running the administration, these women were entirely unpaid. Their green uniform became a familiar sight as they helped out on the Home Front. They played key roles in organising groups of evacuees, running rest centres for the bombed-out, arranging supplies of comforts to the forces and in other traditional female support roles. These activities were not without risk: 241 members of the WVS died in the course of duty.

Lady Reading visited Norwich in 1942. The local press was enthusiastic, commenting: 'Whether it is canteens or cotton that are wanted it is to the WVS that the authorities turn, and never in vain. Its members drive ambulances, serve in canteens and British Restaurants, make woollen comforts for the troops, look after the homeless in rest centres, care for evacuated children and generally make themselves the indispensable maid-of-all-work to the nation at war.'[24]

The WVS also set up nursing centres and War Nurseries, to enable women with babies and young children to go to work. Mothers were encouraged to feel that bringing up children was in itself an essential task – but wherever possible it was hoped that one mother, perhaps the least able to do heavy work, could look after the children of neighbours to free the latter for war related work.

Three

Over Here – The Americans in Norfolk

There were men of many nations in Norfolk during the war, and these gave the county a character that was different from many other parts of Britain. Sally Hamond visited a north Norfolk pub in 1941:

> On Saturday night I went dancing at the *Quisling Arms* (a hotel so called because none of its inhabitants can speak English!), with Herbert & some others. It was great fun & I enjoyed it very much. I saw Canadian, Norwegian, Netherland & Czech uniforms & there were many more civilians – the queerest lot you can imagine. We had great fun guessing who they were![1]

Britain went to war in 1939 to defend Poland, which Hitler had invaded. In the short term, however, this was not a practical possibility: the country was so far away and aeroplanes then had a much shorter range than they were to develop during the war. Poland was conquered and most of its forces surrendered. However, some of its airmen were able to get away and to continue the fight from Britain. A number came to Norfolk.

There were also a large number of airmen in Norfolk from the Commonwealth countries – Canada, Australia, New Zealand and South Africa. The New Zealand men took part in a tragic event:

> One of the most disastrous raids to be carried out from Norfolk was that of no 487 RNZAF Squadron operating from Methwold on 3 May 1943. 12 Venturas set out to attack an Amsterdam power station but during the course of the action, 11 were shot down, and the wing leader, Wing Commander L H Trent, taken prisoner. For this attack he was later awarded the Victoria Cross.[2]

By far the largest group of foreigners in Norfolk for the last three years of the war was that of the American Army Air Force. Germany declared war on the United States in December 1941. America, working together with British forces, naturally used Britain as a base from which to bomb its enemy – and later from which to invade. Norfolk was one of the areas to feel most strongly the impact of this new phase of the war. The 2nd Air Division of the United States Army Air Force arrived in Norfolk on 7 September 1942. Its first mission from England was undertaken on 7 November 1942. Headquarters soon moved to Horsham St Faith and in December 1943 to Ketteringham Hall. It was to remain there until the end of the war. At its maximum, the strength of the 2nd Air Division was well over 50,000 officers and men. This remains the largest air strike force ever committed to battle.

23   *American bombers over the Larkman estate, Norwich.*

The bases eventually covered 100,000 acres of Norfolk: each base might cover 500 acres and house two or three thousand Americans. At any one time between 1942 and 1945 there were about 50,000 American personnel within a 30-mile radius of Norwich. The American approach seemed a casual one to old military hands in Britain. One woman remembered her father who had been in the British army in the First World War: 'He was very disparaging when he saw them marching through our village street, their hands in their pockets, chewing gum. "What a shower. They can't march to save their lives! How will they be able to fight?"'[3]

The Division has a rich archive held in the Norfolk Record Office, which includes impressions of the county by these new allies. Some original letters home have survived in the collection. Here we take just two examples.

Lt Ronald Neumunz wrote a series of letters to his 'dearest Babs', Barbara Doniger of Grantwood, New Jersey in August and September 1944. Some extracts read:

> For the first time I tried a few English beers, worthless that they are – so all the about [*sic*] is just so much stuff to hide one's melancholy sentimental mood. It is you, not the future generations as I've been told, that I'm so called fighting this war. By the way I won $200 at the crap table which is being put away for Junior – I love you madly.
>
> As for me I'm dirty as all of us are. No showers for over a week. Egad – this rugged living – to top it off all my clothes are wet and I'm about to die of a cold.

At present we're really sweating the war out at least in the ETO. Our only news
is gotten from 'Stars and Stripes', the army newspaper, which arrives a day late, and
occasional flashes via the radio. Every night we hope fervently that by the next day
we'll be in Berlin. That plus my Yankees fight for the pennant is causing me terrific
mental turmoil. I'm bragging now! Also the crap games give one headaches. However
they're classified as athletic periods. I told you I'm a little ahead. That money has
been preserved, in fact my aim is $750 by the New Year which will give me close to
$2000 for school and the kiddies. Already I'm worth fortunes so with God's help and
a short war we might not have to wait until you're old and fat.

I always start writing these things with nothing in mind to tell and usually
accomplish just that. However I will merrily continue with lots of nonsense. First
about women on this side of the ocean with whom contact has been practically
negligible.

They're good for chuckles and shocks – by shocks I refer only to my innocent and
well harbored nature. Anyway no subject is barred from the conversation. If you
wish for some love – the question is asked and answered in the plainest of language
and no one's feelings are hurt. It's quite amazing and the price is absurdedly high, up
to ten pounds, and what hurts is that many come across. As for me I'm still waiting
for the real thing. What a delicate subject!!

We live in a small shack that is overcrowded. The rain leaks through the roof, the
beds are hard like stone. Bicycles are the main mode of transportation, that is except
for feet. We walk or ride miles to reach anything including bathroom facilities. Thus
the musty odor of the barracks gives the impression of a pig pen. But it's home and
there's … Beans! I strictly want the facilities of a fifth avenue duplex perfumed baths
and several attractive maids. Ah![4]

In summer and autumn 1944, another American, *Lt Rodney Ives*, was writing home to
his mother, Mrs Carol Ives of Centralia, Washington:

I've seen quite a bit of England so far but I haven't hit any big towns like London
as yet. I'm not supposed to voice any opinions about the English people but the
countryside is a lot like the New England States and in most towns the population
is very crowded – with many tenement sections. All of the richer people live in large
country homes. There doesn't seem to be much of a middle class here – either rich or
poor. There are plenty of pubs (bars) and I'm getting so I like their warm beer – no

24 *Wendling airbase in snow. The 392nd Bomb Group flew over 8,000 sorties from the airbase.*

25 *Debriefing after a bombing mission. At one period the chance of an American airmen completing his tour of 25 missions was just one in three.*

hard liquor. There are no nite clubs except in London which has become somewhat Americanised – at least that's what I've been told.

Our quarters are Nissen huts at this station but they're pretty comfortable in spite of their looks. The food is excellent and we have plenty of laughs with Captain Yak around. I guess I've never told you about him. He was with us at Conopah and Mountain Home and he brought an instructor crew over with us. He used to be a college football player – a great big hunk – but plenty intelligent. He's a typical college Joe and he can really keep you laughing.

(England, Nov 20 1944). I'm thinking about volunteering for some special duties over here so I'll give you the set-up and you let me know what you think.

After our tour is completed we have the opportunity to sign up for some training which would fit us for the job of disarming and demobilizing the German Air Force. It is like the army of occupation but yet wholly different because it would be our job, as each airfield was captured, to go in and clean things up as administrations etc are concerned … of course I can do nothing until I finish my tour so you let me know what you think … I'll probably not be able to mail this until I get back to camp so it may take some time. Love, Rod.[5]

Rod Ives was never to hear what his parents thought of his plans. The letter is postmarked 26 November 1944: he was killed that same day.

Many other American airmen have memories of their time in Norfolk. Rudolph Birsic recalled the first impressions of Tibenham on the arrival of the 445th Bombardment Group (H) on 4 November 1944:

26   *USAAF nose art – 'Wild Hair'.*

> The various living and technical sites were nestled among the fields and pastures of farms and their accompanying thatch roof huts. Cows were pastured behind the hospital, and there was a sugar beet field behind the flying officers' living site. The road leading to the ground officers' living site wound around a rather filthy barn which reeked of various farm smells and from out of which big-eyed cows stared in dumb amazement at the American officers who were intruding on their former peaceful farmland.[6]

27   *USAAF nose art – 'Hazee'.*

Another American in exile, John Truluck, became obsessed with recreating American-style ice cream. His account reveals some things the Americans missed during their stay in England:

> Ice cream had always been my favorite dessert and I could eat a pint at any time. About three months after I had arrived in England, the news went around that we would have ice cream for dessert … In all my life I have never tasted such peculiar food. In the late summer of 1943 I decided I had gone without ice cream long enough and started to make an ice cream churn … Ice was seldom seen in England and our mess officers had some trouble locating some for me. Milk in England was not pasteurized and we were not permitted to drink it so we had to use evaporated and powdered milk. All problems were solved and early one evening I served pineapple ice cream to all of the squadron officers. Fresh fruits and flavoring were hard to find and pineapple was the only canned fruit that would make good ice cream.[7]

The first impressions of Elwin Cross were not favourable. His group first arrived in England on Thanksgiving Day. Hoping for a turkey dinner, they were given spam sandwiches! On arriving at Tibenham: 'It seemed as if it was always raining and there was always mud and it was always cold, and we had plenty to gripe about' – but, as he generously admitted, 'it wasn't really all that bad.'[8]

28 *Sergeant John Dickinson of the United States Army Air Force, killed in action 21 January 1944.*

29 *James Stewart at Tibenham, the base from which the 445th Bomb group operated between December 1943 and April 1945.*

There were some famous names among the Americans, serving their country in war. The actor James Stewart came to Tibenham in November 1943 with the 445th Bomb Group. Another Hollywood actor, James Cagney, was also in the county. Cross was given a briefing by someone who seemed familiar, to be told it was indeed Stewart. Cross was later very impressed by Stewart's leadership: 'What a great leader Mr Stewart was and is. I never heard anyone say anything bad about him. He did not ask us to do anything that he would not himself do. He was truly a great leader and I am glad to have served in his squadron.'[9]

Few of the Americans had ever left their home country before. They were issued with booklets offering advice about England and the English:

30 *Stewart in determined pose. Another Hollywood actor on duty in Norfolk was James Cagney.*

SOME IMPORTANT DO'S AND DON'TS

BE FRIENDLY – but don't intrude anywhere it seems you are not wanted. You will find the British money system easier than you think. A little study beforehand on shipboard will make it still easier.

You are paid higher than the British 'Tommy'. Don't rub it in. Play fair with him. He can be a pal in need.

Don't show off or brag or bluster – 'swank' as the British say. If someone looks in your direction and says 'He's chucking his weight about', you can be pretty sure you're off base. That's the time to pull in your ears.

If you are invited to eat with a family don't eat too much. Otherwise you may eat up their weekly rations.

Don't make fun of British speech or accents. You sound just as funny to them but they will be too polite to show it.

Avoid comments on the British government or politics.

Don't try to tell the British that America won the last war or make wisecracks about the war debts or about British defeats in this war.

NEVER criticise the King or Queen.

Don't criticise the food, beer, or cigarettes to the British. Remember they have been at war since 1939.

Use commonsense on all occasions. By your conduct you have great power to bring about a better understanding between the two countries after the war is over.

You will soon find yourself among a kindly, quiet, hard-working people who have been living under a strain such as few people in the world have ever known. In your dealings with them, let this be your slogan:

It is always impolite to criticise your hosts;
It is militarily stupid to criticise your allies.[10]

A guide to Norwich for the Americans prepared them for the difficulties of shopping – and explained the English Sunday:

> Norwich offers a variety of interesting shops for the purchase of everyday goods to exquisite antiques. The general hours of opening are from 9 am to 5 pm, although in the summer a few keep open a little later. On Thursday they close at 1 pm.
>   Most food, all civilian clothes (except hats), boots and shoes, soap (except shaving soap and dentrifices) or candies cannot be bought without coupons.
>   As a Cathedral City, Norwich observes the typical British Sunday. A few restaurants open, and most of the cinemas give an early evening performance. The Theatre and Hippodrome remain closed. At the YMCA in St Giles a free concert is given every Sunday evening at 7.30. Service Clubs are, of course always open.[11]

The American soldiers brought with them the concept of racial segregation. At first Eisenhower wanted black GIs to operate in those parts of Britain where there was already a black community, but many were needed in East Anglia to build and supply the airfields there. Black and white personnel would be given leave passes on different nights. Sometimes whole towns were reserved for black GIs, such as Diss.

Black personnel rarely became pilots: in fact it took a court case before training facilities were made available to them. Some prominent black figures did serve in the American forces including the world heavyweight championship boxer, Joe Louis. On one occasion he and some friends wanted to see a film in a cinema in Britain: a special 'black section' was hastily roped off for them. Norfolk people have memories of Louis in this county, too. Mr Bradstreet, of the Morley Home Guard, recalled that he often met American airmen in the local pub: 'One night, I was at the *Buck*, when Joe Louis, the world heavyweight boxing champion, appeared. But he would not come into the bar because he didn't want to cause offence to any southern Yanks who might be in there!'[12]

Rachel Dhonau's diary records both sides of the race issue. In August 1943, a woman with whom she got into conversation on a train told Rachel she knew they (black servicemen) were fighting for us but she couldn't help shuddering every time she went near one. However, in the following month her diary records an incident in Norwich where some American soldiers refused to eat in the same restaurant as black soldiers: 'A Norwich woman stood up and said that if they were good enough to fight they were good enough to mix with.'[13]

There were few black people in Britain before the war, and very few in Norfolk. For many people, contact with a serviceman was their first association with a black person. One Hackney evacuee in Lynn recalls an occasion when, from round the corner, line abreast across the whole pavement, came a group of laughing American servicemen:

Americans in uniform were a very common all over East Anglia in the second half of the war, but these men were giants and they were coal-black. I had never before seen a black person and was struck dumb with fear. My only knowledge of black men came from films and comic strips, where they were pictured as brutal savages, whose principal object in life was to capture white people and boil them in a cooking pot for their dinner. I'm afraid I turned and ran away. However, black Americans became quite common, and we all got used to them eventually.[14]

Dorothy Calvert in the ATS had a similar experience, when hitching a lift from an army lorry in the fog:

Then it loomed into view, just giving us enough time to nip clear. It pulled up, and we saw that it was an American lorry, being driven by, and the back was almost full of, black Americans. Now that was quite a tricky situation. We had been told many times on the sites not to accept a lift from anybody at all, and from black men, well that would have been a crime indeed. Which was rather less than cricket, as what difference did the colour of a man's skin make? Men were either nice or rotten swine, whatever colour they were, and I think now it was laughable, as the black lads were the least likely to assault us. (I can say that from experience.) And what gave the white people the idea they were superior I'll never know, as we were all conceived the same, and we will all face the same GOD when the day of reckoning comes.[15]

The Americans were paid far more money than their British equivalents: in 1942, a British private earned 14 shillings a week, an American private almost five times as much. Many of them took to the local entertainment scene, although others preferred to stay on their own bases. The most popular venues in Norwich were the dance halls – the *Sampson and Hercules* on Tombland and the *Lido* on Magdalen Road. The former had a theoretical limit of 1,000 people at a time, but of course this was impossible to enforce rigidly. A popular venue for jazz was the *Jolly Butchers* on Ber Street, where the music was led by 'Black Anna' (the nickname referring to her dress). She was still providing jazz in the pub thirty years after the war had ended, and is remembered fondly by many Norwich people.[16]

Another favourite pub for the Americans was the *Cat and Fiddle* on Magdalen Street. This was much used by men based at Horsham – they could walk home afterwards if necessary. William Jameson recalled that the pub was run by a couple named Matthews. Their four-year-old granddaughter was often in the pub and became quite a pet of the servicemen: in 1944, she was given an American rag doll for Christmas. English licensing hours were a source of confusion. Jordan Utall was one of a group from Hethel who cycled into Norwich in search of beer: 'Due to your very odd licensing hours, the pubs were closed and there were no drinks to be had, so we settled for tea at the *Maid's Head* of all places – tea and the brave little sandwiches and biscuits.'

Glenn Matson was based at Horsham and he recalled that it was possible to leave the base by a path through the woods at the back, thus avoiding the sentries: this was nicknamed the Burma Road. His favourite leisure activities were drinking at the *Castle Hotel*, watching vaudeville at the *Hippodrome* and seeing movies at the *Odeon*.[17]

Country boys among the servicemen favoured more rural pursuits in their leisure hours. Leon Moquin from New England enjoyed cycling in the country and sailing on the Broads in a rented sailboat. When Matson was cycling through the country, he came across a stream that reminded him irresistibly of his childhood days, skinny-dipping in similar streams in Minnesota. He stripped and plunged into the stream naked, only to be surprised a few minutes later by an English couple in a canoe. As he hid his modesty under the water, they greeted him with a phrase forever to be associated with Americans in the English mind – 'Have a nice day!'[18]

Service personnel were eager to contribute to civilian functions, not only by attending, but also by organising and assisting whenever possible. They were also very keen for civilians to take part in their activities. Very many families accepted servicemen into their homes and in doing so created a better understanding between them. Since there was such a large number of Allied servicemen in Norfolk this also did much to help international relations. Some of these friendships were so strong that the servicemen – including several Americans – returned to Norfolk to settle down after the war.[19]

An English teenager, Sybil Neale, recalled the arrival of the 'Yanks' in 1942:

> Soon the city filled with trucks and 'men on leave'. Best remembered as the 'Liberty Run'. 5 April 1943 the 56th moved to St Faiths Airdrome. 9 May 1943 the Officers gave the men a dance party at a local Dance Hall called 'The Lido'. This was a 62nd Squadron Party. John 'Red Dog' Woods and my girlfriend Connie had been dating since the Group moved to St Faiths Airdrome. Red asked Connie to come to the party that night, and I went with her. In the middle of the dance, the Air Raid sirens sounded and I had to leave my blind date Billy Billings and run to my Depot. It was over a month later before we saw one another again.[20]

Love triumphed in the end: Sybil and Billy married on 17 June 1944 and moved to the United States after the war was over. She was just one of many Norfolk girls to marry American airmen. One airman, Philip Litwin, met an English land girl named Dot and proposed on their third date. Another, Louis Bargout, when invited to tea

31 *American servicemen try their hand at cricket. One of the men has written on the back of the photograph, 'Having a ruddy go on the playing fields of Shipdham'.*

32   *Norwich City football ground at Carrow Road was used by the Americans for a rodeo show on 1 August 1943.*

with the parents of his new girlfriend, Marjorie, presented them with a salami. They had no idea what to do with it and after a couple of days gave it to Marjorie's uncle George who fed it to his chickens: even they would not eat it and the salami was eventually consigned to the dustbin.

At the end of the war, some 70,000 English brides were waiting to travel to America to join their ex-GI husbands. Dot joined Philip and settled down in Pennsylvania. Marjorie had more problems in settling down in America: Louis was from a Syrian family and had been brought up by his grandmother who cooked Syrian food and spoke only Arabic. Despite the problems, Marjorie eventually settled, and in 1984 she told a newspaper that she would never have been happy staying in Norfolk.[21]

The Americans did not have the British system of total registration of women for the war effort, but they did have a Women's Auxiliary Army Corps, set up when the war broke out in December 1941. The Women's Army Corps was formed in 1943 and the WAACs were merged into it. At the peak of the war there were over 200,000 American women in uniform: about 10,000 served abroad, including at the airfields in Norfolk, where they almost invariably undertook clerical duties. However, they were always a relatively small group: there were about 200 American servicewomen in Norfolk at any one time.

Sally Reston wrote an article about them for the *New York Times*:

Most WACs here are doing clerical and communications jobs, though each company
has its own kitchen staff as well. There were some problems at first in learning the
tricks of the keyboard on English typewriters, and telephone operators were sent to
school for a week so that they could familiarize themselves with the king's English,
and, for instance, learn that the English telephonist was connecting them with their
party and not cutting them off when she said, 'You're through'.... On the whole,
General Somervell's Services of Supply have done a good job in transportation
across the Atlantic of such things as fingernail polish, face powder, lipstick and other
things which women expect but which the War Department never thought it would
have to worry about before this war. So far, General Somervell has not figured a way
for his WACs to get permanent waves at a post exchange, and that is a problem in a
country where most hairdressers have been called up for more essential war work.[22]

Mary Frances Elder enjoyed the food served at her base in Norfolk, but she did not
appreciate the English monetary system, writing back to her family:

The first night we got here we had french fried potatoes and pork chops. What a
reception. Since then we've had the best food I've had since I left home. For instance,
yesterday we had meat loaf, sweet potatoes candied, cabbage slaw, raisin bread —

33   *Rodeo at Carrow Road: very few football matches were played during the war, as the length of the grass suggests.*

34 *Members of the American Women's Army Corp at work on a US base in Norfolk.*

gravy, canned peaches and coffee for lunch. For dinner we had pork roast and believe me it was good. I've never eaten such food, in all the time I've been in the Army.

Are we having a time with the English money. I wonder who in the world ever thought up such a complicated system. It is rather hard to get accustomed to thinking in pence, shillings, half-crowns, crowns, pounds etc. But the boys say that after [a] while you get so you don't even think of American money. You should see the pennies. They are as large as a half-dollar, only they are copper. The half crown is also the size of a half-dollar but it is silver, you have to look to see which is which.[23]

The Americans were here for a serious purpose: to bring the war to an end by bombing the enemy until they could not continue the struggle. The pilots were the elite – Utall Jordan recalled that for every person who flew, there were ten support staff on the ground.

Missions could involve much loss of life. To take just one of many incidents, on 21 January 1944, planes of the 44th Bomb Group attacked military installations at Escalles-sur-Buchy. Five planes were lost over France and a sixth crash-landed in Kent. Most of the crew of the planes were killed, including Sergeant John Dickinson: others were captured by the Germans. A few men were lucky: they were found by members of the French Resistance and managed to evade capture and eventually return to England. One, Sergeant Reeves, was taken south to Paris and then travelled

35 *WACs and soldiers relax at Ketteringham Hall, the HQ of the American 2nd Air Division.*

36 *A Norfolk girl marries an American serviceman: over 70,000 English girls went to the United States with their new husbands after the war.*

37 *An unidentified 'GI Bride': few English couples could afford a full-scale wedding and wedding dress during the war.*

by train and bus to southern France and cross the Pyrenees into neutral Spain: his guide deserted him in the mountains and Reeves almost died in the snow, but eventually reached safety.[24]

Codes of conduct could develop between airmen of opposing countries. Elwin Cross recalled a mission over Germany in April 1944. Bombers were normally protected by fighters, but on this occasion these disappeared in a cloud bank and German fighters seized the opportunity to attack the bombers: 'I could see the plane on my left wing was on fire, his engines were burning and I saw the tail turret shot off by enemy fighters. This particular plane then lowered its landing gear which was a signal to enemy fighters that they were going to bail out. The enemy fighters did not make any more attacks upon that plane and we saw a few parachutes from the members that were able to jump out.'[25]

In just 30 months of operational work, over 1,500 American planes based in East Anglia were lost. Almost 7,000 US service personnel were killed. Many of them lie together in a cemetery at Madingley outside Cambridge. Their Norfolk memorial is the 2nd Air Division Memorial Library. The first library was destroyed in a fire in August 1994, but it has been replaced on a larger scale within the Millennium Library in Norwich. This collects books covering all aspects of American life and keeps alive the close contact between Norfolk and America which began during those dark days of war. It also has an important educational role in making the young people of the county aware of the American contribution during the war.

Four

Prisoners of War

As in any war, some members of the armed forces on each side became prisoners. The experience of these people was a varied one: some suffered mainly from tedium, others were to die of their treatment.

Germany

Geoffrey Ransom of Holt has left a fascinating series of letters from his years as a prisoner of war. The son of Frederick and Beatrice Ransom of Holt, he was in the RAF: he had been with the British Expeditionary Force in Calais in 1940 when he was captured. His letters home begin with an acknowledgement of a parcel received on 18 October 1940, of another parcel containing Bible, New Testament, Shakespeare and playing cards, received on 8 December, and a parcel containing vitamin C tablets on 11 December. An officially approved postcard of men playing quoits was sent home by him on 10 June 1941.

He was held at first in Lauffen (which he spells Laufen), but by the time that the first letters came home he had been moved to Colditz:

> 10 Aug 41: Very pleased to hear from you. I'm still very fit and cheerful. I've been here more than 3 weeks now and have not regretted it once. The atmosphere is quite different. Laufen was very highly organised, but here by comparison you can do as you like. For instance 8 am and 9 pm are parades and if you feel like it you turn up in pyjamas. The numbers in the camp are about 230 French and Belgians, 140 Poles, 65 Dutch and now there are 59 of us (20 have come in since me). The season is in full swing. There are 3 or 4 Majors here I'm rather sorry for. Laufen since March suited them very well. All was quiet, orderly and tidy. Here the average age is about 25. No one wants quietness, order or peace and that does not seem to go down well with people when they get over 45. In our (British) quarter we've a piano, gramophone, 2 trumpets, several guitars. All we want is some bagpipes to cap it all. On Saturday we had a party with 50 guests. It was a great success. Cheerio and good luck.

The Red Cross Society wrote to Ransom's sister at Havelock Road in Norwich:

> Thank you for your letter of 3 September informing us of your brother's transfer from Oflag VII C/H to Oflag IVC. This camp is situated at Colditz which is half way between Dresden and Weimar and slightly north of a line drawn between the two. This is a camp to which Officers who have attempted to escape have been sent, but there is absolutely no reason to suppose that your brother will come in for any

ill-treatment. The camp is more closely guarded than Oflag VIIC and it is very much smaller, there being only 40-50 British Officers and Men. There are also prisoners of war of other nationalities interned at this camp – French, Belgian and Polish, and you will be glad to know that the British write most cheerfully from there.

We are glad to be able to tell you that during the first half of August, from 1 August-15, 154 food parcels were received at Oflag IVC. 127 of these were packed in Canada, and from letters which we have read we gather that these food parcels are extremely popular.

We think that your letters and parcels addressed to Oflag VII C/H will be forwarded to your brother. We cannot of course guarantee this but in most cases the camp authorities have been very good about it.

We hope that it will not be long before you hear from your brother again and that he will give you a good report of the conditions.

38 *'Curling' – a postcard sent from Colditz prisoner-of-war camp by Geoffrey Ransom to his parents in Holt.*

39   *Colditz – exercise in winter.*

Ransom's letters home were deliberately upbeat:

15/9/41: Here's a card for you Dad. Many happy returns! I know you're not well again yet, but I'm sure you'll be your cheerful self however annoying things may be. Mother says you're apt to be a little depressed occasionally but in the main you're very cheerful. That's what I like to hear! Keep it up! Of the people who've been badly wounded, I've only known one depressed about it. All the others, who may have lost an arm or been otherwise wounded, are as high spirited as us others. Everyone has their ups and downs – we're only human, but I'm mighty proud to be able to think and know that you're able to laugh at your misfortunes. That's the way to treat life, I'm convinced – it's infectious too.

The family were continuing to send parcels to Ransom, but in August 1942 they were told they could no longer do so. Muriel Bromley-Davenport of the POW Department of the Red Cross and Order of St John wrote to Miss Ransom:

I am just writing to let you know that we have forwarded your parcel to your cousin, and I hope he will receive this one safely.

At the same time, I must tell you that our regulations with regard to these special parcels have become much more strict recently, and we are now able to send them only in cases of severe ill-health, or wounds, or on the recommendation of the Senior Medical Officer of the camp.

Since this new regulation came into force however, we have been sending much larger bulk supplies of tonics, remedies and invalid foods to all the camps and hospitals where there are known to be British prisoners of war.

I think therefore that your cousin should be able to obtain whatever he may be needing in this connection by approaching his Senior RAMC Officer, who is in charge of the reserve stores.

I hope that you are getting reassuring news from 2/Lt Ransom and that he is busy with his Library. He does sound as though he were a person of many interests, and this must make all the difference in the world to his peace of mind, even when things are very difficult.

Ransom's flow of letters home continued through 1942 and the following years:

20/12/42: We're getting ready for Xmas. We've made some paper flags of all the countries who are fighting or who are organising themselves to fight and beat Nazi Germany. So far we've 46 flags up and with streamers round them they make a colourful setting. The news is the best Xmas present we could have and I think we'll be home between August and October next.

31/10/43: A number of people still think the war may end this year – I personally think May or June next year is most likely. I've had notification that I've been a full lieutenant for the last 18 months or so strange to be promoted as a P.O.W. One's pay here goes up by 9 marks a month to 81 marks – for what its worth. Like most people

40   *Christmas at Colditz. By April 1945, there were over a quarter million British and American prisoners of war in Germany.*

I've got over 1,000 of the things in my pocket I don't know what to do with! All's well with me – I'm lucky that in the last 3½ years I haven't spent a day in bed.

These letters and cards had to pass the German censor, of course. One card attracted his attention, but rather than scrawl through the text he has merely stuck white paper over the text: it can be read by holding it up to the light! The censored parts have been put into italics:

27/1/44: *I judge from the tone of your letter that you agree with me that the war will be won this year. There's no doubt about it. We'll get that late holiday in September. So get the tent pegs ready! How could we be other than in good spirits.* The Red X shop sounds a fine effort! Expect you're looking forward to when folks start spring cleaning. You'll get plenty to sell then. You want to put a placard up – 'Remember Its Spring Cleaning Time'. Two more *months and your garden will have reached its peak again. I'll have to wait another year to see it. What about my finishing that lawn and planting the whole with proper seeds.* Love to all.

News of D-Day brought a new level of optimism. On 30 July 1944, Ransom wrote home: 'It looks as if I'll be following hard on the heels of this card. And a very agreeable thought it is too. I'm backing the first fortnight in October, but I'm beginning to feel that may be a bit later'. On 29 September he was still optimistic: 'if the post maintains its new turn of speed you'll get this before I arrive home, but I don't think it will be more than a month ahead'. By the end of October he was becoming resigned to the fact that the war was taking longer than he had hoped, but he was still cheerful, at least in his letters home: 'It looks as if we may have another Xmas here, which we didn't expect, but it will be the last all right this time!! And there will be a lot to be said for getting back in the spring, with the larks singing exactly as they were when I left, and that camping cum sailing holiday I've hoped for may yet come off, with weather like May 1940.'

Tomorrow is Xmas Eve (1944), and there is great activity in the cooking line. We are again lucky on our table in having Jerry Hill who is a professional hotel man who has spent 3 or 4 years in ritzy hotel kitchens in England, Paris, Rome, Prague and elsewhere and he has taken on all our troubles and produced two enormous iced cakes, and all sorts of things we've been saving up a month for. By Jove we're going to be full. Your letter arrived saying you had heard from Barnet – it seems strange that he was here only a few months ago – I wonder what he said. This is another day, Xmas Eve, and I've just had breakfast – I wonder what you are doing. Being a Sunday there is a service this morning, a Methodist one this time, by Padre Platt. This evening is a carol service and a Church of England one tomorrow. Then tomorrow is a pantomime at 5.30 and Xmas dinner at 8.45. Boxing Day there is a whist drive which we're having mainly for the benefit of the orderlies. I've volunteered to take charge of all washing up and table scrubbing for the three days – I'm happy so long as I can keep clear of the cooking.

31/1/45: We are in a highly optimistic state and it looks as though I shall see those daffodils of yours this year … Needless to say, I'm rather impatient, but the cause is beautifully reflected in the German communiqué each day. Enough parcels have arrived to see us comfortably through to the end of next month which I feel will be in a week or so of the end of the war – either way. We shall be getting back with all

41 *British airmen at Colditz. The prisoners were finally freed on 16 April 1945 when the Castle was liberated by the Americans.*

the good weather in front of us, be with you all again, bloaters and eggs for breakfast – in fact a return to paradise. My love to you all, keep your chins up – not long now.

Many people tried to help. A friend in Rugby wrote to Mrs Ransom in Holt:

> This week past an article appeared in the Free Dutch paper, which I take, telling the story of a Dutch officer who escaped from a prison camp in Germany. We think it must be the one connected with Geoffrey. He escaped from the heart of Germany with only chocolate and the equivalent of £1 in Dutch money. A long way to go for £1 – cheap travelling I should have thought. He mingled with civilians in towns trains and buses, in some of which he had very narrow escapes for want of tickets. Any more news from Geoffrey? He's best staying where he is now – it may not be so very long for him to wait –the Russians press on – God be with them.

The War Office was also aware of the situation, writing to Mrs Ransom in September 1942:

> I am directed to inform you an officer who was recently in Oflag IVC and has managed to reach this country has offered to communicate with a certain number of the relatives of officer prisoners of war in that camp.
> The further movements of this officer are somewhat uncertain but if you would care to be put in touch with him perhaps you would be good enough to notify this Department, so that your address may be forwarded.[1]

When working on local sources for my book on Norfolk in the First World War, I noticed that, although men were often introspective and depressed in entries in private diaries, they are almost invariably much more chirpy when writing to their loved ones at home. We will never know to what extent Ransom's cheerful letters hid private gloom and despair as the war dragged on, leaving him a prisoner in Nazi Germany for month after month. However, he was lucky: liberation did come and he was able to return to Britain and to resume his career as an architect.

Many planes involved in missions from Norfolk were shot down over occupied territory. Wherever possible the pilot would come down in allied territory, or failing that in a neutral country such as Sweden or Switzerland, where the airmen would be interned until the war was over. If one came down in an occupied country like France, Belgium or Holland, there was a reasonable chance of escaping: sympathetic natives would often help an Allied airmen, in many cases risking their own lives to do so.

However, for many there was no choice but to crash-land or bale out over Germany itself. To have one's surrender accepted there was not always automatic, especially after heavy Allied bombing raids had devastated German cities. There are quite a few cases of captured airmen being beaten to death by German citizens or shot by local minor officials even after they had surrendered. Some of these civilians were themselves tracked down after the war and hanged or sent to prison. Here I look at two incidents that illustrate the mixture of brutality and humanity that make up life in wartime.

Odell Dobson was just one of many Americans forced to land in Germany. He was wounded in both legs. Some local villagers saw him come down: they took him by cart to the nearest small town where he was locked up in the one cell they had. He was lucky: he was taken to a German military hospital for treatment. One of the men working there was even prepared to help Dobson escape: he could hide in the man's cellar except when it was being used in air raids, when he would have to go up into the man's house and take his chances. Dobson discussed the plan with his colonel who advised against: the German would be risking having himself and his family shot, and besides the war would soon be over. Dobson agreed and went into a prisoner of war camp only to face the horror soon after of the Long March. This was when the Germans forced all prisoners of war in camps likely to be overrun by the advancing Russian army to march back into the heart of Germany. These men included many from both the RAF and USAAF who had taken off from bases in Norfolk. Dobson was forced to march for 87 days, covering well over 600 miles and cursing his colonel all the way. At least he survived – for many the journey was too much and they fell behind to die of exhaustion, or even be shot by SS guards. In later years he returned to see the man who had offered to help him: his house had been bombed and several members of his family killed, so perhaps Dobson made the right choice.[2]

The other incident relates to a plane from Hethel, which crashed at Bierstadt in October 1944. Three men baled out: one was soon caught and taken to the Rathaus in Niederhausen. Two German policemen went by truck to bring in the other two. One of the Germans, Willi Crist, wanted to shoot the airmen, saying, 'You don't know what the cities look like, where women and children have burned to death, lying on the rubble and around the streets'. When they got back to the Rathaus, they found that the prisoner already there had been given two cups of tea by Margaret Dulin, a German girl who lived close by. The Chief of Police, Herr Schauer, stormed round to Margaret's house and shouted at her: 'What, you being a good German girl, and bringing tea to an American officer. What do you think if our Kreisleiter should hear that? You should be shot!' Dulin's uncle pointed out that the men were prisoners of war: Schauer said that he had men ready to shoot the airmen. The three men were indeed killed. After the war, Crist, Schauer and another man received prison sentences for their crime.[3]

Italy

Many British soldiers were captured by Italians rather than by Germans in the early years of the Desert War in North Africa. Trooper Gordon Lee of the Royal Tank Regiment was captured in Libya in June 1942 and sent to prisoner of war camps in Italy, originally at Modena and later at Macerata. He was there in September 1943 when the Italians agreed an Armistice with the Allies:

> Immediately the camp guards became very friendly to us. I well recall dishes of fresh figs being handed out. I'd never tasted them before. After a few days many huge German troop transporters were seen flying south, they were obviously strengthening their lines and taking over the complete control of the country. This was a sign for the Italian guards to disappear to their homes and to avoid serving any longer with their late German partners. There were now no guards on the camp and we began to wonder how to make the best of this situation. We were certainly bewildered by the Senior British Officer issuing an order that anyone escaping would be put on a court martial charge when he returned to England! His idea was to prevent thousands of POWs from wandering around the countryside causing strife to the local inhabitants. It would be much easier to hand us all over in one block to the advancing Allies. But, as we later learned, they weren't advancing.

Eventually we four decided that now was the chance to go and there were probably a few hundred more who thought the same but the majority in the Camp preferred to wait and see. Two hours after we left, what we saw was the arrival of German troops who surrounded the Camp, fired shots into the air and took the place over. After several weeks the prisoners were taken to Germany to work in the mines, on the railways and had a rather rough time.

Lee and his three comrades decided to travel west into the Apennines and then south down the mountains to meet up eventually with the advancing Allies. They ate grapes and tomatoes as they walked that afternoon and slept at a farmhouse, where friendly Italians gave them bread and goat's milk. This was repeated many times as they travelled, although a few were less friendly: one villager called in a policeman. The man arrived by bicycle and failed to spot the four men who ducked down behind a hedge. Near Tresungo, one of the four badly cut his leg. They remained in huts on the hills above the village for nine months, looked after by Erbe Petrucci and his family. In the winter they lived in the family's hayloft.

Eventually we learned from the radio that the German forces were in retreat and we watched from our eyrie on the hillside overlooking the main road as they went northwards. It was surprising to see how many were on bicycles or in carts towed by horses or oxen. They had obviously stolen goods on their way and one day passed with a herd of cattle. To our amazement a lad popped out from behind a house, quickly separated one of them from its friends and disappeared with it round the back and out of sight. It was butchered the next day and we helped to eat it!

The flow of troops eventually came to a stop, the last of them blowing up bridges to make Allied progress more difficult and we judged it time to leave Tresungo, to contact the approaching forces and make our way home. It was a sad parting from all those friends who had taken care of us for all those months at great risk to themselves.

Lee returned to Tresungo with his family in 1982, 38 years after his adventures. The Petruccis had died and their children had moved on, but he met many locals who remembered him including the local barman.[4]

The Far East

In the Far East, those who died in battle were the lucky ones. The Japanese could not understand the concept of surrender. To them it was cowardly not to fight to the death. They treated prisoners with unbelievable brutality, using them as slave labour and all too often working them to death. A large number of Norfolk men worked on the infamous Siam-Burma Railway, and many of them died. The railway was a key factor in the Japanese attempt to advance into Burma and eventually India. Over 60,000 prisoners of war and over 300,000 native labourers worked night and day on the railway. The 'Railway of Death' finally opened in November 1943: each one of its 250 miles had cost the lives of 400 men.[5]

Getting one's surrender accepted by the Japanese was the first step. It was not always easy. At Singapore, Becket was beaten with canes by the Japanese soldiers:

I had a split lip and bloody weals for ages. We were ordered to take all our clothes off. They even snatched off my ID discs.

42 *Changi jail, Singapore. All the photographs of Changi in this book were taken by Russell Beckett, who was a prisoner of war in the jail.*

We were then made to go into an old coconut shed, where we were bound with our hands behind our backs, some other POWs were already lying there, some very wounded others looking pretty sick at the way things had turned out. The badly wounded were bayoneted to death and dragged out before our eyes, we wondered what was going to be our fate. We were not allowed to move so toilet relief took place as we sat on the earth floor. Dysentery broke out quickly, for three to four days we were given no rice or water, just the odd green coconut thrown in by the Japs. We were in an appalling state, my lips puffed right up due to no water. At one time we were lined up outside ... Jap machine gunners then came and got down in front of us about twenty yards away, loaded up their guns, we thought this is it some of the lads passed out. I stood with my hands behind my back and said God be with us. After a while they got up and herded us back to the hut, just degrading us all.[6]

The Norfolk Regimental Museum has a diary and other belongings of Corporal Lane of the 5th Norfolks. He was a prisoner of war at Changi. In September 1942, all the prisoners at Changi were told by their captors to sign an agreement not to escape. They refused and were herded together into a barracks courtyard at Selerang to be kept there until they would submit. The Colonel commanding the British and Australian troops at Changi finally told them to sign, in order to prevent them suffering further.

Eric Dack of Dereham was also in Changi:

Arriving at the crowded prison barracks we were crowded into a room with just enough space to lie down, I slept on the floor using my boots as a pillow with a rolled up cardigan in between ... it was not an uncommon sight to see POWs with a heavy duty motor tyre on a thin cord around their necks standing with their arms outstretched in the sun for some form of punishment.

A very few did try to escape from Changi. One group included Gunner George Thompson from Methwold. They managed to get hold of a boat but were recaptured.

43   *Changi – hospital huts. Prisoners of war were sent from Changi across south-east Asia to work for the Japanese: some weakened survivors returned in late 1943 and 1944.*

The entire group was then bayoneted to death in front of the other prisoners.[7]

Lance Corporal Bill Smith, from Yarmouth, was in the 4th Norfolks. The diary he kept while in captivity has survived. His thoughts were with his wife, Ida:

> August 21: Time is passing Ida dear and every day brings peace one day nearer. There have been 167 deaths this month and the record was 28 in one night. It's plain murder.

> Sep 26: According to official figures, over 2000 are dead out of the 7000 who left Changi. It seems it will never end but one must keep smiling. I pray to god it won't be long now.

The last entry reads: 'December 8: at the present having a bad spell with malaria'. Smith did not recover: he died on 17 December 1943. His daughter, Carol Cooper, played a major part in establishing Britain's memorial to those who died in the prisons of the Far East, the National Memorial Arboretum, which was formally opened on 15 August 2005.[8]

More than 16,000 people died of disease or malnutrition while working on the railway. One was Russell Mower from Acle. Captured when Singapore fell, he was taken to the camp at Kanchanburi at the southern end of the railway in May 1943: he died of tuberculosis just five months later.[9]

Harold Churchill of Pulham Market worked as a doctor in the camps along the railway. He has memories of a friend, Leslie Horne: 'If he ever reached home himself, he said, he had many messages to carry to their families. He was memorising the names and addresses, in case the Japanese should deprive him of his notes.' It was not

44 *Changi – POW graves. Of 42,610 British held prisoner by the Japanese, 10,298 died in captivity.*

to be: he died in the Far East. Churchill wrote: 'he was buried by a small sad party of friends who carried his body out of the camp to the prisoners' cemetery. When later I visited the burial ground I could not identify his grave; children and dogs scuffled about in the dust, but the graves were nameless'.[10]

Reggie Burton was another prisoner forced to work on the Burma-Siam railway.

> The labour was at hand, in the shape of prisoners of war and Tamil coolies who could be forced to work for the New Order in Asia. Although all this was logical enough in theory, in practice it became as blundering and lunatic as the routine counting of prisoners.
>
> The Jap high command was feverishly impatient to have the new railway in working order so that the essential fodder for their war machine could reach Burma. Yet they tried to achieve this with an undernourished force of men who were only fit for a convalescent home. Among ourselves it was often debated that the Japs didn't want the railway, but were using it as a means of exterminating their equally unwanted prisoners without any wastage of ammunition. It certainly looked that way; but there was a fanatical driving force which somehow spread right down to the most uncouth Korean guard. All our captors were in a hurry, though it was usually a directionless and senseless rush. Hardly a day passed without some ugly incident, some bestial outrage on a prisoner.

Burton felt this himself when, suffering from malaria, he collapsed while carrying a sack of rice: 'Tears streamed down my face as the Jap sentry came up to me, his face contorted with rage. After barking incomprehensible orders he kicked me, then beat me with a bamboo cane until I was semi-conscious.' Burton suffered permanent

45 *Changi – release at last. Singapore remained in Japanese hands until the end of the war. The Royal Navy ships reached the city on 3 September 1945.*

damage to his groin and a broken rib, which self-healed in a misshapen manner causing a deformity.[11]

Beckett kept a diary on scraps of paper, recording events and attempting to keep his spirits up:

> 5 March 1943: Another birthday has rolled round and nothing much has changed. I had a good meal three of us to a tin of Bully, sharing a tin of pineapple.

> 12 Sept 44: Food is not too good at the moment, quantities being small and not much food value is obtained from it.

> 27 Sept 44: Today I received the bitter blow News that George Sams had died up country, this was indeed a shock to me, as he was so fit and well on leaving, but like him so many others died also, of these terrible Far Eastern complaints.

> 25 Nov 44: Only another month and yet another Xmas will be here, with still no sign of freedom, it seems to be a marvellous dream those care free days that I spent at home and with Betty. But still we smile and try hard to keep our spirits high although God knows how very trying it is at times.[12]

Other prisoners of war were brought to Japan itself to be worked as slave labour. The journey was a risky one as the ships in which they were carried were not marked as bearing prisoners of war. Robert Durrant of Acle was one of 1,500 British aircraftmen shipped to Japan on the surrender of the Dutch East Indies in March 1942. The unmarked ship was torpedoed by an American submarine and Durrant was one of 53 British servicemen killed.[13]

Harry Hill was one of those working in Japan. he was at Miyata not far from Hiroshima on the day the first atom bomb fell. His diary records: 'Aug 6: there was sure a heavy rumble of dull explosions this morning soon after starting work. It was more like a dump going up. The Sirens were on the go, on and off, pretty well all day.' He left the camp on 19 September, and travelled through the city of Nagasaki, devastated by the second atom bomb: 'There are not the shells of half a dozen buildings standing, everything has just been blotted out. The only things semi-standing are the metal frameworks of huge buildings and these are twisted and distorted beyond recognition.'[14]

People in Norfolk knew little of the horrific conditions in which prisoners of the Japanese were kept until the war was over. In October 1942, the first postcards from men held in Japanese prisoner of war camps began to be received in Norwich. The parents of Arthur Harris, who had been captured in Malaya and whose parental home was in Esdelle Street received a card which read, 'I am a prisoner of war, being treated well, and in the best of health'. The parents of Clifford Bailey had a similar card sent to their home in Grove Road: he had been taken prisoner at Singapore.[15]

Elsie Marechal

Women did not serve in the front line and so were not normally captured by the enemy. However, nurses did serve just behind the lines and might risk being captured, especially in the Far East where the Japanese advance was so rapid. British-born people, both men and women, who were in enemy country at the outbreak of war, might be interned. At least one Norfolk woman suffered the ultimate of horrors, a concentration camp. Elsie Bell was born in Acton, but brought up in Yarmouth by her aunt. She went to the Teacher Training College in Norwich and became a teacher in London. She married a Belgian, Georges Marechal, and moved to Belgium. The family were in Brussels during the war and helped Allied servicemen to evade capture and make it back to England. They were caught by the Germans: Georges was shot and Elsie, with her daughter, spent the rest of the war in concentration camps at Ravensbruck and Mauthausen.

Elsie published a small book of poems, written by her in prison. They are in French. Part of the preface to the book says (in translation):

> I should before familiarising you with a prisoner's life, so different to anything
> you could imagine when free, tell you in detail about the Odyssey which was ours
> between the torturing interrogations and the atonement which drove us to Germany,
> first into the convict prisons then into the concentration camps.
>
> I don't wish to do that, I prefer instead to familiarise you with a few poems and
> songs which I used to make up as much to occupy myself as to amuse the people
> with me, but above all to keep up the incredible morale which allowed us to laugh at
> our tyrants, even at the most critical times.
>
> These short poems, humble songs were whispered, hummed even in front of the
> 'Boches', they were the remains of the spirit of this life which 'they' would have liked
> to stamp out with everything else.
>
> About the camps at Ravensbruck and Mauthausen, where I was stranded with my
> companions, I have nothing to say: the indescribable horror in which we were living

46   *Cover of book by Elsie Marechal.*

there allowed no more burlesque parodies. There was no place there for dreams, all there was was the tragedy of each day, the dreadful hours which saw so many of us perish.

She did eventually talk about the conditions at the latter:

> The average death rate was about 200 a day. The crematorium was continually in use and our 'blok' being not far off, we continually had this horrible odour in our noses. The only water for all purposes was a small stream that ran close to the building. The dandelions that grew near were soon uprooted by the prisoners. Our comrades who worked in the potato column brought us a few raw potatoes from time to time, which probably saved our lives at this moment. For a week or more we were fed on soup made from the lights and tripes of exhausted horses coming from the front. Then started a period of beetroot soup and the bread was reduced to a small slice a day, very often quite green and mouldy. The sanitary conditions became worse and worse. The WCs consisted of four large wooden receptacles (with a plank placed across) at the exterior of the building. After a few hours these were overflowing on to the ground, making an awful mud that finally found its way into our little stream. From that moment we licked our bowls clean rather than wash them in the stream.[16]

German and Italian prisoners in Norfolk

The first German prisoners of war were airmen and sailors. Many were sent on to Canada – by the end of the war there were almost 34,000 German prisoners of war there. The number held in Britain was low in the first years of the war, only 2,000 in March 1944. The numbers rose enormously after D-Day and the re-conquest of Europe, and continued to rise even after the end of the war: by September 1946 there were over 400,000 prisoners in Britain.

Leslie Bently witnessed a capture in a field near Clenchwarton:

> One day a German plane got into difficulties over the village and the two man crew bailed out by parachute. They landed in a field where wheat was being cut. The workers surrounded them with their pitch forks, offered them something to eat and drink, gave them cigarettes and managed to converse with them. Someone went off to get the local policeman who took them home and kept them overnight until some military people came the next day and collected them.[17]

There were prisoner of war camps at Hempton Green near Fakenham; Uplands, Diss; Kimberley Park; Redgrave Park, Diss; Marham; Mousehold Heath, Norwich; RAF Snettisham; RAF Seething; RAF Attleborough; North Lynn Farm; Aldborough;

47 *German submariners brought on board HMS* Hotspur *after being depth-charged by the destroyer in the Mediterranean, Christmas 1941.*

and Wolterton. There were also a large number of Italian prisoners of war, sometimes in the same camps as the Germans, sometimes in different ones. The conditions in which prisoners were held was laid down by the Geneva Convention. Officers could not be forced to work, but might choose to do so. Men could be made to work: they were usually used on farms and to mend the roads.[18]

In January 1942, it was announced that Italian prisoners were available to work on Norfolk farms. Farmers living within ten miles of a prison hostel were to fetch the prisoners, those further away were to provide food and accommodation of the same standard as for civilian workers. Employers were to pay the War Agricultural Executive Committee 40 shillings a week for each prisoner for the first three months, rising to 48 shillings a week after that. They could deduct 21 shillings a week for board and lodging and were promised that 'only selected men of 'good conduct' will be chosen'.[19]

Records of the Norfolk County Surveyor tell us about the conditions under which these men worked. In a circular of 15 May 1943 concerning Italian prisoners, he was told:

> Will you please let me know as early as possible the probable number of prisoners which you could utilise throughout the year for roadworks in your County in addition to those which you may have been allocated already, if any.
>
> In considering the matter you will of course take a broad view of the possibility of using prisoners and to the probability that owing to lack of maintenance the road system may deteriorate rapidly if a hard winter should be experienced this year, and that although prisoners may not be an entirely satisfactory form of labour they may be the only source available for the additional work which may become necessary.

There is little doubt that prisoners could be employed permanently where tank training areas exist and probably where continued heavy traffic is expected eg in the vicinity of sources of material, such as gravel pits, also on clearing road ditches and working at a highway authority's macadam plants.

A later circular gave more details:

Hours of Work

Prisoners should work the normal hours of civilian labour. They will not be asked to work on Sundays.

Rate of Pay

Rates of pay will be authorised by the Ministry of Labour and will be those applied to civilian labour, as fixed by the Joint Industrial Council. Payment will be for working time only. The time occupied in transport and meals will not be included. Accounts will be received from and be payable to the Command Paymaster. No payment of any sort and no gifts of cash or in kind should be made by employers to prisoners. Piece works rates are not allowed.

Security

Prisoners may not work in large towns. Where possible they should work apart from civilian labour.

Where an escort is provided he will be responsible for discipline and security.

Parties of up to 12 may be employed without an escort. Escorts will be provided for parties of 12 or more.

Where no escort is provided the employer will be responsible for the prisoners' safe custody. If a prisoner escapes the Camp Commandant and the local police should be notified immediately by telephone. Employers must not use fire-arms to prevent the escape of prisoners. Any case of misconduct or indiscipline, or unsatisfactory work of prisoners should be reported to the Camp Commandant.

A circular of May 1944 shows that the road menders were reluctant to employ the men: 'I realise that Divisional Surveyors are not keen on having Prisoners of War, but we <u>must</u> make use of whatever labour we can possibly get hold of.' The pay rates were a maximum of six pence a day for unskilled labour and a shilling a day for skilled labour. Bonuses were to be in the form of tobacco:

48   *POW camp at Hempton, re-used as temporary housing after the war.*

Where Italian prisoners work for more than 8 hours a day and their employers certify that they have worked well, a special issue of two (large size) cigarettes will be made by the Military Authorities for each complete hour worked in excess of 8 hours actual work on any one day, with a maximum of 30 cigarettes a week.

In May 1945, the County Surveyor was offered 400 German prisoners, which he urged upon his reluctant Divisional Surveyors.[20]

Many Norfolk people have recollections of the prisoners. Christina Ward of the Land Army recalled: 'We had German and Italian prisoners of war working on the land with us. One girl married a German prisoner of war. The Germans did work hard. The Italians were lazier, but romantic; they would pick flowers for the girls!' This cliché about the men of the two nations seems to have been experienced by many: at Diss, women had to be told by the police that it was an offence to take an interest in Italian prisoners of war! However, the Italians were not without initiative themselves. Chris Morter says: 'I remember my parents talking about Hempstead Hall where my mother grew up. She told me a story about the Italian POWs who worked on the farm. They used to take the farm door off its hinges and prop it up with a stick and a stone. When the birds got under the door they'd trap them to eat by pulling the stick away with string.'[21]

Derek Barber worked on the land near Fakenham. There were Italian prisoners here from the camp at Pudding Norton: he remembered them as 'not very efficient, they did some odd things'. They were given more freedom after 1943, when Italy was no longer at war with Britain. Germans replaced them in the camp: 'About fifteen would come out at a time, with a guard. They were given an incentive to pick sprouts, so many cigarettes per bag picked.' Only the trustworthy prisoners would be allowed out of camp as one of them, Hans Wienz recalled: 'Those of us who could be trusted and were not members of the Nazi Party were set to work out on

49 *German POWs at work, Morley Hospital, Wymondham.*

50   *German POWs watch from behind the fence as American servicemen relax.*

local farms and estates, others remained in the camp. There were some nasty pieces of work amongst them.' Wienz was one of a number of prisoners of war to stay in Britain after the war was over.[22]

Of course, there was a darker side. Henry Grinberg, a Jewish evacuee in Lynn, recalled:

> One day a bunch of us, including Henry Woolf, had come from playing football when we met a group of yet-unpatriated German prisoners of war. They were under the casual, unconcerned supervision of an elderly member of the Home Guard. My heart burned with hatred at the sight of them, looking so tanned and healthy from whatever work they had been doing, obviously wholesome and out of doors. News had been reaching us of mass murders and of the human wreckage discovered in the concentration camps. The prisoners called out to us to pass the balls to them, indicating that we could kick them back and forth until their lorry arrived. We were

all to be friends again. Their guard smiled benignly. I said nothing at the time but felt distinctly ill.[23]

It took a long time before the prisoners finally reached home. Many were still here at Christmas 1947, and took part in various local events:

Remembering the Christmas message of 'Peace and good will towards all men', Norfolk and Norwich families entertained half of the total number of German prisoners at Mousehold. The hosts included many ex-Service men. Nearly 300 Germans were invited to sleep at their hosts' houses on Christmas night, and another 200 were entertained to Christmas dinner.

At the Co-operative Hall 40 Germans were the guests for the day of the Co-operative Education Department, which, for nearly a year, has built up a spirit of understanding of the English way of life among the prisoners. In a hall gay with decorations which the men themselves had carried out the old German party games were played and old German songs sung. Heinz Linde, formerly a shipping clerk, told a reporter that the Germans found in Norwich a spirit of friendship and understanding not encountered elsewhere.

Meanwhile, Ukrainians from Hempton camp attended a service at Fakenham Methodist church on Christmas day. They sang a song in their own language and a Ukrainian led part of the service and gave an address.

Repatriation was only completed in July 1948.[24]

'Aliens'

British civilians caught in enemy countries at the outbreak of hostilities were interned for the duration of the war. The same process took place in this country. There were about 70,000 German and Austrian citizens in Britain when war was declared. Some 55,000 were refugees fleeing persecution from the Nazis: the majority of them were Jews. Other refugees had passed briefly through England before moving on to the United States. The most famous of these, as far as Norfolk is concerned, was Albert Einstein. He spent just under a month in Norfolk in September and October 1933, living in a hut on Roughton Heath as a guest of Oliver Locker Lampson. It was the isolation that appealed to Einstein. He said, 'I can live quietly working out my mathematical problems'. Philip Colman recalled the reaction of the local gamekeeper, Herbert Eastoe: 'You won't believe it. Old Locker have got an old Jarmin in the hut, because them old Nazis want him.' Legends have built up around the visit, for example that Einstein visited the local school and handed sweets out to the children. However, according to Colman, these actually relate to a later German refugee to stay with Locker Lampson, Dr Ott.[25]

As early as 4 September 1939, arrests of German citizens began. In theory the refugees should not have been interned but in practice many were. Several camps were set up. The only one in East Anglia was at Clacton on Sea where Butlin's Holiday Camp was used in September and October 1939 as a temporary internment camp. On 15 April 1940, a Home Office order prohibited aliens of any nationality from living in certain coastal areas, none of which was in Norfolk. On 12 May all coastal counties including Norfolk were declared prohibited areas. Male Germans and Austrians over 16 and under 60 in these areas were to be temporarily interned.

No such person could enter these areas without the express permission of the Home Secretary.

On 10 May 1940, Mussolini declared war on Britain. All Italians in Britain aged between 16 and 60 who had lived here for under twenty years were rounded up. Many of the internees, both German and Italian, wound up in camps on the Isle of Man: they included a number of Jews who had fled from Hitler's Germany. Others went to Canada or Australia, but this led to tragedy: the *Andorada Star* was torpedoed on 2 July 1940 while carrying internees from Liverpool to Canada. Over 450 Italians and almost 150 Germans were drowned.

Many British citizens felt that the way in which the Government was treating aliens was a disgrace. One of these was Henry Strauss, the Conservative MP for Norwich. On 30 July he raised his views in Parliament, asking the Home Secretary if he was aware that men as eminent as Albert Einstein, Toscanini and Thomas Mann would be in internment camps if they had happened to be living in England: was Strauss aware that Einstein had actually stayed in Norfolk seven years earlier?

In fact the tide began to turn in the autumn of 1940: many of the internees were released and by the summer of 1942 fewer than 5,000 enemy aliens remained in camps on the Isle of Man. Those who had been living in Norfolk could not return to the county, however, as it remained a prohibited area: they had to pick up the pieces of their lives in other parts of Britain.

Five

Evacuees in Norfolk

The idea of evacuating children from dangerous areas of Britain that were expected to be heavily bombed had been decided upon even before the war started. A leaflet issued in July 1939 set out the government's thoughts. The scheme would be voluntary but parents were strongly encouraged to register their children well in advance. Expectant mothers and those with children under school age would be evacuated. Those children of school age would go not with their parents but with their classmates and their teachers. People were allowed to make private arrangements if they preferred, but were warned that the Government evacuation scheme would have priority on all trains and buses. The leaflet warned that it would not be possible to let parents know where their children had been sent until after they had arrived at their new destination. It encouraged mothers who had been reluctant to register to do so at once:

> Naturally they are anxious to stay by their menfolk. Possibly they are thinking that they may as well wait and see: that it may not be so bad after all. Think this over carefully and think of your child or children in good time. Once air attacks have begun it might be very difficult to arrange to get away.[1]

The country was divided into three areas. The 'danger areas' were the big cities like London and Birmingham: all children would be evacuated from these. 'Reception areas' were those parts of the country that were thought to be safe from the threat of bombs: the children would be moved into these. 'Neutral areas' were those where there was some risk of bombing: children in these areas would not be evacuated but children from danger areas would not be moved into them. Norwich and Yarmouth were classed as neutral areas, the rest of Norfolk as a safe area. On 1 September 1939, rates of payment for those looking after evacuees were announced: 8s. 6d. a week for each child, if unaccompanied. For families the weekly rate was 5s. for each adult and 3s. for each child.

Norfolk began to get itself ready for the newcomers. In Salle, for example, five local women organised a survey of accommodation as early as February 1939. A register was drawn up listing each house, the number of habitable rooms and the number of persons ordinarily resident. The number of rooms minus the number of residents produced the possible number of persons who could be accommodated. The largest house was Salle Park, where there were seven people living in 20 rooms. Thus 13 additional people could be accommodated. However, the report also noted: 'Large house suitable for purposes other than evacuation.' There was room for eight

51   *London evacuees and their teachers in North Walsham, September 1939.*

evacuees at Stinton Hall Farm and six at Park Farm. At the other extreme, 13 of the houses had as many – or more – occupants as there were habitable rooms and so could not take in any evacuees: most of these houses were on The Street.

Mr E. Stimpson, a local Justice of the Peace, was appointed billeting officer. On 27 August 1939 he received a letter saying that 39 evacuees would arrive at 2.15 pm on the third day of the evacuation, and a further 25 at 12.25 pm on the fourth day, without any actual dates being specified. The dispersal centre was to be the village school.[2]

City children might well have different needs from those of country children, as a circular sent to Stimpson in November 1939 recognised:

> It has to be recognised that in the matter of boots and clothes the needs of children in the country are different from those of children in towns, more particularly when, as will often be the case, the children have to do a considerable amount of walking on country lanes and footpaths. The object to be aimed at is protection from cold and wet. In addition to warm clothing, the provision of some form of mackintosh, preferably a cape with a hood, and of stout laced shoes or boots, or alternatively Wellington boots, is important.
>
> The Minister trusts that in the communications with parents the special importance of these needs (which may well not be fully appreciated by those living in the towns) will be kept to the fore, and that this matter will also be borne in mind by those who are collecting funds or clothing to meet the needs of evacuated children in the reception areas.

Some contemporary comments made by the London evacuees of 1 September 1939 have survived in a book recording the evacuation of children from St James' School, Upper Edmonton. The children included John and Albert Beckwith, Derek Potts, Joan Burling, Jean and Marjorie Cole, and Joyce, Gladys and Dennis Stevens. They were evacuated together with children from Montagu Road School. North Walsham was ready for them: the church was opened and the evacuees taken inside to rest. Bags of rations were distributed and many helpers brought drinks of water. After three weeks some of the evacuees were sent on to Aylsham by bus: they described the town as 'larger and quieter than North Walsham, sometimes almost deserted'. They were deposited at Aylsham School. The Stevens children stayed with Mr and Mrs Parker in Cawston Road, Aylsham. They clearly got on well, perhaps because there were children of a similar age in the house. When the Parker's daughter, Muriel, got married in Aylsham church on 6 April 1940, the evacuees took part. Joyce and Gladys Stevens were bridesmaids along with the bride's two young sisters. Dennis Stevens and the bride's brother John Parker acted as pages.

Someone noted down a few of the children's comments on the new situation in which they found themselves:

52 *Waiting in the Market Place, North Walsham.*

(In the train from London to Norfolk): Are we still in England?
We have lovely breakfasts at our billet. My mum at home ain't half silly; she don't give us no breakfast, & then grumbles cos we're skinny.
If my dad comes to fetch me home, I shall tell him I ain't.
(Nightly prayers at billet, told by foster mother): Dear God, B [small brother] has been trying to be a good boy today. I am sorry I cannot say the same for Hitler.[3]

In fact the arrival in North Walsham and the transfer to Aylsham was more complicated – and more controversial – than the children knew. One foster-parent called it a 'gross muddle'. The people in Aylsham had expected a mixed elementary school but received a boys' secondary school. The detraining authorities pointed out that they had had to receive 21,000 people 'of all classes'. The first train at North Walsham arrived as expected and used up all the facilities there. Then 'at the end of the same day another train suddenly disgorged about 200 secondary school pupils with their masters, all from one school, and the only alternative to splitting up this party among a large number of small villages was to send them to Aylsham, where accommodation existed for them all.' After about three weeks the Norfolk Education Committee said it could provide for the boys' education at North Walsham so billeting arrangements were made accordingly. One foster-parent noted the distress caused to the children: 'North Walsham was not so concerned with the inconvenience caused them as they were with the feelings of the children, quite 50 per cent of whom left there weeping.'[4]

Great Yarmouth acted as a transit camp for many of the evacuees from London at the beginning of the war: they arrived by paddle steamer from the capital, just as so many holidaymakers had in the 1930s. For many children this was both their first time out of London and their first trip by boat. Betty Jones, then aged nine, remembered the experience: 'We were put on a bus to Tilbury Riverside Station when we embarked on a Thames pleasure steamer … I remember sitting on deck sniffing a lemon. Mum said this stopped you feeling sick. After a trip of about four to five hours, we landed at Yarmouth.'[5]

Greenacre Senior Girls' School, under their dynamic headmistress Miss Johnson, prepared for the visitors:

Desks were taken from the classrooms, and straw beds and blankets were prepared to receive evacuees who were to come by boat from the London area, and were to stay here for 2 or 3 days before being sent to their country billets. Staff, caretakers, children, parents and friends in the district worked energetically to prepare for the reception of the evacuees and the loyalty and generosity of all who lent blankets, crockery and other necessities must be here acknowledged and put on record.

In the event, fewer came than expected and Greenacre was not used. However, over 7,500 mothers and children did arrive in East Coast towns from London: school-age children came with their teachers, those under five with their mothers. They stayed in local schools for up to three days before going on to their new homes in rural Norfolk. For example, 400 were accommodated in the Church Road school until Monday 4 September. Their teachers and helpers were assisted by the local staff.[6]

The boys of Hackney Downs School were evacuated to Upwell and Outwell, and later transferred to King's Lynn. Leslie Bently (Bernstein) remembered the procedure:

53 *London children negotiate a muddy Norfolk lane.*

When we arrived we were lined up in the village schoolyard in alphabetical order. The local people looked us over and selected the healthiest-looking ones to live with them. As I was skinny and miserable looking, I was one of the last to be selected. For the first few weeks I had to live – in Jubilee Bank I think it was – with a woman whose husband was in the army or somewhere and who had not wanted to take in an evacuee but was forced by the 'evacuee law' to do so. She did not feed me properly, or see that I was washed. I had to sleep on the floor, and kept falling asleep at school. The authorities checked out the situation and removed me from her home.

Obviously the timing coincided with another in-take from London so I lined up in the schoolyard again and this time was fortunate enough to be chosen by the Frushers, a wonderful family, who had a 9-year-old son, Ron, and who lived on a smallholding in Clenchwarton, three miles west of King's Lynn.[7]

To take on evacuees could be a daunting experience. Some people found the very idea too much of a challenge, such as Mrs Dexter of King's Lynn:

We stopped in front of a cheerful, modern brick house.

Mrs Dexter herself answered the door. 'I've changed my mind', were her first words. 'I can't take them'.

She added: 'I can't afford it. I've got to get black-out curtains'.

Mrs Brand replied: 'But the LCC pay for mothers and children'.

To this Mrs Dexter said: 'Friends of mine in Ealing and Liverpool are willing to take my house if they are bombed out. Anyhow, why should I open my house while there are so many other people who haven't got evacuees?'

We were flabbergasted. Even the indefatigable Mrs Brand was non-plussed.

'But you promised us,' she said. 'We've given you all day to get ready for them. What are they to do if you refuse them?'

Mrs Wright clutched my arm. 'I'll have to go back to London she whispered. 'Don't make me go back to that 'place' tonight'.

I reassured her. I listened to the pleading of Father Vaughan and the persuading of Mrs Brand.

'But these people have been bombed! These are the people to whom you owe hospitality!' I said.

'I don't care,' said Mrs Dexter. 'I won't take them'.

And she shut the door in our faces.

The children were bewildered, unhappy. For the second time the people of King's Lynn had turned these little souls away.[8]

The experiences of a billeting officer in North Norfolk have survived. John Hastings Turner, a writer of plays, and his wife Laura had moved from London to Titchwell in March 1939. Turner was asthmatic and could not serve in the forces: he became the billeting officer for the village and recorded his impressions in his journal:

> 3 Sept Children from Hoxton and Shoreditch arrived here and were billeted. One mother told me she had never seen a field. The babies suck openly which is Rubensesque and pleasing.

> 4 Sept Slight trouble with a Hoxton mother. Produced a constable and said a few words. Hope for local peace, but have grave doubts of the situation a little later on when they realise that there are no cinemas etc. I had no idea that these poor folk were so sub-human.

> 5 Sept As suspected our guests from London are proving difficult. They have not even elementary ideas of sanitation. We are considering a scheme for packing the whole lot in the parish hall. But the big problem is that of food. The Government make no allowance for mothers' and infants' food in the hope that their husbands will send them money from London. Some hope!

> 8 Sept A deputation has arrived from the evacuees. They want to go home. Well … why not?

> 9 Sept The ladies from Hoxton decided to stay.

However, three of them left on 11 September, and the husband of another arrived to take his wife and baby home – 'he told me that there were rumours in London that the evacuees were being badly treated in the country'. Turner slowly became more tolerant, however:

> 15 Sept I went to visit our guests. They have turned much more human. Perhaps it is difficult for them to believe that people are anxious to be good to them. By an accident of birth I have never lived in a slum. I expect one's ideas of men and things become rather warped there. Some of Laura's old toys were taken to them. The reception was pathetic in its pleasure.

54 *Evacuee children visit a farm for the first time. This is Gertine's farm in Aylsham.*

By Christmas only two of the London families remained in Titchwell. Turner's wife Laura acted as 'Lady Bountiful' and presented them with a Christmas box each, for which they were duly grateful.[9]

Turner's experience illustrates a pattern common to these evacuees of September 1939. Some remained where they had been sent for the whole war, but many drifted back to London within a few months when the expected air raids on the capital failed to materialise. A school logbook such as that of Great Cressingham shows how this worked out in practice. When the school opened for the autumn term on September 1939 there were no fewer than 47 evacuee children in attendance. The children underwent a medical inspection: three brothers were found to have 'very dirty' heads. One of the teachers took all the London children on a nature walk for several weeks in the autumn term.

The children soon dwindled in number, four returning to London just a week after arrival. In January 1940, there were only 17 evacuees at the school. Two, Mary Kirk and Peter Bear, had problems with their feet: they were given a programme of daily foot movements and were reported in November 1940 to be much improved. Glasses were provided for three evacuees in the summer term – Jean Kirk, José Stone and Joyce Bradley. In September 1940, the school went blackberrying and gathered 11 pounds of fruit. One of the evacuees, Marie Rosenthall, clearly enjoyed this new experience: on the following day she gave in a further three pounds of blackberries that she had gathered in the evening. In another school, the disruption was much smaller. Just two evacuees, both from Walthamstow, came to Hardingham school at

55   *Evacuee and local children acting as bridesmaids and pages at an Aylsham wedding in April 1940.*

the beginning of the autumn term. One returned in late October, the other was back in London before Christmas.[10]

Bed-wetting was a common problem among the evacuees, not surprising in young children without their parents and in a totally strange environment. A circular issued by the Women's Voluntary Service recognised that there might well be serious traumas for these city children suddenly deprived of their parents' care:

> Some children may try your patience by wetting their beds, but do not scold or punish, as this will only make matters worse. In many cases the trouble is due to excitement and nervousness and will be overcome by rest and regular life. Sufficient warmth in bed is important and it may help if the child is got up about 10 pm, but be sure to consult the doctor, district nurse or health visitor if the difficulty persists. If you need advice in cleaning the children's heads or dealing with any minor skin troubles, consult the school or district nurse.
>
> Should you be in any difficulty about the child consult the billeting officer or teacher but do not complain to the parents.[11]

Mrs Riches of Gaywood wrote to the Lynn Billeting Officer in November 1939: 'We, like many others, took one of these children into our home. Before many days had passed we discovered the boy was not very clean in his habits at night.' She asked for a new mattress but expressed a willingness to have another evacuee child, so she had not been totally put off by the experience. Another Lynn foster parent complained that she had two evacuees 'and one of them has been unfortunate enough to break half a tea service'.[12]

However, the relations between evacuees and their host county were generally good. In the first few months at least, and especially over Christmas 1939, many local people provided treats for the newcomers. Miss Maples of Saxlingham wrote in December 1939 to a friend in America: 'Last Saturday I gave six little evacuee boys a Treat. They sang songs – Clementine etc – and carols, whistled, played my piano, beat my drum, had games & stories told them; also had grapes, crackers, oranges, nuts, biscuits, sweets – a lovely party.'[13]

The number of evacuees from London to Norfolk in September 1939 was about 19,000. There were still just over 11,000 evacuees in the county in January 1940. The *Eastern Daily Press* reported in March 1940 that of the 2,354 evacuees that came to St Faith's and Aylsham Rural District Council in September 1939, only 1,085 remained.[14]

1940-1943

The situation changed in the summer of 1940. Once Germany had conquered France, London became subject to nights of bombardment from the air – the blitz. Now, many of the people who had returned to London fled once more to the country. Norfolk was ready, if not necessarily willing. St Faith's and Aylsham RDC sent out 10,400 letters in March 1940 asking householders to place themselves on a register of those willing to take evacuee children. Only 427 offers came in, and 128 of these were from people who were already housing evacuee children. In Forehoe and Henstead, 7,550 letters were sent out: just 247 positive replies were received. However, house-to-house calls to 18 parishes in the district found promises that 607 children would be given a house if necessary. This was nowhere near enough. By February 1941, there were between 1,500 and 1,600 evacuees in the district. Houses were found for most of them, but some had to live in hostel accommodation such as the Dell Hostel in Aylsham and the Winston Hostel in Foulsham. The latter was overcrowded, with 30 people living in a house made for ten. The sanitary arrangements were insufficient, cooking facilities were inadequate and there was no provision for the washing of young children.[15]

The Chief Billeting Officer sent a letter to all the local billeting officers, including Stimpson at Salle, on 18 September 1940:

> The Council have been requested by His Majesty's Government to give immediate consideration to the question of providing accommodation for mothers and young children who have been rendered homeless by the recent indiscriminate bombing of the civilian population of London.
>
> Billeting allowances at the rate of 5/- per week for adults and 3/- per week for each child will be paid and the Council are authorised, if necessary, to requisition unoccupied houses and to purchase the equipment necessary for the essential purposes of the daily life of the occupants.
>
> The experiences through which the mothers and children have recently passed may mean that some of them will arrive in an exhausted condition and some will have been unable to maintain their accustomed standard of personal appearance and cleanliness. Such steps as are possible will be taken in London to enable the mothers and their children to wash and be re-equipped, but in the present situation

the facilities of this kind which can be made available are, in some areas, extremely
limited. It will, therefore, be of the greatest help in restoring their courage and self
respect if cleaning arrangements could be made available for them at some suitable
place in the village as soon as possible after their arrival.

Naturally, there were last-minute changes to arrangements. On 5 October, Salle
was told it would be receiving ten people, three days later that it would not be taking
anyone, and finally that seven evacuees would be coming to the village. Among
those arriving at Salle in October 1940 was Mrs Burke with her child, Patrick, who
was just 8½ months old, and also her mother, Mrs Marie Morgan, all from Queen's
Park, London. Mother and child were billeted with Mrs Harrison, but Mrs Morgan
was accommodated with the house of Miss Williamson. Another family of three
generations arrived in Salle at the same time. Mrs Winifred Goulder, with her daughters
Audrey aged 12 and Janet aged four, was also accompanied by their grandmother,
Mrs Anne Woodall: they lived in Edbrooke Road, Paddington. The entire family was
billeted with Mrs Brown.[16]

The papers of the billeting officer for Winfarthing survive and show how much
work was involved in the process. A roll of householders for 1940 shows that out of
about 110 houses who had received a Ministry circular asking people to take evacuees,
only two replies had been received: Mr Smith of Lodge Cottages and Mr Howlett of
Ivy Farm were each willing to take two girls. The officer visited each house and found
rooms for another 23 children. Many houses were deemed to be unsuitable for various
reasons – 'both husband and wife out at work all day', 'old and infirm', 'reserving for
relatives' or in some cases simply 'not willing'. Ten houses already had evacuees.

There is a register of evacuees among the records of Docking Rural District
Council, giving names, home addresses, the address to which they went, and the date
they returned home. Unfortunately the last column is left blank in most cases. There is
enough information to recreate the stories of some individual families. Mrs Chapman
arrived from London on 23 April 1941 with her three children George, James and
Violet. Their address was 11 Vittoria House, N1. A week later, near neighbours from 8
Vittoria Place arrived – Mrs Coxhead with her children Linda and Barry. Both families
went to the Harrisons at Snettisham Holiday Camp. The Chapman family went back
to London in August 1941 and the Coxheads followed in January 1942. Some left
for London while other families were still arriving from the city. Mrs Judge and her
family of five – Doris, Willie, Florence, Vera and Pauline – from the Isle of Dogs
were billeted together at 'Kelso' in Neville Road, Heacham: they arrived in May 1941
but left for home after just two months.

At Lynn, the Infirmary was used as a staging post and a register of evacuees
survives: they usually stayed for two nights and then moved on to one of the district
councils, either Lynn itself, Heacham, March, Ely or Docking. In January 1941, for
example, two families called Sicklemore were admitted on the same day: both came
from Clarence Road, Lower Clapton E5. Alice brought two children and Lilian
brought three: after two nights in the Infirmary they moved to Docking. In fact, all
the families that arrived together on 21 January 1941 seem to have been assigned to
Docking, including Harriet Lancaster and her children Doris and Raymond. Their stay
was brief, however: a terse note in the register reads: 'Returned to London. Refused
to stay.'[17]

56 *Thurne school admission register showing evacuee children who have left London because of the rocket attacks on the capital in the summer of 1944.*

Because homes were being bombed out, it was more common for mothers and children to come together in these years, rather than children in their school groups as before. These London mothers could be feisty. Maud Eagleton of Gaywood Road wrote to the Lynn Town Clerk in March 1941: 'I have had an evacuee mother & child with me for nearly 4 months & I am now asking to be relieved of them. Recently the mother has been abominably rude to me on 3 occasions, I refuse to have the atmosphere of my home ruined by her.' As always, there were clearly two sides to the dispute: the mother had been to the Billeting Officer and put 'her version of the case' to him.[18]

The idea behind children being evacuated with their teachers was to enable their education to continue with as little disruption as possible. This could only work in cases where the children stayed in their place of evacuation for a period of years rather than just a few months. North Runcton school saw the usual pattern of frequent movement between London and the country. However, some of the children did stay for a longer time, and for one child at least, there were positive results. On 3 March 1944 it was recorded that one evacuee was taking the Metropolitan Test. In July the result came through: 'We have today been notified that Maurice Micklewhite, an evacuee billeted here since he was 11 years old, from London, has passed the LCC scholarship exam which he took from this school last March.' Micklewhite went on to become one of Britain's best-loved actors under the name of Michael Caine.[19]

In many other cases, however, children were moving so frequently that all continuity in their education must have broken down. Holme Hale school admission register records cases of children who came as evacuees, went back to London only to return at a later date, sometimes more than once. Jenny Fivans (13) and her brother Gerald (eight) from East London were admitted on 26 May 1941. They left just five days later but were admitted once more on 14 July. This stay lasted just three weeks before they returned to London. The Poberefsky sisters from Clapton had three stays at the school. Minnie was admitted on 26 May 1941, followed by Aubrey on 4 July. Both girls left on 2 December 1941. A fortnight later they were readmitted, this time staying until April 1942. They came back for a third time on 1 June, this time remaining at the school for six months before returning to London in December. Maureen Bailey from West Ham was just seven years old when she was admitted in October 1940: she was in the guardianship of Elsie Hunt. Maureen stayed for 30 months, leaving for London in June 1943. A month later she was back, and this time did not return home until October 1945, well after Germany had surrendered.[20]

New arrivals came to Titchwell too, as Turner recorded in his diary:

> 23 Jan 41: In the afternoon Marjorie came with Laura and myself to see to evacuees who arrived by omnibus about five o'clock.
> 1 curly-haired ultra-smart mother with two neat boys.
> 1 depressed mother, probably anaemic, who belonged to a slightly lower category in the amazing system of class. Her husband had not been so continent. She had three girls and Sidney Harold who is one year and a half old.
> But they are much easier people than the last lot which came here, and look, at the moment, as if they might settle down happily.[21]

As well as the official groups of evacuees, many families made their own private arrangements. Members of the Hamond family came to Norfolk from their London home in 1940. Anthony Hamond told his son in December: 'Muriel and her sister Susan, Michael & the dog all appeared a few weeks ago & rang up to say they were at Holt station one night at 7.30 and could I fetch them please. They had had a pretty bad go the night before, with incessant bombing & a good deal of wreckage all round, & Muriel has left them here though she has gone back herself & has not had too bad a time since.'[22]

Roy Barnes came to Norfolk in September 1940, with his mother and brother and also his aunt and her three daughters: by this time the bombing in London was severe. They were found accommodation in a tiny cottage in Walpole Highway: 'No gas, no electricity, no running water, no toilet, no bathroom, just a pantry in the corner under the staircase and a seat over a hole in the ground in an outside shed for a loo … And it was cold in those bedrooms. In winter there were icicles on the insides of the windows.'[23]

A circular letter sent from the Senior Regional Officer for the Ministry of Health to the clerks of District and County Councils in September 1941 suggested ways to improve relations between residents and evacuees:

| LIST OF CHILDREN OF SCHOOL AGE AND UNDER. | | | Parish—WINFARTHING. |
NAME.	DATE OF BIRTH.	TYPE.	ADDRESS OF BILLET.
BANGS—Joyce	19. 3.36.	Y.C.	Mr.Chamberlain,The Cottage,
BANGS—Paul	6. 7.44.	Y.C.	" " " "
CHRISTMAS—Evelyn	8. 6.41.	Y.C.	Mr.Holman,Heath Farm,
CHRISTMAS—David L.	17.12.42.	Y.C.	" " " "
DAVIES—Leslie	9. 9.31.	Y.C.	" " " "
DAVIES—Joyce	4.10.33.	Y.C.	" " " "
DAVIES—Jean	26. 7.36.	Y.C.	" " " "
DAVIES—Maureen	28.10.38.	Y.C.	" " " "
PEARCE—Brian	24. 6.33.	U.C.	Mr.F.Barham,Eaton Road,
WATSON—Christopher	9. 2.33.	U.C.	Mrs.Chamberlain,The Cottage,
WATSON—Roy	6.11.38.	U.C.	" " " "
BOURNE—Margaret	10. 1.42.	Y.C.	" " " "
ANSTEY—Frederick	11. 6.37.	Y.C.	Willow Farm,(Req.House)
HOLMAN—Ann	5. 4.44.	Y.C.	Dove Cottage,(Req.House)
HOLMAN—John	26. 1.36.	Y.C.	" " " "
HOLMAN—Alan	21. 9.41.	Y.C.	" " " "
HOLMAN—Yvonne	31. 5.40.	Y.C.	" " " "
HOLMAN—Jean	13. 8.37.	Y.C.	" " " "

TYPE:- U.C.—Unaccompanied Child.
       Y.C.—Young Child with Mother.

57 *List of evacuees in Winfarthing, summer 1944. The youngest, Paul Bangs, was just six weeks old.*

The lines we are trying to pursue in this work are many, and will of course vary from time to time, but the obvious ones are:

1. To show householders the sort of conditions from which evacuees from the cities have come.
2. To impress upon the householders and evacuees alike that they can only get along by 'give and take'.
3. To give descriptions of hostels etc, showing what has been done and thereby stimulating efforts elsewhere.
4. By giving examples, in story form or otherwise, bringing home to householders the great work they are doing, the fact that those in authority appreciate it, and that they are serving the country just as much as those in uniform.
5. Generally by articles and examples to stress the fact that evacuation is, and must be, always with us under present circumstances, and that continued effort is required. By precept showing to those who have not responded, all that they might be doing for their country if they played up as others have.[24]

In April 1942, new rates of payment for unaccompanied children were announced, ranging from 8s. 6d. for a child under five to 16s. 6d. for a 'child' aged 17 and over.

The County Education authorities had a great deal of responsibility for evacuee children: they issued a stream of instruction and advice. As early as April 1940, they were concerned at a breakdown of communications between children in Norfolk and their parents in London: 'Instances have come to light where parents have not been informed when their children are ill, and a few cases where children's illnesses have had fatal results before the parents in London have been aware of the illness. Head teachers will wish to reassure themselves that parents are made aware of anything

58   *Evacuees visit a Norwich Pantomime.*

that concerns the health of their children.' In September 1940, they considered the question of clothing: 'On ascertaining that a child is not provided with the boots and clothing which it [*sic*] needs, teachers, voluntary workers, or others interested in the children, should first get into touch with the parents, drawing their attention to the items required. When this fails to produce the desired effect the needs should be reported by the teacher or voluntary worker to the Relieving Officer in the reception area, ie the Rural District, Urban District or Borough.'[25]

1944-1945

By the summer of 1944, the tide of the war had clearly turned. After D-Day most people thought that Hitler would be too busy defending his European conquests to bomb London. They were wrong: Hitler had secret weapons in reserve. In July 1944 the flying bombs struck London and a new wave of evacuation began. Norwich was deemed safe from this threat and made preparations for new visitors. Some 4,000 were expected. Thirteen houses formerly occupied by the military were found, including four in Unthank Road and another four in Grove Avenue.

For the rest, the best that could be offered was 'accommodation in Nissen hutting erected at the sites of barrage balloons'. These huts included sites in Bowthorpe, Tuckswood Lane, Newmarket Road, and at the Greyhound site in Sprowston. They were pretty grim. The hut at Bowthorpe was on the playground at the municipal school. There was no water or electricity: the balloon station crew had 'obtained water from the school and used school ablutions'. The hut on Newmarket Road was on an army vehicle park. There was no electricity and water had to be fetched from a well outside cottages twenty yards away. Nevertheless, by 10 August three huts were occupied and a further five were about to be filled.

Some of the new refugees had nothing. The Ministry of Health Regional Office took on responsibility for providing essentials but they had little to spare:

> Equipment must be issued to billetors only where and to the extent it is actually needed. The normal maximum provision is 1 camp bed (or pallet), 2 coloured blankets and jaconet [bed-covering] as necessary. This maximum should not be exceeded. Pillows and pillow cases are not in the ordinary way to be provided.

In the end, 350 evacuees were billeted in huts and empty houses. Over 3,200 evacuees – just under 2,000 of them children – were housed with families in the city, 1,400 of them in working-class terrace houses and 1,100 in council houses.

In September 1944 the Norwich officials noted that about 960 schoolchildren had arrived from south-east England. Teachers, however, were in short supply. London County Council had sent seven teachers and promised four more; Essex had promised to send teachers but none had yet arrived.[26]

Norwich Education department sent out a letter to its schools on 19 July 1944: 'As you are aware, numbers of mothers and children are being evacuated from London to the City and will be billeted here. Children of school age billeted in your district should be admitted to your school on application if you have accommodation.' Half a dozen children from various schools in Dagenham were admitted to St Mark's senior boys school Lakenham on 9 September 1944 and others followed throughout the month.[27]

On 24 July 1944, another 800 evacuees arrived in Norwich and were taken to disposal centres in Sprowston and Hellesdon, and then scattered throughout villages in the district. The arrivals included 254 children (39 unaccompanied) and 125 mothers for St Faiths and Aylsham: the youngest was Roger Pigram, just two weeks old. All the arrivals for the district were found homes within two hours.[28]

The *Eastern Daily Press* on 9 August 1944 reported that there were about 20,000 evacuees in Norwich and the district, of whom about 5,000 were 'unofficial' evacuees. The arrivals continued – 640 by special train on 29 August alone. They went to the villages as well as to the city. A group of evacuees arrived in Salle in July 1944: again, most stayed only a short time. They included Mrs Dyerson and her two children. They were billeted with Mrs Wright but returned to London before the end of the month. A few cases were more complex. Dorothy Whiting arrived with her three children June, three, Iris, seven, and Eileen, twelve. They were from Finchley and were billeted with Mrs Tubby at 32 Salle Street. However, in August Dorothy wrote

59 *Christmas party for Aylsham evacuees and local children, 1942.*

60   *The evacuees go home.*

to inform Mr Stimpson that she and her two youngest children were moving to the house of Mrs Rowe at Norton Corner, Wood Dalling: Eileen remained at Salle. No reason was given for her action, and the facts behind it may well never now be known.[29]

The people of Winfarthing also responded to the needs of evacuees from London. Mrs Holman of Heath Farm, for example, rose to the crisis. On 18 August she took on two families from London, Dorothy Davies with her four children, and Marie Christmas (!) with two. The *Fighting Cocks* found room for Mrs Chopping from Beaufort Place, Chelsea, and her two sons David and John. Several other families arrived in the village at the same time.

The rector continued to concern himself with the affairs of these families. On 19 August he pointed out to Mr Johnson that both families at Heath Farm 'are very short of essential furniture and are in urgent need of two camp beds and a cooking stove of some sort, and one or two cooking utensils'. He procured from him two camp beds, two mattresses and four blankets, also lending Mrs Davies six of his own cups. She acknowledged receipt of two blankets and a camp bed from the rector, and wrote to him: 'Did you enquire about a lamp for us. It is awfully dark & miserable here at night with only one lamp. If you can get one could you let the postman have it to bring to us if he doesn't mind & that would save us that long walk.' Wynburn duly lent Mrs Davies one of his own lamps.[30]

In Docking, there were so many arrivals in the summer and autumn of 1944 that the clerk was overwhelmed, failing in most cases to record even the city from which they came. Again it was not uncommon for three generations of the family to arrive. Mrs Threadwell came with her son Ronald and the boy's grandmother, Mrs Bentley in July: Mrs Smith of Shingledene in Heacham came to their rescue. Mrs Crabb came in August with her daughter Carol and Mrs Terry, aged 70: Mrs Ellworthy of Ingoldisthorpe supplied accommodation for them.[31]

John Turner was also experiencing a new wave of evacuees in Titchwell:

> 12 July 1944: Brancaster is to get thirty of these child evacuees, without their mothers. Most of the women are working on the land all day, and I should imagine that the children would be all over the place. It is their mother's job to look after them, but I suppose they scented a nice holiday from domestic cares, and refused to come.
>
> So like the Government! Evacuate the dear children and pose as a sort of Father Christmas, and to Hell with what may happen at the other end of the railway journey.
>
> 15 July There has been great trouble in all the districts about the larger houses refusing to take the children and especially, the mothers. This is not always as selfish as it appears. In Mrs Green's case, at Brancaster, for instance, her Cook has already announced her intention of leaving at once should any evacuees be billeted upon them.
>
> No doubt this is not the only case. We shall struggle, however, to take two of them in here. I can't help feeling that people would be a little different in their attitude towards them if they were called refugees instead of evacuees.

16 Nov: Learnt that the Brancaster evacuees are already drifting back to London, just as ours are. Strange people, difficult to understand. But I believe the root of the matter is not lack of cinemas, fish and chip shops and the rest of it, but a lively suspicion of what their husbands may be up to. After long conversations with the evacuee women at Titchwell, I came to this conclusion a long time ago.[32]

The evacuees of 1944 were very different from those of 1939. Evacuation was an immediate flight response to a new danger, not an action that had been planned many months in advance. Individual responses were varied – in some cases parents sent their children away to safety, in others the mothers came with them and in yet others the whole family came. One such family was Tom and Gwen Major of Cheam who had three children, the youngest of whom, John, was just a year old. When a V1 exploded near their house, scattering glass over John's cot, Gwen insisted the family moved somewhere safer. They came to Norfolk and Tom got a job working at an American base near Thetford. They stayed for a year before returning to Surrey. Forty-five years later, baby John Major had grown up to become Prime Minister of Great Britain.[33]

1945 – The Return

On 2 May 1945 the evacuation scheme was brought to an end. One instruction told the local organisers: 'If the evacuee states that she cannot return home because of shortage of bedding or because her home will require opening up and airing she should be informed that she will be accommodated for a few days in a Rest Centre in London while she attends to these difficulties and that bedding will be provided.' However, the letter recognised that not all families could go home at once: 'Where the home is uninhabitable and requires repair the evacuee must not be given facilities to return home until the home has been made habitable.'

At the same time a notice was sent out to evacuees.

> The Government have decided that persons evacuated from the Greater London evacuation areas who have homes to which they can return should now make arrangements to return to their homes. Free travel will be provided.
>
> If you have no home, or if for any reason you are unable to return to your home, you should explain the circumstances to the Billeting Officer. If your difficulty is a temporary one, eg if you are short of bedding at home, or if your house needs airing, and you cannot get a friend to do this for you, you will be given help when you get back to your home town and temporary accommodation until your home is ready for you. You should not delay your return on this account, but if your house has been damaged and still needs repair, you should not return home for the time being.

Those billeting unaccompanied children also received their instructions:

> Special trains will be provided for the journey, but it will take a few weeks to make all the arrangements and it is essential that the evacuees should remain billeted until the arrangements have been completed.
>
> Some will not be able to go home for the time being, either because they have no homes, or for some other good reason. They must continue to be billeted until other arrangements can be made for them.
>
> The Government is most grateful to you for the care which you have given to these children and asks you to be good enough to continue to care for them until they are

61 *'Don't Do It, Mother'. A warning against bringing children back to the cities after bombing raids had failed to materialise.*

sent home under the plans now being made or until other arrangements are made for them.

One such child, Frank McArdell, was billeted with Mrs Horner at 2 Cawston Road, Salle: he came from Lichfield Grove in Finchley. On 25 June Mrs Horner received a letter informing her that Frank would be returning to London on 29 June: a bus would pick him up at 7.45 am to connect with the 10.15 train from Norwich. Instructions for the journey included:

Please see that each article of luggage is securely packed and labelled with one of the labels that are enclosed herewith. The child's name and home address, in full, should be written in ink on the blank side of each label. Let the children take with them what they can conveniently carry, including their sleeping garments, necessary toilet articles and a change of underwear.

Give the billeting officer particulars of the remaining luggage which the children cannot carry so that he may make arrangements to send it.

Please also write the name and home address of each child on a sheet of paper and place it inside his luggage.

One of the coloured luggage labels should be attached to each child's outer garment so that it can be seen. This will help the escorts in assembling and marshalling the children for the journey.[34]

The evacuees at Winfarthing began to go home in the spring of 1945. Mrs Davies wrote to the rector:

I am writing to inform you that we are returning to London tomorrow, 15 April. We are sorry that we haven't been able to come & see you, but it is such a long way & there has been such a lot to do. We have left everything in order & your things are ready for you to collect.

Many of the evacuees stayed until early June 1945 when they returned home by special train. They were followed by unaccompanied children who returned at the end of June. The city authorities thought of everything, putting six 'Elsan' lavatories in the former air-raid shelter at the station on both occasions. A few evacuees stayed, which could cause problems. Once the evacuation scheme was over they were supposed to pay an economic rent for any property they occupied. In October 1945, three families had come to the City Engineer saying that they were 'quite unable to pay the rent asked'. However, by March 1946 the crisis was over. The City Engineer reported that he had 40 small hanging cupboards, small folding tables and dressing chests. They were no use 'owing to the rather poor state they were left in by the persons who used them'. He hoped that the Equipment Officer in Cambridge would take them off his hands.[35]

The Evacuee Experience

The experiences of evacuees, and of those who received them, remained in people's memories for their entire lives. Joyce Brooks was the daughter of a village billeting officer. Writing 60 years later, she remembered the difficulties involved:

> It was a thankless task as there were never enough people willing to take them. Often our house sheltered several families, mothers and children, until homes could be found for them. Eventually isolated cottages, many uninhabited for some time were used, dreadful places, down muddy country lanes miles from shops and buses, a local official remarking that these people were not used to anything better! My mother was horrified and with friends tried to clean up & make the places a little more homely, even transporting fuel & blankets on a handcart. Some people could not tolerate the conditions and went back to London, where some were killed.
> We did have a family of wife & disabled husband & child in our own house.[36]

Nancy Nuttall recalled the evacuees in Fincham:

> The one event I shall never forget was the arrival of the evacuees from London's East End, Hackney and Stepney … They brought a male and female teacher and used the village hall for lessons. It didn't last for many weeks and some ran wild through the village, causing havoc. The most notorious were the three King brothers. Several families had accommodated them for a day or two, but couldn't cope with their swearing, fighting and general chaos. One Sunday the parson (a nice new one) had appealed from the pulpit for somebody to be charitable and take them on. Getting no response, he said he'd take them on himself, so they were installed at the rectory. I think it lasted for two weeks: the crunch came when he was entertaining some church dignitaries to dinner and had asked the boys to go to bed early and be good chaps. They all three slept in the bedroom above his dining room, and he told Mother afterwards that bedlam broke out above during dinner. Fighting, banging etc. And eventually there was a loud crunch and a leg of the bed appeared through the ceiling.[37]

Freda Morse in 2003 had memories of evacuees at her cottage in Salthouse 60 years earlier:

> They come from East London. They weren't too bad, we didn't have them wet the bed like our friends did. The mother and father came over to visit the little boy and, Oh, she'd got him all in flannelette because she thought he'd be cold. They weren't too bad, but they didn't know how to eat did they? They didn't like anything – only fish and chips.[38]

Looking back, the evacuees themselves had contrasting memories of their experiences. Nine-year-old Margaret Webb was evacuated from East London on 1 September 1939. She was taken by train to Thetford and then on to her new home at New Buckenham:

I took to the life like a duck to water. I would feed the hens, muck out the cattle, brush and groom the three beautiful shire horses. The largest was Captain and he was huge. Next was Blossom and then my favourite, the smallest one John. I helped with the haymaking and harvest and the threshing and adored every minute.

It was not so easy for Eric Court from Camberwell, who was eight years old when he was evacuated:

I went to school in Norwich but was never accepted by the rest of the class because I was a Londoner. I had a good mate, Derek, who was also from London, and because he was a big boy he prevented us from being bullied. There was an air-raid shelter near the school and if the siren went off we had to wait for our Mums to come and pick us up out of the school and take us there.[39]

Roy Barnes was one of a small group of evacuees at Walpole Highway. The village children sat out late at night in the bus shelter on the corner of the road by the blacksmith's shop, most of them keeping a wary eye for their fathers coming out of the *Bell*, or their mothers coming to get them:

At first the evacuees weren't very welcome at these nightly trysts, where a fair bit of shenanigin went on ... We were eventually accepted mainly because we could fight. 'Get the evacuees – Bash the Londoners' was a kind of fighting cry from the locals. Every break at the village school we would find ourselves with our backs to the wall re-enacting the Battle of Dunkirk. I was fortunate in being big and quite experienced in the art of fisticuffs. Acting like a latter day Henry V defending the breach, I often led the counter-attack and had the local louts running for shelter in the boys' lavatory at the other side of the playground.[40]

Nigel Quiney was evacuated from London as late as January 1945, together with his brother Tony: 'For me the ensuing experience was my first taste of real horror.' They stayed not in a family home but in dormitories at Eccles Hall. There were separate dormitories for juniors and seniors: as Tom was four years older than Nigel, the brothers were placed in different dormitories. There were seven or eight boys in the junior dormitory and about twenty in the senior one. Nigel's main memory was of terrible homesickness. Tom became ill in March and the parents came down from London to visit him: 'I was overjoyed to see them, literally throwing myself into my mother's arms and sobbing with relief, somehow believing that they had come to take us home.' In fact Nigel stayed at Eccles until July.[41]

Was the enormous effort made to evacuate children from dangerous areas worthwhile? In its main aim, it was undoubtedly a success. Just one evacuee child of all the many thousands in Norfolk died in an air raid: eight-year-old Jean Miller left Walworth in London to stay at Northcote Road in Norwich, only to become a victim of the Baedeker raids. Its greatest importance was the way that it transported people to new situations and an experience of a way of life that was completely unfamiliar. In many cases this led to an increased tolerance to other ways of living.[42]

Six

Evacuees out of Norfolk

In September 1939, Norfolk seemed a safe place to live. However, by the summer of 1940 the county was a place of danger: the coastal towns were thought likely to suffer from bombing and even, perhaps, from invasion. In 1940, the towns along the coast were declared an evacuation area. Over 47,000 children were evacuated to the Midlands in 97 special trains on just one day – 2 June 1940. Almost 800 left from Cromer Beach station but the largest group came from Yarmouth and Gorleston.[1]

Children of school age went with their teachers not with their parents. The head teacher at Greenacre Junior School recorded: 'We are closing down this afternoon & preparing for Evacuation. 30.5.40.' Church Road School also closed on 30 May: the logbook notes that the children were going to Birlcotes in Nottinghamshire. Admission registers put flesh on the bones by providing the names of individuals. One girl, Heather Nutman, was admitted to the school on 29 May, the day before the school closed: she was evacuated with the rest of the children. She was just six years old, as were several others including John Lake and Elizabeth Symonds.[2]

On 2 June 1940, 3,400 children together with 295 teachers and helpers left Yarmouth for safer homes in the Midlands. Almost three thousand came from elementary schools in the borough: the remainder were pupils at the Grammar School and High School, with 87 children from private schools. Maureen Elvin recalled the moment of departure:

> Many buses arrived at the school which were there to take us to the railway station at Great Yarmouth. As we said our goodbyes to our Mum and Dad and boarded the bus I remember mixed feelings of excitement, panic (a little bit frightened) then tears, triggered by seeing our much loved brother Dick cycling so fast to wave goodbye.

They took the train for many hours. Eventually it came to a stop and the children thought they had reached their destination: 'We scrambled up and got out of the train, bags in hand, gas masks hanging across small tired bodies. To our dismay we were all directed on to another train marked North. By now we were beginning to feel rather tired, our excitement waning, the sandwiches and goodies lovingly prepared by our Mums had long ago been devoured.'[3]

There were 116 children from Greenacre Senior Girls' School: this number included young children travelling with elder sisters. They were accompanied by six assistant mistresses from the staff together with two from the Infant School and one outside helper. They went to six small villages in Nottinghamshire, including East Markham and Ragnall.

Some children did not take part in the evacuation, and some of the evacuated children did not stay away for very long; by the autumn term there were at least 1,300 children in Yarmouth and 50 teachers were recalled so that some schools in the town could re-open. At first the authorities were reluctant to open schools as this might encourage more children to return to the borough, but they soon revised their opinion. Greenacre Senior Girls' re-opened on 18 November with three staff, Church Road School two days later with just two staff. However, other schools such as Greenacre Junior School did not re-open until the summer of 1944: by this time Yarmouth was no longer seen as a target.[4]

We can see what life was like for evacuated schools by looking at Yarmouth High School for Girls and Grammar School for Boys, both of which were evacuated to Retford. One teacher, George Rook, wrote back:

We've settled down here – Oh! The terrible heat. Starting school tomorrow – couldn't start before as there were no tables or chairs for our children. As it is, we are packing the local school to capacity.

We do not appear to be away from aeroplanes. This is a <u>safe</u> area. Air raid warnings all round us on Friday! Planes about all day and all night. There are two or three big aerodromes within a few miles so you'll understand that we get a good deal of noise every day for the whole of the 24 hours.

I hope Yarmouth is still on the map, although there are all sorts of wild rumours about Piers being blown up etc, etc, etc.

62 *'Women Wanted For Evacuation Service'.*

There were many wartime shortages. The head teachers, Mr Palmer and Miss Kerr, had an enormous struggle to obtain even basic footwear for their pupils. Miss Kerr asked for more size threes for her younger girls, but was told by the Clerk to the Governors that all he had were men's size tens. In November he was able to supply 40 pairs of shoes to the new intake of pupils at the Grammar School. The Headmaster's reply pointed out practical difficulties in daily school life:

I am afraid that, if we merely handed over the new gym shoes to the boys, they would be used for a great many uses for which they are not intended, and the difficulty of keeping a check on them would be very great indeed. Most of the school cloak-rooms have pigeon holes for shoes, but they do not lock, and in the normal way we do not use the cloakrooms. The chief reason for this is that the boys have to carry their overcoats with them from lesson to lesson since if there were an alert they would need them in the shelters. As the

63 *Evacuees from Greenacre School, Yarmouth at East Markham, Nottinghamshire.*

overcoats are the chief things which they would normally leave in the cloak-rooms, it has not been worthwhile to use them. This was the practice in war time even in our buildings in Yarmouth. The only exception made is in wet weather, when alerts are less probable and obviously coats must be hung up to dry. The other reason is the overlapping of the two schools, made possible by the fact that the school hall is quite separate from the classrooms: thus our classes do not dismiss until Retford are in the hall having their assembly in the morning, and vice versa in the afternoon. The overlap lasts about ten minutes and greatly helps the daily timetable.

In November 1942, the Grammar School asked for 230 pairs of plimsolls and the High School for 169 pairs. These were delivered in January 1943 in wooden boxes – which the Clerk to the Governors asked to be returned to him undamaged! The Head Mistress of the High School was still having problems: the smallest size she had asked for was size three, but 'the unfortunate position is that the girls without gym shoes are last year's entries, and most of them have very small feet'. The Clerk had none, but thought he might be able at a later stage to provide some used ones in exchange for some shoes of the larger sizes – 'they will of course be fumigated before being sent on to you'. In April 1944 the Grammar School again asked for plimsolls but was told there would be no further allocation until after the war.

In 1943, the Grammar School sports master had his football boots and socks and his gym shoes stolen from the school gymnasium. The Yarmouth Education

Committee could not supply him with clothing coupons for replacements: they could only suggest that he make a formal appeal to the local Board of Trade.

In the summer of 1943, difficulties about billeting conditions in Retford surfaced. The Retford Billeting Officer, Mr Philips, had been paying an extra week's billeting allowance when a boy left his foster home for the holidays provided the home agreed to take him back in the following term. The Regional Evacuation Officer was now trying to stop this payment. Mr Palmer complained that the billeting allowances were far too low: 'I am quite sure that the allowance falls considerably short of the cost of feeding a child, quite apart from other expenses.' Palmer thought it was important to match the class of the pupil to that of the foster-parent. He wrote to the Clerk to the Governors: 'I hope it will be possible for you to let me have notes on the social standing etc of the new scholars, as requested by the Billeting Officer: a misfit in a billet is so apt to lead to the total loss of the billet.' The Evacuation Officer in Cambridge, however, was certain that the Government would not be increasing allowances, and told Palmer that there had been 'very little agitation for increasing the allowances in recent times'.

The year's intake of pupils had travelled to Retford on 28 September 1943. In October, the *Yarmouth Mercury* published an article saying that one boy had been housed in a bathroom. The authorities admitted that this had happened, but claimed that they had acted as soon as the boy had written to his mother about his situation: he was found a new billet on 2 October. They strongly refuted allegations that fee-paying pupils were being treated better than pupils on scholarships: 'The Billeting Officer does not know one from the other.'

In November 1943, 99 parents who between them had 111 pupils at the two schools, got up a petition that 'in view of the difficulties existing in the Reception Area now and likely to continue in the future, and because of changed conditions in Yarmouth itself, that secondary school provision be once more provided in the town'. The petition was organised by Mrs Strowger of Beatty Road whose daughter Margaret was at the High School. However, not everyone agreed with her criticism of the situation in Retford. Mr Marjoram of Manor Farm, South Walsham, wrote that his daughters seemed 'very comfy' in their billet, but he accepted that other children were less fortunate. The Clerk to the Governors simply replied that the schools had been closed by order of the government and could not be re-opened without the government's consent.

The situation grew worse rather than better. In February 1944, Mr Palmer pointed out that some boys were unable to return to the school after the Christmas holidays because of a shortage of billets. At least nine boys were in unsatisfactory situations but a new home had been found for only one of them. He quoted one example at length:

> The case of Goss, who is in the 6th form is an outstanding one. He is a very capable and willing boy and is being exploited by his foster-mother. He lays and cooks the breakfast, takes his young foster-brother most of the way to school and then comes to school himself. On returning to his billet he washes up the breakfast things, often prepares dinner, and washes up afterwards. It is the same story with tea and supper. His foster-mother frequently does not get up to breakfast and on one occasion she left town for a week, leaving Goss to run the house.

64 *Yarmouth Grammar School holding their 1941 sports day in Retford, where the school spent the entire war. Mrs Pereira faces the camera, Mr Whitehead holds the megaphone.*

This is just the headmaster's view, of course. It would be interesting to have a reply from the foster-mother – and the view of Goss himself. All records need to be interpreted and not just accepted at their face-value. In this case, the billeting officer agreed that the case of Goss was not satisfactory but pointed out that he had since been found a new home. In all the other eight cases mentioned by Mr Palmer, it was the foster-parents who wanted rid of their children.

Parents might be in difficult situations themselves. In August 1944, Mrs Swainson wrote to the High School asking that her daughter Stella be withdrawn as she could not afford the fees because her husband was ill. The couple were living in a cottage at Lowdham, Nottinghamshire, and Stella was billeted in Retford. The Governors would not accept this but offered to arrange for Stella to go to a school near Lowdham so that she could live at home. Mrs Swainson was unhappy with this idea. She pointed out that she only earned 25 shillings a week and her husband had been unable to work since having had a stroke two years earlier. Stella could not live with her: the cottage was too small and there was no secondary school for miles. She wanted Stella to stay in Retford and go to the local school there: 'Would I have to pay for her if she went to Retford High School?' Mrs Swainson reported on a visit home in August 1944: 'I came to Yarmouth last week to see when our house will be made habitable & and I am afraid not for another 6 months.' However, by this time it was clear that the danger of air raids in Yarmouth was over: both schools moved back to Yarmouth in September 1944.[5]

Other schools along the Norfolk coast also moved away. Gresham's School, Holt, moved to Newquay in Cornwall in 1940 and stayed for four years: its pupils won a prize for the quality of their coastal patrols. Lydgate House in Hunstanton moved to Ogston Hall in Derbyshire and the Headmaster and pupils of Lynfield School, also in Hunstanton, were taken in by Wellingborough School.[6]

Special-needs children were also evacuated from the area. Children from Melton Orthopaedic Hospital School went to Cawston Manor on 2 September 1939. They remained there for six years, returning to their Yarmouth premises for the autumn term in 1945.[7]

The East Anglian School for the Blind and Deaf in Gorleston also moved: there were 130 children at the school in 1940. They first thought of relocating to Burghley House, two miles from Oakham. Many of the rooms had 'valuable tapestry' and furnishings so that only 20 rooms could actually be used. The pipes had burst, so there was no running water. The School looked at Icklingham Hall in Suffolk and Shadwell Court near Thetford, but decided eventually to move further afield. They spent the war at Apergwm House and Maesyffynon in Glynneath, South Wales. Some parents withdrew their children from the school rather than see them go so far away. The number of pupils from Essex remained constant, but those from Norfolk and East Suffolk fell significantly. In 1944 there were 101 pupils at the school. The school buildings in Gorleston were taken over by the War Department in April 1941. The Headmaster's house was demolished by enemy action in June 1941.[8]

It was not just children who were evacuated from Great Yarmouth. Two hundred elderly bedridden and infirm from hospitals and care homes were taken to Lichfield by ambulance train in July 1940: the eldest person on the train was a man aged ninety-nine. There were several about the age of ninety and many octogenarians. One woman of 86, on leaving the ambulance in which she had been brought to the station, refused an offer of a lift on a stretcher. Another elderly evacuee made the remark, 'I haven't had a rest for seventy years, but I am going to get one now'.[9]

As well as the formal evacuation from the coastal towns, many families suffered agonies as to whether or not they should send their children to a safer part of the country. A few were there already, children away at boarding school. One was Elizabeth, the daughter of Tom Copeman of Unthank Road in Norwich, who was at school at Ackworth in Yorkshire. In September 1939, she wrote to her father: 'I do hope there is not a war. If there is please let me come home I could not live here I should keep thinking that you had been bombed.' In another letter, she commented: 'They are digging trenches in Great Garden and all over the place and gas masks have been issued. Is not war awful. I do hope there is not any.'

Her parents decided she should stay where she was, and her letters home illustrate her wartime life:

Last Thursday morning at 12.30 we had an air raid we were in the cellars for 3¼ hours it was terribly boring there was nothing to do and it was awfully stuffy. We could hear aeroplanes all the time and some shooting, no damage was done though … Oh! if you have any old scraps of wool you don't want please can you send them because we are making a form blanket to help the Friends who are evacuating people from London into the country if they have lost their houses. They have asked us to help as they have not enough bedding etc.[10]

John Turner, living in Titchwell, wrote to his sister in June 1940 about his uncertainty as to whether to send his younger daughter away. She replied:

> You say you are in nine different minds about Ursula. I am in ten! This isn't like the last war, when one could hit on many places in England to which to send a child in comparative certainty of her immunity. I just don't know where it _is_ safe in England now. Even far country places with no aerodromes may get parachutists. I think I should feel inclined either to keep her in Norfolk or let me have her in Brighton either in a school or in my flat, because she is then near someone to whom she will be a first consideration, and in the best 'strange' places if a panic arose she might not come first. At present London seems peaceful, and it might be all right at Nannie's while arrangements were made. There are aerodromes or factories nearly everywhere that I know people – even near Nannie, but I suppose some risk must be taken.

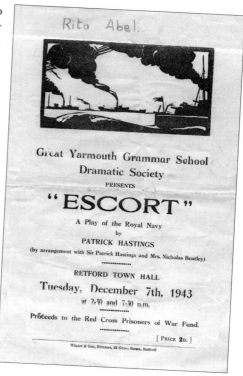

Rita Abel.

Great Yarmouth Grammar School
Dramatic Society

PRESENTS

"ESCORT"

A Play of the Royal Navy
by
PATRICK HASTINGS
(by arrangement with Sir Patrick Hastings and Mrs. Nicholas Bentley)

RETFORD TOWN HALL

Tuesday, December 7th, 1943
at 2-30 and 7-30 p.m.

Proceeds to the Red Cross Prisoners of War Fund.

[PRICE 2D.]

Winter & Son, Printers, 24 Grove Street, Retford

65 *Programme of a play staged in Retford by the pupils of Yarmouth Grammar School in 1943. Appropriately, the play is set on board a naval cruiser.*

On 20 June, Ursula travelled from Hunstanton to Nannie's house at Hillingdon in Middlesex with her elder sister, Ann. Ursula wrote home the next day:

> My dear Mummy and Daddy
> It was a very long journey from Hunstanton to London. We had a carrige [*sic*] to ourselves to begin with, then a little evacuee boy came in all by himself and was put in Aunt's care, his name was John. Then later on some Air Force men got in our carrige two sat down and one stood up in the corridor then he sat in the same seat as me so I was squashed in the corner.

Five weeks later, Middlesex was no longer safe: Ann rang up to say that nearby Kingston had been bombed: two days later Ann and Ursula returned to Titchwell. Nannie and her husband Walter were themselves now having a bad time in Hillingdon as the bombing grew more severe. In October, they came to stay at Titchwell: 'Poor souls! They could talk of nothing but bombs and noise and sleepless nights, not with any self-pity, but as if it was something which Fate had always had in store for them. They didn't know that their nerves were rattled to pieces, nor that their courage was anything to be commended.' They stayed for three weeks and then returned to their home in Hillingdon.[11]

As the air raids increased in Norwich and Yarmouth, many families moved to the homes of friends or relations in the county, or sent their children there. Others

66   *'How to identify the enemy': from a Home Guard leaflet. Fear of invasion reached its peak in September 1940.*

had no choice but to move after their homes were destroyed by bombs. We can take just two examples of families moving from Norwich to north-west Norfolk: in May 1942 three generations (all female) of the Smith family of Esdelle Street in Norwich arrived and were billeted with Mr Thompson at the School House in Snettisham. In August 1942, Mrs Lake and her child, known to the records only as 'Boy Lake', from Rosary Yard in Norwich, were found a home with Mrs Harwood in West Rudham.[12]

One possibility was to send children abroad for their safety, most commonly to Canada. In June 1940, the Government asked schools to help examine applicants. Between 900 and 1,000 children in the county of Norfolk (this excludes Norwich, Yarmouth and Lynn) were examined at a rate of 20 to 30 a day. However, of these children only seven actually went overseas. On 17 September 1940, the *City Of Benares* was torpedoed, with almost 100 evacuee children on their way to Canada on board: 77 were drowned. The scheme came to an immediate end.

The 'seavacuees' as they were called included Nancy and David Dyson of Spynke Road, Norwich. They stayed in a small village called Carp, 20 miles from Ottawa, and were looked after by Mr and Mrs Anderson. Nancy wrote to the Blyth School in Norwich with a description of her experiences:

> On 31 October, we celebrated Hallowe'en. At school we had a party, with peanuts, apples and sweets. In the evening, we dressed in old clothes and put on false faces. I went with another girl of my own age, who also comes from England … Canadians are just like our people. The language is slightly different. They call jumpers 'sweaters', and our gymslip is called a 'jumper' here.

In August 1945, the Dysons returned, arriving by train at Thorpe station after five years in Canada. Nancy, now 17, praised the Canadian schools system: she hoped to go to a college in England and train to become a teacher. Another returning evacuee was Alan Carey, now 13, whose parents lived on Drayton Road, Norwich: 'Living on a farm with a horse of his own and as much swimming, tobogganing and skating as he wanted, he looked the picture of health and 'guessed' he was a foot taller than when he had left Norwich.'[13]

In one area of Norfolk, whole families were forcibly evacuated from their homes, and after 60 years the resentment is still felt. In 1942, the government requisitioned 18,000 acres of land in the heart of the county for training purposes: 800 people were evacuated from the villages of Tottington, West Tofts, Stanford and Langford. There were about 30 farms, 150 houses, three schools and two pubs in the area, which also included the church at West Tofts, a fine Victorian building designed by Pugin. People were given five weeks to leave. Almost all moved into nearby villages so that they could move home when the war was over and the land was given back.

Despite promises, the land never has been given back. There are two sides to every story: some claim that the Battle Area has become a *de facto* nature reserve, where wildlife is undisturbed. Nevertheless, it is quite clear that the people of the area made the sacrifice on the clear understanding that the area would be restored to them after the war was over.[14]

Seven

The Threat of Invasion

On 10 May 1940, Germany invaded Belgium and the Netherlands. In Gorleston, a mere ninety miles from the battle, the sound reached across the Channel. Cecilia Ebbage recalled: 'In the early hours of the fateful May 10 we were woken up at about 4 am by the rattle of the windows and doors. Even with the subsequent bombing of the town I have never experienced that feeling of horror – the Germans had invaded Holland.' On 2 June, France agreed an armistice and Germany occupied the north of the country. Britain stood alone. Invasion was a very real possibility and Norfolk was one of the most likely counties where the enemy might land. People in the county had to think seriously about what this would mean to them. Turner confided to his diary:

> 23 May 1940 Heard astonishing suggestion, following doubt cast by myself on probability of Volunteers remaining at posts in action with their wives and children in cottages between them and the enemy, that it was possible all wives and children would be evacuated from coast-line.

> 5 June It seems strange to be hoarding in one's car a two-gallon tin of petrol (almost impossible to get in tins, now) against the possibility of sudden invasion and the removal, if practicable, of wife and children inland. But I am told it is by no means an unnecessary precaution.

> 30 June 1941: If there is to be an invasion I am, frankly, terrified about what might happen to Laura and to Ursula. I don't see how I can protect them or evacuate them. I find myself waking in the night and wondering about this.[1]

Anthony Hamond was more optimistic, writing to his son in February 1941: 'I can't see into the future further than any one else but though I can't see how Hitler can avoid having some sort of dart at invasion at the same time I don't see how he can hope to get any results from it & every day it gets worse for him. We are now building 125 camps in this country each to hold 1000 men at least, to be ready this summer.'[2]

Alan Colman, in far away Liberia, also thought about invasion. He wrote to his family at Carrow Abbey in Norwich:

> The Wireless news is playing up the Invasion attempt as nine parts of a certainty nowadays. I suppose my odds would be 15 to 1 on it being tried and 10 to 1 against it coming off well enough to knock England out of the War. If this tenth chance

should come off England joins the Occupied Zone and the war is carried on from Ottawa largely with the drive of the USA, who will be so worked up by then that they will be all set to really get down to things in their thorough way and we should eventually win about 1945. This little period will be a tricky one for you at home who will probably have the Gauleiter billeted on you – a difficult man doubtless. If this happens you must just assure yourself that its going to be d-d interesting – and no worse than having J to stay – and that you'll save up the best incidents for me, remaining all the while in your sweetest and most co-operative mood. He should have the Lake Room I think – what a lark! The thing to remember is that its worth just any sacrifice to beat up the little blighter – except the sacrifice of being depressed if he should beat you!

On 16 Feb two American missionaries came to dinner: they were vurry [sic] sweet and earnest and American and expressed a most unholy delight in the tale which they swallow (as do all the French out here) about 60,000 Germans drowned in the supposed trial invasion last October. A fantastic yarn – but it shows the right spirit.[3]

Fear of invasion led to rumours of German spies: any stranger might seem suspicious in the atmosphere of the summer of 1940. Turner recorded several:

27 May: Mrs Ringer reports in awestricken way that two Norfolk clergymen have been arrested, the machinery for their espionage being found in their vestries. Mrs Ringer appears not so moved at possible danger to life and limb from these men, as shocked that they should have the intelligence to hide incriminating material in the vestry – 'actually in our English churches, Mr Turner!'

1 June: During the afternoon PC Cushing arrived in great state of excitement about green car and tall moustached occupant, who has apparently been asking questions at Bircham Newton, and has now given them the slip.

An ammunition lorry charged the barricades at Thornham last night. The placing of these obstacles on the roads, if it achieves nothing else, has made the villagers realise that there is 'something doing'. They stand about, looking rather awed, and gaze at the overturned wagons, old harrows, and rusty iron. I am afraid they may not sleep so well now this has been done!

12 Feb 41: Learnt that in Newmarket(?) area parachutists had dropped in British uniform with device which was squirted over people and gave them some kind of skin disease. This apparently is true as antidote for disease was found and described. Disgusting form of warfare. All the parachutists, am glad to say, were captured.[4]

There were plenty of rumours and false alarms, such as this one recorded in the county war diary for 13 August 1941:

16.49 Parachute seen 16.15 G 7322 believed man attached height about 200 feet.
17.45. Parachutist landed Bergh Apton Rectory.
48.48. Parachutist Bergh Apton now ascertained to be deflated balloon which came down at Surlingham.[5]

Practical measures were taken in face of the new threat: by October 1940, 1,697 miles of wire, 73 miles of anti-tank mines and 440 miles of anti-tank obstacles had been set up in the area covered by Eastern Command. Pill boxes were erected along the coast and at key inland points such as Thetford and Diss railway stations. Other defensive points were cleverly hidden, but a few can still be discovered in the county like that built into the ruins of the medieval monastery of Bromholm

67 *Eccles Home Guard practise defensive duties: the high fence is to make it difficult for seaplanes to land.*

in Bacton village, and the one at the Manor House, Acle, disguised as a small outhouse.[6]

Invasion Committees

Invasion Committees were set up in towns and villages. That at Thetford was especially concerned with supplies of food in the town if it was cut off by German troops. On 18 June 1941, the Food Executive Officer asked the Divisional Food Officer in Cambridge if he could 'have a reserve store of canned meat which could be used as an iron ration in times of emergency ie air raids or invasion … it would certainly allay local misgivings, apart from the fact that the use of such commodity may become very necessary'. The reply was not positive:

The only stores we have in Thetford are sugar and some canned milk in White Hart Street, managed by Mr Palmer.

We do not propose putting any stores for emergency in towns like Thetford as it is considered there is plenty of food in them in case they were cut off during invasion. For instance the population of Thetford is 4845, but the buying population is 6,646; this shows that 1801 people come into the town to buy but will be unable to do so under invasion conditions. I am afraid in any case there is no canned meat available as it is all wanted to build up reserves.

I really do not think there is any need for misgivings as if cut off, Thetford should be able to exist for 14 days in the same way as other towns of the same size. If it were a case of an air raid, we can rush food into the towns as required.

Thetford Invasion Committee was not satisfied, laying out its case at greater length:

Theoretically, on the basis of buying population and resident population Thetford should be able to maintain itself for a period if cut off. But, with every respect, I would point out that in practice this would not follow.

Thetford has 6,576 registered customers for meat, but it is entirely dependent for its fresh meat upon sources quite remote from the Borough. There are no cattle farms in Thetford. If cut off the town would, therefore, be debarred from meat supplies. It might well occur that the town would be cut off on a day when the butchers were entirely without meat in their shops. This happening is not infrequent today.

Further, under the Thetford Defence Plan, which has recently been prepared by the Zone Commander of the Home Guard (Major General E.M. Steward) in conjunction with my local Committee, I am held responsible for feeding the Home Guard when fighting in the town and unable to return to their homes. To provide them with a suitable iron ration can only be satisfactorily done via some method of compressed meat.

Under this scheme, also, plans to provide Communal Feeding for at least 500 people have to be made. General Steward is of opinion that a reserve of Corned Meat of not less than two weeks' supply for 6,000 people should be provided.

Mr Palmer, White Hart Street, informs me he has a store of 10 tons of sugar held on your behalf, but no canned milk.

I quite appreciate your point that in the case of an air raid you could rush food into the town as required, but it seems to me that the same set of conditions would not apply to an invasion cut-off.

If the town has to be self-contained for a period then it would appear essential that it should be provided with an Emergency Store of suitable foods to cope with it, otherwise the Food Executive Officer will be placed in the unenviable position of having to make bricks without straw!

Six months later, in January 1942 – when many might think the danger of invasion had largely passed as Hitler was now fully occupied on the Russian front – Cambridge came round, and was almost showering Thetford with offers of supplies:

The survey of stocks held in your retail shops has now been completed, and we are in a position to compare the results with similar stock returns from other towns …
In my opinion, our assumption that your main need is for reserves of meat and milk is borne out by these figures, but I should be glad to have your opinion on them.

The only other figure which is noticeably low is that for bread. It may be that special circumstances in the week of the return unduly depressed stocks of flour and wheat, or it may be that the baking resources of your Borough are not very extensive. Unless you are satisfied that the return does not really represent the true position, I think it would be wise to include a reserve of biscuits (iron ration type) in your emergency stores. These are packed in sealed tins, and may be expected to keep in good condition for about a year.

Other foodstuffs are available if you consider that you require them, and if you are able to find storage for them. I have given you the figures of the maximum quantities available for your Borough, and should be glad if you would indicate any supplies which you would like to have, up to these maxima.

However, the Thetford Food Control Officer was still not happy. He also, rather late in the correspondence, raised the question for the first time whether there was to be any payment involved for the food. He agreed that the main needs were for meat and milk, but added biscuits to this list of essentials. However: 'It is observed that you have provisionally fixed an Emergency ration for 4,600 people. Thetford's food population is 4,900 and I am strongly of opinion provision should be made for at least 5,000 people. After careful consideration, I would suggest that you make available sufficient Beef, Milk, Biscuits, Soup and Tea to provide a ration for 5,000 people on the same basis per head as set forth in the allocation sheet to me.'

In fact, the total food came to 20 tons, with each ton intended to supply 250 people, and was stored in thirteen different centres around the town. The authorities issued a flyer explaining the plans:

BOROUGH OF THETFORD
IMPORTANT

Emergency Arrangements

In the event of invasion, arrangements have been made to make a distribution at specified points in the town, the location of which will be notified [to] householders by the Police, Wardens, Air Training Corps, etc of an emergency ration to every civilian in the Borough comprising:

3¾ lb biscuits	1 tin corned beef
1 tin pork and beans	1 tin condensed milk
1 lb sugar	4 ozs margarine
	2 ozs tea

This ration will be distributed in bulk for eight people consisting of:

2 tins biscuits	8 tins corned beef
8 tins pork and beans	8 tins condensed milk
8 lbs sugar	1 tin margarine (2 lbs) and
	1 lb tea

The reason for distributing the rations in units each sufficient for eight people is that the biscuits and margarine are contained in 15lb and 2lb sealed tins respectively and cannot be split before distribution. Residents, therefore, must arrange to draw their rations in parties of eight and for the bulk to be divided by the leader of each party when he gets them home. The cost of the rations will be 6/- per person and all ration books will have to be produced. In view of the weight the person collecting the rations should bring with him sufficient means to carry them away, viz a wheelbarrow, handcart, perambulator, cycle etc, or, alternatively for two or more persons to go to carry the food. During the distribution period all the shops would be closed for stock-taking, but would re-open after a few hours for the sale of goods on a basis of equitable distribution. These emergency rations are a last line of defence and should not be consumed immediately but should be kept until all else fails.

The conserving of the water supply will also be of vital importance. Notice will be given by loudspeaker vans, wardens etc that all consumers are immediately to fill pails and any other receptacles they may have for water for use in case of shortage or failure of the supply from the mains. After the limited period allowed for the filling of receptacles the water in the mains will be turned off in order that the reservoir

may be filled. As it may not be possible to obtain a further supply from the mains, the water stores on consumer's premises must be carefully husbanded and used in as small quantities as possible. The same water should be used for as many purposes as possible, with waste water for hand flushing of lavatories. Alternatively, householders having the use of WCs must provide temporary facilities in their back gardens to bury the excreta. Pail closets and privies will continue to be emptied by the Borough Surveyor's Department so long as practicable. Should the piped water supply fail, arrangements have been made for water from the river to be supplied. This will be carted to certain points in the town of which notice will be given. From these points householders will be required to collect their ration of water of not more than one gallon a day for each person. It will be necessary for householders to boil water not drawn from sources in normal use before using it for drinking, preparation of food or washing up. Boiling kills all dangerous bacteria.
By Order,

G. R. BLAYDON,
November 1942 Town Clerk and Food Executive Officer.

This leaflet should be carefully read and taken care of for reference should the necessity arise.[7]

In a market town such as Reepham, preparations were just as thorough – if on a smaller scale. The Parish (Invasion) Committee was formed on 25 June 1941. Its chairman was Mr Owen, who was already chairman of the parish council, senior warden and parish food organiser. Mr Kendall Chapman, clerk to the parish council, was clerk to the new committee. Six other people were present at the first meeting, including Mr Thompson, the deputy senior warden, Inspector Wilkin for the police and Mrs Luscombe representing the local First Aid Point. They decided to call in extra help including Major Campbell with responsibility for refugees and Mr Thompson's 'older boys' to act as runners; he was the school teacher, so that the reference was to his pupils rather than his sons! Mr Curtis took charge of fire-watching.

A meeting with the town tradesmen followed: they were willing to maintain heavier stocks to act as emergency supplies for the town, but pointed out that they could only do this if they were authorised to have increased buying permits. It was agreed to set up a Food Dump, and to assign all non-registered customers to particular food shops who would supply them in an emergency. The scale of issue from the Dump was soon agreed. Each person would be allowed two pounds of biscuits, half a pound of sugar, one ounce of tea and two ounces of margarine: at this stage no meat in any form was included in the emergency ration.

Two lengthy meetings in November and December 1941 showed that Reepham was ready for the worst. Major Campbell had left the town but he was replaced as billeting officer by Captain Gentry, who reported that arrangements were in hand for up to 80 evacuees. Lieutenant Bass said that the Home Guard was 150 strong. However, Mr Thompson had realised that most of his boys could not actually help as they were not from Reepham itself but from neighbouring villages. Mr Curtis was also less positive saying that he did not have enough fire-watchers.

The committee issued a statement on 27 January 1943 showing that all points had been covered:

WARDENS: 30, with about 12 Auxiliary Wardens.

MESSENGER SERVICE: 4 Motor Cyclists of the CD Messenger Sce, 40 St John's Amb and Red Cross Cadets (including 6 enrolled CD Telephonists) and 12 Royal Artillery Cadets.

CASUALTY SERVICES: Part of one Church, the Wesleyan Chapel, and the Band Hall and Town Hall earmarked for expansion. Sanitation anywhere not good for crowded use. About 60 being trained at Depot, and 30 at point.

DRINKING WATER: Reepham's supply chiefly from pumps on each occupation or adjacent thereto, or wells (covered).

FOOD: the official dumps will be augmented by shop supplies, and the total equally distributed. A voluntary staff of about 60 will assist in the distribution. Each householder has been allocated the shop from which he will draw his shop supplies, full details as to procedure having been printed on the card entitling him to supplies. A form for stocktaking the shopkeepers has been issued them. No provision for communal feeding.

EMERGENCY LIGHTING: everyone has been advised to lay in stocks of candles, and where possible, parrafin [sic].

PROVISION FOR HOMELESS: Shelter; To PIC Headquarters as a Clearing House, thence to Billets as available by the Billeting Officer's record. Food will need some consideration.

LABOUR: A mixed force of 319 men and women (chiefly women) divided into 9 groups, each group having its leader, who has become aware of the strength of the group in personnel and equipment. The Emergency Labour Master will instruct the leader of any group needed as to what equipment and service is desired, and the group leader will carry out his directions.

RESCUE PARTY: Leader, Mr H. Collison, Cawston Road, Reepham. Tools, his builder's equipment. (Note: the official Rescue Party is understood to be located at Aylsham. The local rescue Party has been recruited from our builders and bricklayers chiefly.)

CLEANSING AND D/C PROCEDURE: none available locally.

MORTUARY: Officer, S.P. Eglington. Mortuary at *Duke of York*, Reepham. Burial Ground, the Cemetery, Whitwell Road.

COLLABORATION WITH MILITARY ETC: The PIC are fully conversant with the necessary procedure.

CO-OPERATION OF PUBLIC: we have tried to educate our public.

The PIC will be immediately summoned to Session on receipt of Invasion Warning message.

The Food Committee met on 2 February. It had good news. The Dump had received many more supplies:

Original supply
220 cases of 15 lb biscuits + 490 tins extra
18 cases of 48 tins meat + 42 cases extra
18 cases of 48 tins soup
10 cases of 96 tins milk
32 cases of 28 lb sugar
6 cases of 18 ¾ lb margarine + 12 cases of 20 lb tins extra
2 cases of 25 lb tea + 7 cases extra

As a result they were able to increase the amount to be handed out:

Biscuits; ½ tin each person (1 tin between 3)
Meat: 1½ tins each
Margarine: 6 oz each
Tea: ¼ lb each.

The Committee met again in August 1943 to consider exercises planned for 24 August. It was pointed out that the Reepham Home Guard had now combined with those of Booton and Salle to total 150 men. Two spigot mortars had been set up at the railway station. In fact by the summer of 1943 the danger of invasion had long passed. Indeed, in July 355 tins of biscuits were returned to the Ministry of Food. The final meeting was called on 9 November 1944, where the Committee was formally wound down.[8]

Villages also responded to the threat: at Fleggburgh, as in many other villages, a handout went to every household with advice in case of invasion. It advised everyone to keep a fortnight's supply of flour and a week's supply of groceries in the house, and gave the addresses of four emergency food supplies placed so that 'NO ONE NEED CROSS THE NORWICH-YARMOUTH MAIN ROAD'. The ration cost ten shillings and had recently been increased. It consisted of seven and a half pounds of biscuits, one pound of sugar, three quarters of a pound of tea, seven ounces of margarine, two tins of meat, one tin of soup, one tin of condensed milk. The handout ended with three tips in case of invasion; 'KEEP YOUR CHILDREN INDOORS. STAY PUT. HELP ONE ANOTHER'.[9]

The War Emergency Committee in Stoke Holy Cross held its first meeting on 23 May 1941 – as was common, the vicar was chairman. The committee looked at the voters' list to see which men might be enrolled in the Home Guard or Civil Defence Services. A list of 'women who could bake' was compiled. A rota of farmers and wardens was drawn up to watch at night, although it was noted that Mr Green of Upper Stoke 'refused to serve'. Emergency supplies were delivered to various points in the village, including the Vicarage. The supplies consisted of two cases of corned beef, one case of pea soup, half a case of tinned milk, nine tins of margarine, three packets of sugar, 12 packets of tea and 22 cases of biscuits. The same supplies were stored at six other dumps, and it was agreed that in the event of an emergency one dump should be opened every three days. The group were prepared to take all kinds of power if necessary: 'The Committee expects to function as a government while the emergency lasts, and is prepared to shoulder responsibility for action taken.'

As the danger of invasion faded, the Committees met less and less often: in October 1944 they were stood down. The County Council thought about their records: 'The Schemes prepared by your Invasion Committee should either be destroyed as Secret waste or retained within the Local Parish Council archives as being of some historical interest.' Most committees chose the former course: only a very few of these records have survived for Norfolk.[10]

Invasion Exercises

Invasion exercises were held in many towns and villages to see how the emergency services would cope. One of the first in Norfolk was organised by Anthony Hamond in March 1941 as a test both for the Home Guard and for soldiers in training in North Norfolk. Hamond described the events to his son:

CIVIL PARISH OF FLEGGBURGH.

Please Read this carefully.   Keep it for reference.

The Parish Invasion Committee has its Headquarters at Burgh House. The Heads of the various Services are :—

Chairman and Food Officer	...	Rev. W. E. Reeve, The Parsonage.
Home Guard	...	Mr. F. Drake, The Garage.
Wardens' Service	...	Mr. H. B. Claxton, The Laurels.
Labour Party	...	Mr. G. F. Curtis, Town Road.
Casualty Service	...	Dr. T. W. E. Royden, Roby Lodge.
		Mrs. Drake, The Garage.
Billeting Officer	...	Mrs. T. W. E. Royden, Roby Lodge.
National Fire Service	...	Mr. W. H. Woolston, Broad Road.
Fire Guard Service	...	Mr. L. F. Harrison, Tower Road.
W.V.S. and Secretary	...	Mrs. W. E. Reeve, The Parsonage.
Police	...	P.C. F. Harwin, Police House.

In an emergency take orders from no one excepting the Chairman of the P.I.C., the local Home Guard, the local Wardens, and the local Police. NOTICES will be posted on the Official Notice Boards at the Police House, and at the Post Office. ALL OTHER NOTICES MUST BE IGNORED. The FIRST AID POINT is at the Coffee Tavern.

The SCHOOL is scheduled as a REST CENTRE for homeless people until billets can be found for them. Be ready in an emergency to take in people driven from their homes, or to offer beds for casualties. Keep by you old sheets, linen, etc., for emergency bandages. See that your Gas Masks are always in order and ready to hand for immediate use. Get from the Chemist a supply of Anti-gas Ointment No. 2, Price 6d. Notify the Chairman when there are any changes in the number of persons in your household, so that the parochial record can be kept up to date. Make sure that everyone in your household has an Identity Card, and have the address corrected if you move to another house.

In an emergency instructions will be given about digging slit trenches.

Please fill in the attached form. It will be called for.

NAME & ADDRESS OF HOUSEHOLDER...

....

NUMBER OF OCCUPANTS.	Under 16	16—65	Over 65

State how many of the following articles you have :—

Stirrup Pumps...............   Shovels.......................   Axes ....
Ladders...........................   Wheel-barrows..............   Ropes ....
Picks..............................   Crowbars ....   Jacks ....

Sign your name opposite any one or more of the following Services to which you already belong, or which you are willing to join :—

Fire Watching Parties   ....
Stretcher Parties   ....
Casualty Service   ....
Labour Party   ....

THE COMMITTEE EARNESTLY REQUESTS THAT THIS FORM SHOULD BE FILLED IN.

68   *Invasion precautions at Fleggburgh. Every town and village in Norfolk had its own Invasion Committee.*

On Sunday we had a most terrific battle here. A neighbouring brigade asked me if they had an exercise would the Home Guard play? Yes of course, so the attack was to drive E through Warham, Wighton, Gt and Lt Walsingham & Houghton with the main thrust at Wighton. I stipulated that at least one vehicle should act as a tank at each place & the 'bombs' were prepared. Paper bags of soot and chalk, yellow ochre etc, not to mention ½ ton of rotten apples at Hindringham and 300 rotten eggs at Houghton. Battle was joined at 6 am Sunday morning & the defence was really remarkable. Bottles and stones were banned also bayonets & everyone had to be searched for live SAA [small arms ammunition]. Quantities of fireworks delighted the troops from 'Little Demons' to 'Thunderflashes' which were powerful enough to blow anyone to pieces. It was a foggy morning exactly as it always is in war. The troops being strangers got lost & rushed madly ahead unperceived in the fog & were 1½ hours ahead of schedule when they got to Hindringham where they were fallen upon by the populace & forced into a very small room as prisoners. Only on the tearful representation of an umpire that they were dying of thirst did the ancient South African veteran allow them to be marched away.[11]

Several large-scale invasion exercises under the title of Scorch were held in December 1941, including one at Thetford. The scenario that the civil defence volunteers had to deal with was a complicated one:

Between the hours of 15.00 and 24.00 on 6 December 1941, enemy aeroplanes dropped High Explosive, Gas and Incendiary Bombs on the centre of the town, causing great damage, many fires and heavy casualties. Two large Hotels, seven Food Shops, a Nursing Home, the Cottage Hospital and the Girls' Grammar school were destroyed. Outside assistance was sought and rendered by the Regional Fire Services and Ambulance Services attached to the County organisation. These services were dismissed and returned home in the course of the night, although in actuality they would have remained in action.

At 06.30 hours on 7 December was informed by Southern Area Control centre they were unable to get help to Thetford as all roads impassable and advised Invasion Committee to take control.

At 07.20 hours the Guildhall was burnt down, the control Centre and Food Office blown up and the SubController killed. I contacted the Mayor as quickly as possible, who instructed me to call the Invasion Committee together to take control of the town. Under the Mayor's chairmanship the elements of the Committee available operated from the office of the Thetford and Watton Times, at the junction of Raymond Street and Cage Lane, from 09.00 hours.

Emergency Hospitals were set up at the Boys' Grammar School and St Barnabas' Hospital. Casualties were dealt with as far as humanly practicable by the limited resources available. Owing to all bridges being blown, other than the Melford Bridge, road damage and intermittent street fighting, conveyance of casualties to these hospitals was a somewhat lengthy and difficult operation and at times extremely dangerous. On three occasions during the day the enemy penetrated the town and were not finally expelled until 16.30 hours.

A temporary food office was set up at the Salvation Army Hall, Magdalen Street, and the Rest Centre, Council School, was open all day. In the prevailing circumstances, little use of them could be made by the public.

Having received a message from the Regional Control, Cambridge by DR at 16.15 hours that communications with Cambridge had not officially broken down, sent back a brief picture of the Civil and Food positions to the Regional Commissioner and Divisional Food Officer, Cambridge, respectively by DR.

Of course the defenders did not know this scenario all at once – it was fed to them gradually in messages sent by the planners of the exercise. Unusually, these messages still survive among the Thetford Corporation records in the Norfolk Record Office, so that it is possible to recreate the event moment by moment. Not everything went smoothly. At 16.05, Thetford Control reported to the Gas Identification officer at the

Grammar School: 'Gas reported dropped King Street & Market Square please take necessary action.' Ten minutes later the Control Centre informed the Police Station: 'HE dropped King Street & Market Place. Mustard Gas reported.'

The response was not satisfactory. Two hours later, at 18.00, Southern Area at Attleborough complained to the Control Centre: 'Reported by Senior Police Umpire that lack of information passing through Melford Report Centre is holding up civil defence operations – owing to lack of Police Personnel roads which are impassable are not guarded by barrier so no decontamination has been affected although an attack of mustard gas was made on the town at 16.00.' Southern Area raised the issue once more an hour later, at 18.58: 'Reference report of mustard gas please state action taken, the time of the occurrence, the time the decontamination squad ordered out. Time DC squad took to attend to the job. Was the Gas Identification Officer used? This matter is urgent.' Clearly, the defenders had failed to respond adequately to the threat of gas, but otherwise they seem to have coped well.[12]

Invasion exercises were also held in villages but on a smaller scale, typically lasting about 90 minutes. One was held at Fleggburgh on 22 March 1942. In this case the comments of the Umpire survive so that we can see how the amateur soldiers of the village coped with crisis. At 10.45 am it was announced that a bomb had fallen on a house at the corner of Marsh Road and the main Yarmouth Road. There were casualties. The Umpire noted that the casualties were promptly dealt with and men turned up to clear the roads: however, a delay then occurred as no one seemed to know who was in charge of the men. At 11.05 an enemy aircraft dive-bombed and machine-gunned the area, wounding five members of the Home Guard, two seriously: these were also dealt with promptly.

Five minutes later, the defenders were told that the *Live and Let Live* was on fire and that there was gas in the vicinity. The fire pump turned up promptly but the attempts of the organisers to set up the gas attack did not work out, as the Umpire reported: 'Unfortunately the wind was too strong for Lt Pakenham's tear gas, which dispersed before the fire party arrived. He managed to gas himself however, so his well-meaning efforts were not entirely wasted.' When rumours of gas reached the Invasion Committee, everyone there put on their gas masks, which the Umpire thought was an over-reaction: he noted that respirators were not provided for the casualties and that no one actually tried to locate and deal with the gas.

The pressure was kept up by the organisers: the Committee were told at 11.30 that 20 refugees had turned up from Rollesby. Temporary accommodation was given to them in the local school, and light refreshment was made available. Less satisfactory was the fact that, although there was a list of available billets, it was kept in Acle, several miles away!

Twenty minutes later, the Committee faced an even more severe test – they were told that a bomb had fallen on their Headquarters and killed the Chairman. The aim was to see whether the Committee had thought of this possibility and arranged for a back-up headquarters. They had – the school was heated and ready for use. The Deputy Chairman took over and everyone moved to the school, including the Umpire, who 'made the journey safely only stopping to admire a gallant defender who, although under point blank fire from one machine gun and six rifles stubbornly refused to 'lay down' '.

At 12.00 it was planned to announce that a garage had been set on fire and tear gas released. This had to be abandoned as the 'attackers', Home Guard men from Martham, came into the village earlier than planned.

In general, the Umpire was reasonably satisfied. His main criticisms were with the buildings – the Coffee Tavern was not suitable as an HQ as it had no protection from blast and no telephone. The school was not a suitable alternative as it had no blackout. The other complaint was that village boys kept popping in and out of the HQ to see what was going on.[13]

The village of West Rudham was tested on 7 May 1942. The Committee had to imagine that the enemy had landed at Stiffkey the previous night and that all the roads out of the village were closed to civilian traffic. The incidents, in this case devised by Lt Col W.M. Campbell, were spread over just 35 minutes:

> 19.15: Fifteen refugees arrive from Syderstone.
> 19.23: Crater 50 yards east of church – main road blocked, 12 casualties. Crater 50 yards south of church. Fire north of First Aid Post and three isolated cottages to west.
> 19.23: Stick of bombs church to smithy on Harpley Road – six houses demolished, four killed, 16 wounded, 25 homeless. Main road blocked.
> 19.30: Four casualties from machine gun fire at Dr Fleming's.
> 19.50: Message received to say that enemy is working west of Tattersett.[14]

The Home Guard

Most people's idea of the Home Guard comes from the BBC TV programme *Dads' Army* and there is nothing wrong with that. Not only is it a hilarious show, but it conveys all sorts of aspects of wartime life such as the blackout, rationing and spivs, which are easily forgotten. Many episodes of the show, incidentally, were filmed in Norfolk. No doubt there *was* a good deal of buffoonery, pomposity and red tape, but also – as the programme does acknowledge in several episodes – these very ordinary men were the people on whom Britain would have to depend to resist any enemy invasion. Men in the Home Guard, in Norfolk and elsewhere, died in fulfilling their role, as we shall see.

On 14 May 1940, Anthony Eden made a radio broadcast explaining that every man would be needed in case of invasion (he did not mention women). He told his listeners: 'Now is your opportunity. We want large numbers of such men in Great Britain who are British subjects, between the ages of fifteen and sixty-five, to come forward now and offer their services in order to make assurance doubly sure. The name of the new force which is now to be raised will be the Local Defence Volunteers.'

Over 250,000 men volunteered within 24 hours: by the end of May no fewer than 30,000 men had enrolled in Norfolk alone. Guns and uniforms were in short supply at first, though the men of Norfolk were better off than many as a large number of country dwellers would have owned guns and been familiar with using them.

On 22 May, the aims of the LDV were set out by the Secretary of State for War:

1. **Observation and Information**. The first duty was to stay alert for possible enemy attack and in the event of such an attack, to provide details swiftly to the local regular army authorities.
2. **Obstruction**. They were to prevent movement of enemy groups landed by air, by providing road blocks, so such groups would be hemmed in. They were also

69   *King's Lynn platoon, Women's Auxiliary Home Guard, standing down, Tuesday Market Place.*

to ensure there would be no access for the enemy to motor vehicles, by removing spark plugs and distributor plugs and distributors.

3. **Patrol and Protection**. They were to ensure that all vulnerable spots in their area – bridges, crossroads, railway stations, telephone exchanges etc – were guarded at all times.[15]

Armbands were issued in May but battle dress was not generally available until the end of the year. There were very few guns at first – an appeal produced some very ancient ones from places such as the Royal Palace at Sandringham and Norwich Castle Museum! However, things slowly improved: by the end of 1941 all units had rifles and at least some ammunition.

Winston Churchill never liked the name of Local Defence Volunteers: on his insistence the name was changed on 24 July 1940 to that of the Home Guard. A handbill issued by the Eastern Command in August 1940 included the following paragraphs:

The Home Guard is an integral part of the land forces engaged in the battle of Britain. The importance of its part in that battle cannot be exaggerated. The resistance that it will put up in towns and villages will disorganize enemy forces landed by sea or air, isolate their detachments, and prevent co-ordination of effort. Of no less importance will be small parties, or even individuals, who knowing every square yard of their country, harry the enemy with skill and determination by day and by night. The Germans will be well trained and equipped, but they don't like opposition, counter attack or night work. They like to rest at night, and all successful efforts to disturb their rest will have the greatest effect.

Remember that during their move through France in many parts they met little or no opposition. The Home Guard will see to it that this sort of thing cannot happen in England. Also remember that every successful defence of a village, every offensive act carried out by day or night will reduce the area temporarily occupied by the enemy, and the numbers of old people and women and children who will have to suffer the indignities or worse of such occupation.

When the battle of Britain is won and its history is written, the part taken by the Home Guard will stand out with the achievements of all the other services as evidence to all that Britain refused to be beaten whatever the forces arrayed against her.[16]

Many Norfolk Home Guard units took part in training weekends at Moreton Hall near Lenwade. Victor Bennett of the Sprowston Home Guard recalled:

Divided into groups we went through the first days syllabus all being routine stuff. It all changed when the two Sprowston doctors, the Carlson brothers, made an appearance and gave a lecture on the medical aspects in a battle area. It all made sense when red cross boxes and stretchers arrived. Volunteers for the next stage – the injured, attendants, the bearers. Soon the 'injured' covered in tomato ketchup, bandaging, then strapped onto the stretcher, the bearers dashing off with their charge to hospital. The patients would be cleaned up and surely remember the bumpy ride they had experienced on the way to hospital. It would now be their turn next as bearers, making it bumpier.[17]

In December 1941, it became compulsory for men not already involved in some form of home defence such as fire-watching to join the Home Guard. Some of the volunteers did not like the introduction of compulsion, and some of the older men resigned in protest. Under the new regulations, men were required to put in 48 hours a month: most of the volunteers had been giving a lot more time than this to the Home Guard.

A record of the names of the men in the Syderstone Home Guard was kept by the vicar, Norman Foudrinier, himself a founder member. Twenty-two men enrolled in August 1940, two more in September, and another six in 1941. A few subsequently left, of course, usually for health reasons, although one, Douglas Havers, departed when he was old enough to join the regular army in 1944. With the introduction of compulsion, 17 men joined in 1942 and six in 1943. Sprowston Home Guard was a much larger organisation, with a maximum of 190 members: no fewer than 36 men passed through the unit prior to joining the armed forces.[18]

Women could not join the Home Guard. However, many units did admit women to make up the numbers. From April 1943, Women's Home Guard Auxiliaries could be formed: the women were to be between 18 and 65, and preferably over 45: they were not be trained in the use of weapons.

Although the Home Guard never had to face the enemy in battle, there were dangers and even fatalities. Barbara Smith of Norwich recalls that her father had served in the Home Guard: he told her that one of his unit died after developing pneumonia following an exercise in very wet weather; another was killed in an accident during bayonet practice. The latter was Terry Wasley, who had worked at City Hall.

Joy Hayward knew him and wrote to John Heading:

> On Thursday evening there was something for 'Salute the Soldier' held in Chapel Field gardens. I don't know quite what it was, but I know the Home Guard were there doing demonstrations. An unfortunate accident happened, and when two men, the best performers of it, did a combat or something, something happened and one of them got stabbed in the thigh with a bayonet. Next morning at the City Hall the news got round someone had been killed, almost as soon as we were on the doorstep and then I was told it was a man in our office – Terry Wasley.[19]

Wasley is buried in the Rosary Cemetery, his membership of the Home Guard recorded on his tombstone. Others who died on duty in Norfolk included 44-year-old railwaymen, Sydney Crown of Heacham, killed when a mills bomb blew up during bomb practice, and George Spilling, killed by a gunshot wound in a Home Guard and Civil Defence exercise at Aylsham in 1944; Spilling was only 17 at the time of his death.

Other members of the force distinguished themselves by their courage, as this newspaper report makes clear:

> HM THE KING has been pleased to commend Corporal FRANK JAMES PAGE, 9, Brabazon Road, Hellesdon, a member of the Home Guard, in recognition of his services at Horsham St Faiths on the 22nd November 1941, when, showing initiative and gallantry in the face of danger and after a determined search, he rescued a child from an upper room of a smoke-filled and blazing house on which a British aircraft had crashed.[20]

70 *John Turner in his Home Guard uniform.*

In June 1941, the Germans turned east and attacked Russia. Many people thought that the Russians would be defeated in a few weeks and that Germany would then turn its attention to Britain. This was not to be. Fighting with immense bravery, and making an incredible sacrifice in terms of lives, the Russians retreated for months, but were eventually able to hold their enemy. The real fear of invasion was over, and by 1944 there was little doubt that Germany would eventually lose the war. After D-Day, there was no need for the Home Guard. John Turner, one of its members, noted in his diary:

> 19 Aug: There is a rumour that the Home Guard is to close down in October. Certainly I cannot see that the expense of it is any longer justified.

> 5 Sep: We learnt that the Home Guard is on the verge of 'standing down' (the preliminary to disbandment). I actually saw the War Office letter and the book of instructions for the moment when the code word is received from Whitehall. So, in a week or so, the Home Guard will come to an end. I shall not be sorry, having no inclination towards arms. But I am much afraid that the Major Whitakers and Major Watsons will find their occupations (and their trumpery importance) gone for ever.[21]

The Home Guard was stood down in November 1944. It has left few memorials in the county. One is on the pillbox beside Diss railway station, where a plaque reads:

> This pillbox was one of some 1800 pillboxes, almost all constructed to War Office designs between June and September 1940, at a time when Winston Churchill was MP and the German armies had reached the coast of Holland some 160 miles from this spot. This plaque is placed here as a reminder of those times, and as a memorial to the Home Guard, formed originally as the Local Defence Volunteers and finally disbanded 50 years ago in May 1945.[22]

Eight

Death from the Air

Pre-war Precautions

As the situation in Europe darkened in the 1930s, there was increased pessimism about the effect of heavy bombing on cities. Stanley Baldwin told Parliament in November 1932: 'I think it is well for the man in the street to realise that there is no power on earth that can prevent him from being bombed. Whatever people may tell him, the bomber will always get through.' By 1936, people were planning ahead: the Norfolk County Air Raid Precautions Committee first met on 10 February. In December, it suggested that the County Council should select four or five institutions in different parts of the county which could be used as hospitals for between 100 and 150 cases each. It was also said: 'Since Norwich is an obvious target for air raids and the Norfolk and Norwich Hospital a conspicuous and indefensible building, we advise the evacuation of all patients fit to be moved. It is therefore suggested that the County Council should be asked to reserve for our use an Institution near to the city, capable of accommodating 100 patients. This Institution would be staffed by the Hospital and would be used for cases of disease and accident not resulting from air raids.'

By October 1938, almost 4,000 Air Raid Wardens had volunteered in the county (that is, excluding the boroughs, which had their own organisations); only 49 were fully trained but over 2,500 were in training and the remainder waiting for their turn. By February 1939, 10,630 had been enrolled and over 6,000 were fully trained.[1]

Dress rehearsals began to be held. An ARP test at Reepham in June 1938 was a fiasco. An aeroplane dropped 'bombs' and smoke candles were lit to represent burning buildings: 'For some minutes nothing happened. Then a warden patrolling a short distance away, attracted by the smoke clouds, came to the scene. He studied the situation and then came on to the road and walked over a section that had been liberally sprayed with a mixture that he should have recognised as mustard gas. This was the first big mistake. He not only ignored its presence – for which he ought to have been immediately marked as a casualty – but was allowed to continue – he even neglected to go to his station or report anything. Consequently the fire brigade remained in ignorance of the fact that a fire was in progress and that there was also mustard gas to contend with.'[2]

A rehearsal at Wells in March 1939 appears to have been more successful. The local press reported:

A 'bomb' was exploded at the north end of the town and this was immediately reported by two patrols, and within two minutes of the report leaving headquarters the Fire Brigade were on their way. Twenty minutes later a report was received of another 'bomb' having exploded, quite near the headquarters, and again the Fire Brigade were promptly on the scene and averted all dangers.

The thick fog which hung over the town to a great extent hindered operations, but in spite of this everything was carried out in a most satisfactory manner. Weather conditions prevented the appearance of aeroplanes.

At the conclusion of operations Captain Chamberlin had a talk with all the wardens and stated that he was pleased with the manner in which they had carried out their duties. He said they learned many lessons. All the wardens showed willingness in their duties and went about their work seriously.[3]

It was the foreign situation that made people prepare for war. Ralph Mottram wrote:

The Munich crisis brought disillusion. Then began the feverish digging of trenches in public places and the little less heating [sic] discussion of the rival merits of open trenches or deep shelters. No one knew what would be the effect of the rain of high explosive which the most pessimistic prophesised [sic] would be showered on our devoted heads on the very morrow, at latest, of the outbreak of war.

Munich, however, not only carried conviction of the practical certainty of war. It gave the public at large its first experience of the usefulness of the wardens' Service through the distribution of more than 126,000 respirators – or gas masks as they were called. Shelter construction, too, was carried on, so that by the time war really did break out, 17,000 Norwich citizens could take underground refuge if the need arose, and if they had the warning and the time to reach the open spaces where in the main public shelters were dug. By the time the big raids came in April 1942 there was room for 122,000.[4]

On 22 September 1939, the *Eastern Daily Press* reported that 27,000 gas masks for St Faiths and Aylsham Rural District had arrived at Aylsham Town Hall. Within a week about 5,000 had been delivered throughout Sprowston.[5]

A county-wide blackout rehearsal was held in June:

IMPORTANT NOTICE
NORFOLK COUNTY COUNCIL
AIR RAID PRECAUTIONS
Night of 13/14 July, 1939

The County Council have agreed to hold a 'black-out' on
the night of 13/14 July 1939, and it is desired to secure that
no lights are visible from the air between 12 MIDNIGHT and
4 am in the MORNING of the 14 July, 1939.

HOUSEHOLDERS AND ALL OCCUPIERS OF
PREMISES ARE ACCORDINGLY ASKED TO ASSIST BY
ENSURING THAT LIGHTS IN THEIR PREMISES ARE EXTINGUISHED, OR SCREENED BY DARK
CURTAINS OR DARK
BLINDS, BETWEEN 12 MIDNIGHT AND 4 IN THE EARLY
MORNING OF THE 14 JULY, 1939. IT IS PARTICULARLY

DESIRABLE THAT EXTERNAL LIGHTS AND OTHER LIGHTS
DIRECTLY VISABLE FROM THE SKY SHOULD BE EXTINGUISHED
OR SCREENED.
All lighting in streets will be restricted, vehicles should, so
far as possible, keep off the roads during the darkened period.
It is emphasised that there is no intention, in connection
with the 'Black-out', of cutting off lighting or power supplies
at the mains.[6]

As well as the community shelters, smaller shelters for individual families became available – the Anderson and Morrison shelters. The Anderson shelter came first; it was made of curved metal plates and could be put up in a garden, where it would be protected further with earth. A few still survive in Norfolk, now used as garden sheds. The Morrison shelter was a later idea, introduced in 1941 to help people who had no gardens. It was basically an immensely strong steel cage, 6 feet 6 inches in length and 2 feet 9 inches high: it could accommodate two adults with two small children. The sides were mesh, with the top a steel plate one eighth of an inch thick – it was strong enough to resist the collapse of two floors above. An Anderson shelter for six people cost about £7 10s. to produce, a Morrison shelter cost £7 12s. 6d. to buy. Anyone could buy these shelters, and people in danger areas could get them free. People in other areas were subjected to a means test: if you earned less than £250 a year you could get an Anderson shelter free – if you had a garden to put it in. If you earned less than £350, you could get a Morrison shelter for free. However, they could only be erected only on the ground floor because of their weight, so they were not much use to people living in flats or apartments. Rachel Dhonau wrote: 'I don't much like Morrisons because you can't sit upright in them – mothers had found a marvellous new use for Morrison shelters: they put the children inside, hooked on the sides and went out for the evening.'[7]

Both forms of shelter undoubtedly saved many lives. An Anderson shelter would not survive a direct hit but provided protection against flying glass and debris. When a 1,000-kilogram bomb fell in Miller's Lane, Norwich, in 1942, it left an enormous crater. Anyone in a shelter at the centre of the explosion would have been killed, but of the 27 people in five shelters on the edge of the crater, only two died. Some people in Norwich also died in their Morrison shelters: in one case a couple were trapped in theirs in a burning house, in another a shelter was hurled out of a house by the force of a direct hit, with fatal results for the occupants. However, there are many cases of people emerging unharmed from the shattered rubble that was once a house, thanks to the protective strength of their Morrison shelter.

As the bombing became more serious the demand for shelters increased. There were 1,349 Morrison shelters in Norwich at the time of the Baedeker raid in April 1942; another 600 were at once ordered and soon delivered. Boulton and Paul in Norwich built 85,400 Anderson shelters during the war, turning out over 2,000 a week when demand was at its peak.[8]

Sybil Billings recalled the year before war broke out:

For me, it began late 1938; talk was of war. Our government issued the parts for the Air Raid shelter (Anderson). Having only a small back garden, half was dug up to sink the shelter part way in the ground. My brothers and neighbours worked together to complete this task of setting up the shelter.

71   *Anderson shelter. Although the shelter would not stand a direct hit, it protected its occupants from blast and from flying glass.*

At the age of fifteen I volunteered for Civilian Defence. I studied First Aid and later I was assigned to an Ambulance Depot. At this time gas masks were issued to all civilians.

On September 3, 1939 we listened to the Declaration of war on the radio by King George VI. That night the sirens sounded for the first time. We left our bed running for the shelter, sitting there with our gas masks in our hands, wondering how we would know when to put them on. Next morning we were told it was a false alarm sounded in panic.[9]

The rain of bombs expected in September 1939 did not come. However, once Germany had occupied Belgium, Holland and northern France, their air bases were only 100 miles from Norfolk. From the summer of 1940, the county suffered many air raids. As might be expected, the large towns were the chief targets, but the countryside was far from immune.

The Towns

The first raid on *Norwich* came on 9 July 1940. At 5 pm two planes attacked Barnards Ironworks on Mousehold Heath, killing Harold Dye and Arthur Shreeves. One plane then dropped a bomb on Carrow Hill, killing five 'Carrow girls' leaving work at Colman's mustard factory. Further bombs killed ten people at Boulton and Paul engineering works on Riverside and caused more fatalities at the engineering sheds by Thorpe railway station.

Twenty-six people died in this first raid. It was the Carrow Hill incident that brought home the new horrors of war to the people of the city; innocent girls pushing their bicycles up the steep hill after a day's work were caught unawares, with fatal results. Brief obituaries were put into the next issue of the *Carrow Works Magazine*, although the cause of death was not given. Two women had been killed instantly. They were Bessie Upton, who had worked at Carrow for 23 years, and risen to become forewoman of the Mustard Packing Department, and Maud Balaam, who had worked at Carrow for 26 years. Three others were taken to the Norfolk and Norwich Hospital where they died. Bertha Playford, 19, and Gladys Sampson, 18, had both worked at Carrow since leaving school at the age of thirteen. A fifth woman, Maud Burrell, lingered for three days, dying at the Hospital on 12 July.[10]

In January 1941 the Norwich ARP Committee issued a card of instructions to be hung up in every home. Its instructions included:

LIGHTS. Be very careful of your lights whether from windows or opened doors, skylights or torches. If you go out to a shelter, be sure to turn off the lights in your house before you leave. Turn off your gas at the main if there is a raid on the city.

GAS MASKS. If you want advice about your gas mask, go to your Warden's post, but if you wish to exchange or replace it, apply to one of the undermentioned Wardens' Divisional Headquarters:

1, Rackham Road. 2, Milverton Road. 3, West Parade

PROTECTION AGAINST GAS ATTACKS. Carry your gas mask always.

If you have been in contact with Gas and your clothes are contaminated go home quickly or go to a friend's house, discard your clothing before going indoors, have a bath and put on clean clothing.

If your eyes are affected by gas, or if you have inhaled gas or if any part of your body is affected by gas spray or vapour, go to one of the First aid posts mentioned in paragraph 6 [that on Casualties, below]. The best way to protect yourself from gas is to stay in your shelter (if you have one) or remain indoors. If the shelter or room is not gas proof, wear your gas mask. Everybody who has no other duties to perform should adopt these precautions when gas has been used. The wardens will endeavour to warn you of the presence of gas by using their rattles.

CASUALTIES. If you have received injuries but can walk, go to one of the under-mentioned First Aid Posts:-

Bertha R. Playford   *Maude E. Burrell*

72   *Carrow girls, victims of Norwich's first air raid on 9 July 1940.*

Norfolk and Norwich Hospital
Colman Road School
Sussex Street ARP Headquarters (Entrance Baker's Road)
Thorpe Hamlet School, St Leonard's Road

INCENDIARY BOMBS. Keep a look-out for these on your house or your
neighbour's. Deal with them promptly either with a stirrup pump or with sand
or soil. If you have none of these things at hand, call the wardens or the nearest
voluntary Fire Party or a neighbour who has a stirrup pump or other means of
putting a fire out. Everyone, ordinary householders as well as owners of business
premises, must learn one of the great lessons of war. The first protection against
fire is not the brigade, it is themselves. Only by the united work of ordinary men
and women, not by fire services alone, can we be saved from the enemy's worst
weapon. Fires are beacons which tell following planes where to drop their H. E.
Bombs.

FATAL CASUALTIES. Information as to casualties will be available as soon as
possible at the Public Libraries. If you are anxious about any of your relations or
friends you should consult the lists which will be exhibited at the Libraries.

IMMEDIATE FEEDING AND SHELTER. If you are rendered homeless and
cannot make any arrangements with friends, you should go to the nearest premises
shown below, where food will be provided:-

Maud P. Balaam

Gladys Sampson

Colman Road School, South Park Avenue
Lakenham Council School, City Road
Bignold School, Crook's Place
Larkman Lane School
Nelson Street School
Norman School, Mile Cross
Catton Grove School
St Augustine's School, Aylsham Road
George White School, Silver Road
Mousehold Avenue School
Wellesley Avenue School
Thorpe Hamlet School, St Leonard's Road
Crome and Stuart Schools, Telegraph Lane

Other feeding centres may be established later. You will be told about these. It is also intended to post bills close to bombed areas indicating the nearest place where a meal of some sort will be available.

If you need shelter after you have had food you will be told, before you leave the feeding station, where to go.

If possible make plans now to stay with friends in case your house is destroyed and arrange for them to come to you if their house is knocked out.

Bessie G. Upton

73   *Caleys Chocolate Factory, Norwich: Chapelfield Shopping Centre now covers this site.*

If you have a few clothes to spare pack them in a suitcase and either keep it on your ground floor or deposit it with friends. If you have to evacuate your house, try to take blankets and, if possible, a knife, fork, spoon, plate and cup, with you.

HELP YOURSELF! If the city suffers a heavy attack the available services will be working at high pressure and under difficult circumstances. So be patient; help yourself and your neighbours as much as possible, and keep your chin up.[11]

The greatest damage to the city was done in the two 'Baedeker raids' on the nights of 27/28 and 29/30 April 1942. These were ordered by Hitler in revenge for British raids on Rostock and Lubeck. Cities rated highly in the guidebooks for tourists by Baedeker were selected to be bombed, including Norwich. Of all the people killed in air raids in the city during the war, about 60 per cent died on these two nights: 162 people were killed in the first attack and 69 in the second. Caley's chocolate factory, St Benedict's church, the Teacher Training College in College Road and Curl's department store were among the buildings destroyed in the raids. Most of the dead were buried in the Earlham Road cemetery; at the same time a large number of graves were prepared for the victims of future raids.

Betty Crouch (formerly Jaques) described the bombing of the Training College:

The sirens sounded at just past eleven and shortly the raids began. There were anti-aircraft guns in Heigham Park on the Avenues and although I had seen them under camouflage netting I had never imagined the ear-splitting noise they would make in action. We went on to the recreation ground and into an air raid shelter. It was like a large rabbit burrow with wooden forms against the walls. Pit props held up a planked wooden ceiling. The heavy thud of bombs falling nearby caused soil to drip through the gaps in the planks. Miss Duff called the register and asked if we had any injuries. She had a first aid box. We were all present and amazingly unhurt. I have to own up that all our knees were knocking and we felt clammy cold … It suddenly dawned on me that eight months paperwork was gone for ever as well as my new shoes, dress and coat, which I had hoarded coupons and money to buy. The noise of bombing faded and at 1.15 the all clear sounded. We left the shelter and were marshalled into a crocodile to walk to a rest centre on Colman Road, still in our nightwear and slippers. We passed small groups of people who either wept at the sight of us or waved miniature Union Jacks and cheered us on.
    At the rest centre there were more tears at the sight of us from the white-coated ladies who gave us each a very large mug of very sweet cocoa and a huge doorstep of bread overspilling with golden syrup. I presume all the sweetness was an antidote for shock. We were given a grey army blanket to wrap ourselves and we lay on the classroom floors, hopefully to sleep.

Betty's parents lived at Aylsham and on the next day she got a lift there with her uncle: 'In less than an hour I was home, being hugged by my mother and father. They had watched Norwich burning from Aylsham Market Place. And, having two daughters living in Norwich, wondered if they would survive the Norwich inferno. Cousin Bill had checked that my sister Angela was safe after a traumatic night in her Aunt's house in Essex Street. They had an shelter in the garden. When they came out, the chimney stack was on Angela's bed, half the roof was missing, there was no glass in the windows and no front or back door. I remember weeping over my

74 *Caleys and the surrounding area, taken the day after the Baedeker raid.*

75 *All Saints' Green, Norwich. The buildings here, which included the Thatched Cinema, were destroyed in the air raid of 27 June 1942.*

brand-new coat, lost in the fire and mother said, "We can always buy you another coat, but not another You!" '[12]

Records list only the civilian dead, not military personnel, even if the latter were at home on leave with their families at the time. This can create a misleading impression. For example, Lilian Potter, aged 30, is recorded as being killed in her house in St Mary's Road on 28 April, along with her children 10-year-old Brian and three-year-old Nova. Her husband, Royal Potter, was in the RAF. In fact, he was on leave at the time and was killed along with the rest of the family: however, he does not appear in the lists of those who died as he was not a civilian. A 20-year-old soldier, Paul Glendinning, was staying with his mother in her house in Southwell Road on the night of the second raid: both were killed but only her name appears on the list of civilian dead.[13]

The photographer George Swain was in Norwich on the night of the second Baedeker raid:

> I was in my studio, in St Giles, loading my camera when the *Hippodrome*, next door, was hit. Esmond Wilding was taking over the management of the *Hippodrome* that week, and he and the retiring manager were standing on the stage-door steps when the bombs fell. The stage manager and the owners of a troupe of performing sea-lions were in the indoor shelter of a one-storey building near the stage door. The bombs killed the stage manager and the sea-lions' trainer, blew the two house managers down the steps without hurting them, ripped the back out of my studio, and lifted the stage of the theatre into the air. The stage supports fell, but the stage remained four inches above its normal level. From inside the theatre came a terrible sound – a wailing worse than the whistle of a bomb. It was from one of the sea-lions which the bomb released. I shall never forget the noise it made, flapping its ungainly way through the dark, empty theatre, crying for its master.[14]

76   *Terraced houses in Norwich after an air raid. This photograph was taken by an American serviceman visiting the city.*

The other raid that caused an enormous amount of damage occurred on the morning of 27 June 1942. Some heavy explosive bombs were dropped, but it was fire bombs that were the major threat: 20,000 incendiaries poured down on the city in a raid that lasted just 45 minutes. Buildings destroyed include Bond's department store, St Michael at Thorn and St Paul's churches and the Jewish synagogue off King Street. Sixteen people were killed that night.

May Houghton wrote from the lodge of Thorpe St Andrew's Hospital to family in Yorkshire describing the June raid:

> We have been quiet round this area lately, so have had some good nights sleep.
> Those raids & disturbed nights one after the other make one feel a bit weary. Jerry
> did a good bit more damage in Norwich, mostly by incendiaries. He seemed out to
> destroy everything. All Bonds shops of Ber St are burnt out & Loose's of Magdalen
> St our nice china shop, Colmans is partly burnt & also the N&N hospital, some
> of the N&N patients are up here on the other side of the Rd which was the men's
> side where the wounded soldiers have recently been, that too had a narrow miss.
> They dropped a basket of incendiaries which did not all disperse. It fell between
> the piggery & the hospital & an oil bomb fell the other side of the hospital. We saw
> the fire & also heard the bomb whistle down – it broke some branches off a tree.
> The case which holds the incendiaries is a huge thing ever so heavy, they had it here
> in the workshops, it would give you a nasty old bump. Thorpe Stn too was hit &
> several other places, they tried for the Cathedral – so I hope now he thinks he has
> done enough to Norwich. Some people say for the size Norwich is nearly as bad as
> Coventry (Caley's factory was burnt out in the previous raid).[15]

The bombing raids left a large number of people with nowhere to go: Rest Centres, usually staffed by the WVS, helped as many as they could. After raids on

77 *The Duke of Kent talks to city housewives. Royal visits were intended to lift morale.*

the Long John Hill and Barrett Road area of Norwich on 17 May 1941, 61 people turned up at Lakenham Council School and 35 stayed overnight. Breakfast was provided next day for 46 people and dinner for thirty-nine. The school was filled to overflowing during the Baedeker raids in April 1942. No fewer than 173 people were at the school on the night of 27/28 April. On 28 April, the centre supplied 163 dinners and 120 teas, on the following day 126 breakfasts, 164 dinners and 127 teas. The streets from which these people came were Goldwell Road, Southwell Road and Ashby Street.[16]

Trekking

The Baedeker raids, like most of the raids on Norwich, occurred during the night. This led many people to take up 'trekking' – taking their family out of Norwich to sleep. Ralph Mottram deplored the practice:

> We witnessed, during those long light evenings, the melancholy spectacle similar to that which London and Portsmouth knew in 1940, of small groups, women with young children, aided by such relatives as were not otherwise engaged, pushing a pram, barrow or handcart, making their way out into the fields, in which some few of them spent the night. Others reached neighbouring rest centres, or relied on the kindness of friends in surrounding villages. This in itself was pitiful enough, but a more serious matter was, that many a father of a family found it hard to refuse the appeal of his dependants to be taken to such safety as could be found, and this depleted the fire-watching services.[17]

It was natural for people to escape to the country in the immediate aftermath of air raids. Mr Dack of Wymondham rang the civil defence authorities at 22.40 on the night of 1 May. He reported that 250 refugees had arrived by bus without notice and required instructions as to whether they were to be returned to Norwich in the morning or billeted in Wymondham. The next day it was reported that no Wardens were on duty on the Thorpe Road the previous night to direct people to the Hillside Avenue Rest Centre. The temporary rest centres at Wymondham and Saxlingham were closed down on 4 May as the immediate panic blew over.[18]

Diary entries record similar events. Agnes Podd lived at Doris Road: she was 76 years old and had a sick husband and an invalid son to care for. In her diary, she wrote: 'April 30 42: went to Tharston, everyone leaving the city that could get away, hundreds sleeping in the open. We were fortunate to get in a farmhouse at Tharston at Mr Palmer's, we stayed there till 26 of May. There was a raid on Poringland on the next Friday night after we went and a lot of damage done and several killed and injured and much damage to property.'[19]

Mary Pettit travelled through Norwich on the day after the Baedeker raid:

> I had to pick my way up Prince of Wales Road through the rubble, go past the castle and through more rubble to reach the Bus Station. I had to stop on my way to visit a toilet that was reasonably intact. There was a notice there to say that all water must be boiled. Nearing the Bus Station, I came to my favourite department store and tearoom, or rather, what was left of it. It had taken a direct hit and was a smouldering ruin. The Bus Station, normally busy, was absolutely heaving. Masses of people there, some carrying blankets etc. I did manage to get on a Coltishall-bound bus, packed to the gunnels. After four or five miles outside the city, most of these people and blankets left the bus. They were going out into the country to sleep. After that the bus quietened down and I got off as usual at Scottow Cross. That night I went to bed very grateful for having a bed to go to. I knew nothing about the name 'trekkers' but I had been in the middle of them.[20]

Other people travelled into the country by evening train, returning the following morning. Rachel Dhonau travelled from Sheringham to her work in the city: she noted in her diary on 12 May 1942: 'The train is still crowded with people who have slept out of Norwich.'[21]

78   *Norwich Teachers' Training College destroyed in the Baedeker raid. The street name 'College Road' is the only memento of this building.*

Sporadic raids continued throughout the year, but with nothing to match the great raids of April and June. Agnes Podd wrote:

> Mon Sep 4 1942: wakened at 3 o'clock in the morning by sirens but false alarm all very upset.

> 19 Oct. Winnie's birthday, sent card. Raid warning 7 o'clock in morning. Bombs dropped Carrow woodyard, Pottergate Street, Bullards, Willow Lane, Edward and Holmes Boot Factory, Moores and bakers shop in St Benedicts, windows out of Sid's shop again. Another warning 9 o'clock at night but no raid here. Made Bullace Jam in spite of all.

In October 1942, it was reported that there had been 27 raids on the city since the war began, with a total of 331 deaths. Almost 400 were seriously wounded and over 650 suffered minor injuries.

Although people could not know it at the time, the worst was over. There was only one death in the city in 1943 directly due to bombing: Harriet Flood died in her house at 19, Pottergate, on 19 March 1943. Her body was not recovered until 22 March. The last raid in the city was on 6 November 1943, when houses in the Unthank Road area were set alight; one man had to go to hospital and another was slightly injured.

Occasional bomb-related deaths still occurred. Albert Ashfield was injured in an air attack at Scottow on 22 February 1944. He was rushed to the Norfolk and Norwich Hospital where he died that night. The last bomb-related death in the city occurred on 10 June 1945, a month after Germany had surrendered. Charles Coates died at the Lodge, Bowthorpe, where he had been since his spine had been fractured during a bombing raid on a Norwich restaurant.[22]

The coverage of air raids in the press varied. Often an event was described as happening in 'an East Anglian town'. However, the raids on Norwich were given full coverage in local newspapers. The *Norfolk Chronicle* reported:

Savage Raid on Norwich
MUCH DAMAGE AND MANY CASUALTIES

Norwich was the target of Germany's 'revenge raid' during Monday night. For nearly an hour the city was dive-bombed indiscriminately by a large number of bombers. The Air Ministry and Ministry of Home Security stated that early reports indicated that damage was widespread, and there were a good many casualties. A number of fires broke out.

A hospital received a direct hit, and another hospital was damaged. Streets of small houses suffered much from HE and incendiary bombs, and scores of people were rendered homeless. British fighters went up during the raid, and the Germans admit that three of their bombers are missing.

The defence services did splendid work, and amongst those who lost their lives were many of their number, several fire watchers and ambulance workers.[23]

The *Eastern Daily Press* stressed the part played by women:

Women played a prominent part in extinguishing fire bombs which fell in the city.

At one place where they received direct hits with high explosive and incendiary bombs firewatchers had a narrow escape. One man was blown 20 yards against a wall, but was only 'winded'. One or two of the men were sent home with slight injuries.

Most of the damage in this area was done by incendiary bombs. Women in one street rushed into action, armed with sandbags, when a shower of incendiary bombs fell in the roadway and on the houses.

It was only when high explosive bombs started dropping in the vicinity that they were forced to seek shelter.

The newspaper focused on one woman's story. Mrs Sadd was alone with her five-year-old son and twin babies, when her house was destroyed. An incendiary bomb actually fell on to the cot of one of the twins. Mrs Sadd grabbed her children and tried to leave the room by the door. She was met by a wall of flame but managed to break a window at the other side of the house and get through it. She and the children were given eiderdowns and blankets by neighbours and stayed in a rest centre for the night. She then went to her mother's house in a nearby village.[24]

Naturally, people worried about their relatives in different towns, especially as raids on a place like Norwich could be seen from miles away. 'Biddy' Ransom in Norwich wrote to reassure her mother in Holt in October 1942: 'You may have heard that we had another raid this morning. We were down our shelter this time. I believe some of the bombs fell on parts which had already been demolished & some more down Pottergate direction. Anyhow I thought I'd let you know I am all right. Expect you had lots of sirens too, I hope Holt was all right.' Anthony Hamond in Morston wrote to his son: 'We run in much the same groove here, being occasionally jumped out of it by a bomb or a machine gun bullet, but of course we can hear the blitz on Sheffield & the Midlands – it sounds like a continuous rolling or a very large and distant drum when they are really having a heavy raid.'[25]

Yarmouth suffered very badly from raids between 1941 and 1943. Mr Newstead in Gorleston wrote to his son Peter:

79 *St Nicholas' church, Great Yarmouth, gutted by incendiary bombs on the night of 25 June 1942. Approximately 1,500 incendiary bombs were dropped on the centre of the town in this raid.*

Mother has told you about the second alarm and as I am writing this 6.40 pm a third alarm has just gone. Jerry came over during the second alarm quite low it seemed almost within rifle shot the 3 or 4 bombs were dropped at the end of the RNH [Royal Naval Hospital] some on Barrack Road I think. Shryane & I rushed down but Admiralty Road was blocked off halfway, as was the approaches from the Drive etc but I understand the only results were hundreds of broken panes of glass.

Unusually we have a second account of the same incident, this time in a letter to Peter from Shryane himself:

You left a little too early on Sunday because Jerry had a pop at the RNH about 5 pm. He dropped one just inside the wall of the grounds at the SW corner. He didn't damage the RNH, but removed an enormous amount of glass from the windows of houses, in Admiralty Road and on the barracks Estate. Dad and I cycled to the scene of operations a few minutes after the bomb dropped.

The Italian fighter brought down at Corton was a tiny little 'Fiat' and the pilot is alleged to have said that he thought he was over Germany! Perhaps he mistook the Home Guard for Brownshirts.[26]

The raid that did most damage in Great Yarmouth was that on the night of 7/8 April 1941. One bomb destroyed a Special Constabulary Sub-Station at the Seagull

80 *Cromer High Street and churchyard after bombing, July 1942.*

Garage, killing five special constables. They were Herbert Davy, William Harrison, Percy Smowton, George Willsmore and George Brown. C.G. Box wrote four years later:

> Human memory is short but I shall never forget the appalling sight that Yarmouth presented that night and, with the additional fires that continually broke out, it seemed that nothing could prevent the destruction of the centre of the Town and

South Quay, but when day broke, owing to the untiring efforts of all concerned, all fires were under control and the situation, although bad, saved from becoming any worse. It is estimated that 4,000 incendiary Bombs were dropped during this night. [27]

The air raids continued. Northgate School was being used as a first-aid post when it was bombed on 7 May 1943: two of the first-aiders, Olive Riches and Dorothy

Wilson, were killed. Five people died at a coffee stall at Vauxhall railway station in an attack on the same day: they included the manageress, Ethel Wright, who lived at Swirles Buildings.

A total of 49 people died in the air raids on Yarmouth on the night of 11 May 1943, including the ATS girls mentioned in chapter two. As it turned out, they were to be the last bombing casualties in the town. In fact there were only two more attacks, on 23 October 1943 on Gorleston, and on 1 June 1944 when four bombs fell on the foreshore at the South Denes.

The total number of civilians killed in air raids in Great Yarmouth was not as great as might have been expected, no doubt because so many citizens had been evacuated. The number of fatalities was 217, nine in 1940, 109 in 1941, 27 in 1942 and 72 in 1943. These figures do not tell the full story as they do not include military personnel such as the ATS girls already mentioned. To take another example, Stanley Smith and his wife Victoria died together at their home at 6 Whittleton Place on 7 July 1941. He is listed among the civilian dead but she is not: she was in the WRNS. The damage to the housing-stock in the town was enormous: 2,639 houses were totally destroyed or so badly damaged that they had to be demolished. Another 1,500 houses were so badly damaged that the occupiers had to be evacuated while they were repaired.[28]

King's Lynn was less severely hit than the other two large towns: a total of 59 civilians died in bombing raids. There was a serious attack on 12 June 1941. The dead included eight-year-old twin boys, Derek and Donald, together with their mother, Leath Grace Brittain; they died at 4 Boal Street. Two young sisters, Brenda and Marie Stringer, aged five and eight, died at 11 Whitefriars Terrace in the same raid. There was another major raid exactly one year later: four members of the Adams family died at the *Eagle Hotel*, Norfolk Street. Many RAF servicemen drinking in the pub were also killed: a total of 42 people lost their lives, by far the worst single incident in the town. The attack happened at 21.59: four bombs fell, one directly hitting and demolishing the pub. First casualties were reported as four killed, 20 injured. Two days later 28 bodies had been recovered but a further 20 were expected to be found. By 17 June the figure was revised to 43 dead and 17 taken to hospital.

Some of the military victims were buried in Lynn. Six men who were not from the town are buried in Gayton Road cemetery: John Campbell, David Killelea, Edward Mallett, Joseph Milligan and Brian Swaffield were all sergeants in the RAF, Reginald Martin was an army private. William Holmes of the RAF, whose parents lived in Lynn, is buried in King's Lynn cemetery.

As the bombing threat grew, some towns felt they were not being given adequate protection by the county authorities. *Sheringham* was one such town. In April 1941, the County Architect reported to the ARP Emergency Committee:

> No public shelters have been provided in Sheringham since no recommendations for such shelters have ever been received, but some eight Communal Domestic Shelters have been approved and now erected under the supervision of the UDC Surveyor.
>   Some time ago it may be recalled that according to press reports some criticism of the County Council was made on account of delay in providing the communal shelters and at that time I sent an account of the correspondence etc to the Chairman shewing that such delay was certainly not caused by the County Council …
>   The matter was discussed fully with the result that the Assistant Regional Technical Advisor will approve, subject to the Committee's confirmation, of obtaining tenders

81   *Damage to the* Eastern Daily Press *offices in Cromer High Street, 1942.*

for the following brick surface shelters, in view of the recent enemy actions which
have taken place:

(a) One 50 person shelter in High Street near the Clock (Actual position to be
decided by the UDC in collaboration with the Police).

(b) One 25 person shelter at North end High Street adjoining public conveniences.

(c) One 25 person shelter on Hill's Land, Station Road.[29]

There were in fact four raids on Sheringham that had fatalities. One person had
been killed on 22 September 1940. Four were killed on 19 January 1942, one on
8 March 1942 and nine on 22 July 1942, including three generations of the Hannah
family. In January 1942, Rachel Dhonau was working in an office in Sheringham with
Peggy Smith. Her diary tells the story:

Mon 19 Jan: We were sitting peacefully over our tea today when suddenly there
was a loud bang, which we presumed to be a bomb, there having been a zooming
of aeroplanes beforehand. Timothy [Rachel's son] and the kitten bolted into the
cupboard under the stairs, while eventually Mummy and I went to see if we could
see anything. There was a wisp of smoke in the sky, but the streets were quite empty.
Timothy wept and the kitten refused to come out of the cupboard for a long time.
We learned from our next door neighbour that the bomb had fallen not far away and
brought down four houses. It is in this street that Peggy lives, who works in the food
office with me. I am wondering whether she is all right.

Tue 20 Jan: My forebodings were realised. Peggy, her father and her mother were
killed by last night's bomb, which was dropped from a very low level. The bodies
weren't found till much later. The office was in a state of great dejection all day – and

I felt quite dazed. Peggy and I had
worked together since the beginning
of the war, and I liked her. It seemed
incredible that I should never see
her in the office again. People were
feeling very revengeful – if only
they could get their hands on the
airmen that did it – and they were
glad to hear our bombers going out
at the same time to do the same to
Germany. But we went on with our
work and our life. It reminds me of
the waves of the sea.[30]

Eleven people were killed at Cromer in
an attack on the night of 22/23 July 1942.
One woman recalled:

We had several small but frightening
raids on Cromer but one night in
1942 the central pattern of the
town was changed. I saw the effect
next evening. The church with
shattered windows was surrounded
by the debris of Church Street and
uncanny noises came from inside
the building as the organist tried to
play the damaged organ.[31]

The Country

Although the towns bore the main brunt
of the attack, villages suffered too. Eighty
civilians died in bombing raids on the
countryside of Norfolk during the war.
People who lived close to aerodromes
naturally felt themselves to be especially
vulnerable. In August 1941, the County
Architect reported:

Home Protection has been
authorised around R A F property
at Weston Longville (Attlebridge),

82 *Searching through the rubble, Cromer 1942.*

Spixworth and Catton (St Faith's aerodrome). Applications for protection have
been received from a number of persons living in timber constructed bungalows
etc to which Home Protection is impractical, and in some cases the householders
have undertaken to build themselves shelters with free materials which have been
supplied. Others, however, are unable to do this, and after consultation with the
Assistant Regional Technical Adviser, I have placed proposals before him for the
following shelters:

Weston Longville:
4 four-person domestic shelters, estimated to cost £32 each
4 nine-person shelters – £45 each

Spixworth:
1 twelve-person communal domestic shelter, £45

Catton:
1 four-person shelter, £32.[32]

German bombers were no respecters of council boundaries, and people living on the fringes of Norwich had to cope with the effects of the Baedeker raids as well as those within the city. A report of the ARP Emergency Committee in June 1942 said:

> The fringe area of Norwich in which Morrison Shelters had hitherto been available on conditions governed by income was extended on 18 May 1942 and the free issue to householders, irrespective of any income limit, within the newly prescribed district, authorised by the Ministry.
>
> The announcement of this concession following the air raids to which Norwich had been earlier subjected created an immediate and abnormal demand for Shelters, taxing to the utmost limit the resources of the Department responsible through whose energetic action the whole of the 2328 applications received since 27 April 1942 (as compared with a total of 1060 for the preceding 9 months) have been promptly dealt with and the Shelters in most cases delivered to the applicants within two days from the receipt of the request.[33]

Air-raid shelters were built in towns, not in small villages. For example, in April 1941, the question of protection for the First Aid Depot at Blofield was raised. The County Architect replied: 'Recently a circular has been issued by the Ministry of Home Security indicating that personnel of ARP Depots "should be provided with the same standard of protection as that provided for householders and members of the public generally in their area". Blofield is, of course, very rural in character and is a district in which no protection for householders or members of the Public has been given. There is no military objective in the vicinity as far as I know, and I doubt whether proposals for protection of householders and public in Blofield (and the great number of similar villages in Norfolk) would receive approval.'[34]

The first bombs fell on Norfolk on the night of 24/25 May 1940. Thirteen fell in fields north-east of Raynham aerodrome just after midnight. At 1.30 am, a bomb caused slight damage to a bungalow at Burgh St Peter. Two more bombs fell on Langley Marshes, killing a pony and a cow, and injuring two other cows. The first human casualty was at Strumpshaw on 2 June: a soldier had a foot blown off by a bomb that fell on a searchlight unit. On the evening of 22 June bombs fell at Pulham and at Diss where a woman was killed, the first fatal casualty.

The fear of gas attack was always present in these first air raids, and could lead to individual panic. On 27 June 1940, Mr Goodeson, air-raid warden at Ditchingham reported that he had heard spluttering on leaves at 1 am in the morning and that his skin began to tingle. A gas van was sent from Bungay driven by Mrs Sprake. On arrival she collapsed, and both were taken to Bungay in an ambulance. There they were examined by a doctor, who said that they were not gas victims. However, there was still some doubt: a local Special Constable reported that his nose itched. A second doctor also found no evidence of gas and by the afternoon it was concluded 'that incident recorded at Ditchingham was pure nerves'.[35]

The worst single incident was on 26 April 1941: 23 people were killed and another eight injured when the *Horning Ferry* inn was bombed just after closing time. The Civil Defence War diary tells the story of the dramatic events of the night. Information was passed to them at 11.04 pm that the Aylsham rescue party had been sent to the inn. Central rang Eastern 15 minutes later: they had no definite information but

83 *War in the country:* Horning Ferry *inn was bombed on 26 April 1941. One theory is that it was the victim of a deliberate scheme to decoy bombers away from Norwich.*

believed the inn had been hit. At 11.45, the caretaker at Aylsham depot confirmed that the inn had been hit and that the North Walsham rescue party had been sent out at 10.23: the bomb had fallen at exactly 10 pm. Four injured people were taken to hospital, but the dead could not be counted until the morning. At 8 am it was said there were 20-30 casualties, including two RAF personnel. By 9.30, the latter figure was given as six. The casualties were later announced as six RAF men, 11 male and four female civilians (including one of the wounded, who had since died in hospital). Three other civilians were seriously wounded and two more slightly injured. It was established that five HE bombs had been dropped: two were direct hits, one fell on the boatshed and two on the lawn.

Next day, Newstead wrote to his son Peter:

> It was a terrible affair at Horning Ferry. The place was apparently packed & it is said that there many motor cars outside with lights on, have just heard there were also 15 of the RAF killed including S O Tuck the well known DSO etc, also Mrs Adlington is not expected to recover but that I am not sure of, there are so many rumours.

The rumours were half right. Katherine Adlington was indeed badly hurt, and suffered from her injuries for many years. She told her story to *Norfolk Fair* 40 years later. According to her, two men had entered the bar. The barman asked them: 'Have you put your car lights off?'

> The next thing Katherine saw was a flash of light similar to a Catherine Wheel firework in what was otherwise complete silence and darkness. Looking up she saw stars in the night sky, and thought: good gracious, we've been bombed. She felt

nothing but the thought flashed through her mind: 'underneath are the everlasting arms'. After being rescued she was unaware of her serious injuries, or that she was in a state of shock, because she felt no pain at this time.

The dead included three pilots from Coltishall; their names are now recorded in a plaque in the bar. The 'S O Tuck' mentioned by Newstead was Squadron Leader Stanford Tuck, a Battle of Britain hero based at Coltishall. He was not killed or injured in the bombing; in fact on the night of 27 April he was attacking a German plane trying to bomb shipping off Yarmouth.[36]

There were a large number of air raids in the countryside around Norwich on the night of 8/9 May 1942, as Agnes Podd noted. A bomb at Hellesdon damaged 20 houses in Links Avenue, trapping some people in their houses. A man died from shock in a shelter on the corner of Reepham and Cromer Roads. A Rest Centre was established in Hellesdon on the next morning dealing with 46 people, 16 of whom had been made homeless.

However, most of the damage was done south of the city. A bomb at Long Road in Framingham Earl killed one person, injured two others and blocked the road. An enemy plane crashed in flames. More bombs in Caistor and Stoke Holy Cross burnt out French Church Farm, Valley Farm and two bungalows. A WVS Mobile Canteen was sent round the villages next morning. Rest centres were opened up in a ring around Norwich at Rackheath, Drayton, Costessey, Easton, Cringleford, Hethersett, Trowse and Poringland, with the schools at Thorpe, Sprowston and Hellesdon made ready to be used to provide more accommodation if needed. Some of the bombs dropped were delayed-action, which created further hazards. Three bombs exploded at Caistor during the following day and other unexploded bombs led to road closures: one or two near the *Gull* in Framingham exploded the following evening.

By 11 May it was possible to assess the casualties on the night of 8/9 May. They were surprisingly light: one man had died in Poringland, one in Framingham Earl, and a woman in Caistor. Fifteen people had been injured that night.

There is some uncertainty as to why so many bombs had fallen on the villages south of the city that night. Angus Calder says that an attempted raid on Norwich 'was frustrated either by a hastily assembled balloon barrage or by the presence of a decoy site near the town'. Joan Banger says that the first enemy aircraft was chased by an RAF fighter and dropped its marker flares over Poringland: the following planes bombed on the flares.[37]

Most of the incidents were much smaller than this, and recorded laconically in the county war diary:

> 8/9 July 1941. 06.43: 4 HE on marshes West Caister. Damage to farm house. 1 heifer killed, 1 house [sic] injured, must be destroyed. 1 man, 1 child slightly injured.
>
> 21/22 July 1941. At 0340 8 HE and 1 UXHE N and S of Ferry Farm Reedham which received direct hit. Owner (Charles James Mutton) broken arm and numerous minor injuries. Mr and Mrs Bertie Fox, late of Lawn Avenue, Great Yarmouth killed; UXB approximately 80 yards SW from Farm in marshes.[38]

Unexploded bombs caused enormous inconvenience in both town and country. This could be a risky business, as demonstrated at Themelthorpe where a bomb exploded while being dismantled on 8 May 1943:

8/9 May. 1030. Mr Gladden Div Officer, North Walsham reported explosion of bomb while being dismantled by LIS. Mine in a ditch. Rope put round mine and she began to tick. LIS dived into ditch. Mine exploded. Nobody hurt. Railway Authorities, although warned, apparently ignored advice regarding precautions. Had train been passing at the time it would have been blown off the line. Excellent turn out by CD Services following explosion.

1038. Explosion damaged Church windows, windows and tiles in cottages and telegraph wires on railway.[39]

V1s and V2s

The summer of 1944 saw Hitler's secret weapons unleashed on England – the V1s and V2s. These were short-range weapons aimed mainly at London, but some did reach Norfolk. More than forty V2s were fired at Norwich: 51 people were hurt but no one was killed. Norwich was targeted because it was close to the bases in Friesland from which the rockets were fired. Faster than sound, they struck without warning, causing enormous craters. Churchill did not reveal what they were until 10 November, by which time they had ceased to fall in Norfolk.

The new weapons were the subject of much speculation, as shown in the correspondence of the Heading family of Norwich:

> Mother to John, 6/10/44: I think we can take it for certain that they are 'rockets' we have been having round about here lately, they go off with an awful bang, & of course there can be no syren [sic] for them, because they travel faster than sound, so there are no means of warning people, but thank God (and I really do thank Him) most of them have fell on open fields & ground.
>
> Joy to John 7/10/44: so far today we have had no V2s. But Tues, Wed & Thurs we had three each day and one yesterday at 9.25 am. None have actually fallen on Norwich, but on areas round about eg Hellesdon, and somewhere near Costessey and Ringland. The Tuesday evening one at Hellesdon was the loudest I think.
>
> Sister to John, writing from Reydon near Southwold, 5/11/44: I hope you don't get much evidence of V1 or V2 round you. A doodle-bug was shot down into the sea near here a few minutes ago.

Agnes Podd recorded in September 1944: 'Auntie May came here to sleep, had been in Norwich 1 month, came here because of the awful time in London with flying bombs, slept at Auntie Alice's. Could not keep there any longer so came here. After 5 nights here she said it was worse than London, so has gone back this morning, 5 Oct, as these flying bombs and rockets are coming out here and our shelters are not so good as London ones.'[40]

The air-raid warden's logbook for Fleggburgh survives. It records the first flying bombs in the area on 24 September: two passed overhead, one apparently exploding at Swainsthorpe, the other said to have reached Ely. Two days later, the first rocket bomb in the area exploded at Ranworth: a man was seriously injured after his horse bolted as a result of the explosion. By 27 September it was recorded that rocket bombs were now a daily occurrence: 'Many appear to explode in the air close to us and missile is then carried some miles further inland before reaching earth. Passage of these missiles cannot be heard.' Two or three rocket bombs were recorded on

11 October, and flying bombs on 4 and 9 November: these were the last to trouble the Fleggburgh wardens.[41]

After this, there were a small number of conventional raids, but the war was clearly coming to its end. The last German bomb to fall on Norfolk was at Swanton Morley on 20 March 1945.[42]

Machine-gunning

The image of death in the Second World War is of bombs dropped from a great height, but sometimes the danger could be more personalised, with a plane swooping low and using its machine guns. Sybil Billings recalled:

> One night, I was machine gunned in our back lane. The plane came over the house tops spraying bullets. I heard bullets hitting the ground beside me … then the plane was gone.[43]

Anthony Hamond had a similar experience, but from a greater distance on the north coast in October 1940:

> A Hun elected to fly round here and machine gun fields of sugar beet near the sluice & thence to the Point, Salthouse, Cley etc. Very few people appeared to notice it. Tilly was propelling her bulk per velo [that is, she was riding her bicycle] along the Chase but was unmoved by a hail of lead discharged over her head. Charles Dale being of a nervous temperament took refuge in a ditch and did not budge till dark.[44]

There was a similar incident in Colney. David Glister recalled that he and five school friends were walking home along School Lane:

> As Miss Wilson and Miss Cobbett were about to overtake them on their bicycles a German plane suddenly appeared and started to machine gun them. The teachers ordered the children to run into the T-Wood, Milestone Plantation for shelter where they hid until the plane circled and went away. They cheered and waved when a Spitfire appeared in pursuit but they did not know whether he 'got him'.[45]

Plane Crashes

In an area like Norfolk a large number of planes, both enemy and allied, crashed or were brought down. These incidents were frightening and could cause fatalities, especially if the plane had bombs on board, or desperately jettisoned them in an attempt to save the plane. They are recorded in the Civil Defence War Diary, as these examples show:

> 4/5 July 1941. 10.47. At 0005 WELLINGTON bomber crashed at G 1112. Machine wrecked, 5 killed and 1 injured of crew. Plane contained DA bombs. Houses evacuated and Feltwell-Southery road closed by Police.

> 11.00: RAF in charge of incident and informed police they would not accept responsibility for DA bombs unless Feltwell-Southery road closed and houses evacuated. 2 DA bombs have already gone off. Not considered that road will be closed long.

12.50: Police have reopened road at users' risk. Peat soil where machine crashed. Fire will burn for some time.

16.32: Police have now decided to close road.
8/9 July 1941. 12.49. Feltwell-Southery road now open to traffic and persons evacuated can return home.[46]

On the night of 22 April 1944, the German air force struck at bombers just as they were about to land at their Norfolk bases on their return from a mission. It appears that security had become lax at this relatively late stage in the war and that the bombers were in the habit of putting on their navigation lights once they had crossed the English coast. The War Diary received several reports of crashes that night: a plane came down at Cantley at about 10.20, followed by Liberators at Horsham and Rackheath and an unidentified plane at Ashby. At 11.35 it was reported that an American plane had crashed at Langley Marshes, and also that an enemy plane had come down killing everyone on board. Later in the night, another plane was reported to have crashed, this time at Swanton Morley.

Seething airfield suffered most. As the first Liberator came in to land, with its landing lights on, the landing lights on the ground lit up, providing a perfect backdrop for the waiting German planes. One plane was hit while landing and crashed beyond the airfield at Worlingham. A second plane caught fire as it landed and its smoke blew across the airfield, causing problems for the three other planes that had to land: the last plane slammed into the tail of the previous one. According to Simon Parry, nine planes were blown out of the sky that night, and another three forced to crash land at Rackheath, Hethel and Seething.[47]

On 24 November 1944, a Liberator struck the tower of St Philip's church in Heigham and flew on to crash in the Corporation Yard off Barker Street. Many people witnessed the crash. Joy Hayward wrote to John Heading:

Last Friday about 4.45 pm an American Liberator crashed at Barker Street somewhere near Heigham Street. Mummy saw it apparently in difficulties when she was blacking-out. There was an account of it in the paper, & it hit the tower of St Philip's church where it lost a wing & then fell on a Corporation Depot at Barker Street. Poor Corporation! Firemen fought the fire, but the crew were killed, but no civilians, apparently. Daddy said if it had been any other night the men would have been there, but they were out getting their pay.

Mrs Brett of Sprowston also saw the incident:

I had just left the Lazar House on Sprowston Road & noticed the bomber flying very low. At first I did not realise any danger, so fascinated was I in watching the skill of the pilot & his efforts to gain height. A girl just passing me with a pram screamed 'It's coming down, run'. Snatching her baby out of the pram, she ran up an opening, her pram meanwhile tumbling into the gutter (which I hope she retrieved). Watching it out of sight I breathed a silent prayer for its safe landing & a 'thank you' to the crew. Later, calling on a dear friend, an invalid of years, I found her very distressed, saying she had been so frightened she had forgotten to pray, which might have saved the 'poor dear brave boys'. Lying in bed near her open window, she had felt sure it must have come into the room.[48]

The people of the area were sure that the airmen had sacrificed their lives to save those of civilians. They raised money for a plaque, which was unveiled on 196 Heigham Street on 6 November 1945. The area has seen much rebuilding: the plaque is now at Freeman Square.

On 4 March 1945, the Germans launched Operation Gisela, a desperate attempt to disrupt the bomber offensive against their homeland. The War Diary reported crashes of Allied aircraft at Oulton, Fulmodestone, Buxton (a Mosquito), East Rudham, South Lopham, Horstead Hall, and perhaps others; because the record is of telephone calls hurriedly noted down as they came in, it is not always clear how many planes were involved in a particular incident. The Mosquito came down in the Avenue in Buxton, killing the crew and slightly damaging a house: there were no civilian casualties. The plane at East Rudham was the only one specifically stated to have been shot down by an enemy intruder: there were no survivors.[49]

Plane crashes continued right into the last weeks of the war:

> 15/16 April 1945. 10.04. Plane crashed on Old Hall Farm, Mattishall Burgh. Liberator, completely wrecked, no. 129593, from Weston Longville at 06.10. Crew of 9, 2 killed, 7 injured. Loaded with incendiaries, all burned out.

In any war there are always some victims of 'friendly fire', as it is now called – accidental attacks on one's own side. On 16 December 1940, a British plane dropped bombs on the Dereham Road area of Norwich: one fell on Howes' garage in Bond Street. Civil defence records mention other such incidents, for example:

> 5/6 August 1941. 22.46: report from Mundesley Police received via North Walsham at 18.55: at 12.55 2 Hurricanes and Blenheim over Mundesley. One Hurricane, apparently mistaking Blenheim for hostile aircraft, fired 8 rounds into one bungalow and one into a second. Damage to walls and a table. No casualties.

> 1/2 May 1943.11.50 At 10.43 at Hunstanton G 134599, member of CD FA Post Service shot in leg by gun fire from aircraft passing Northwards. Believed Liberator or Fortress.

> 12.10: Ascertain and report in writing whether casualty was on duty and also whether any damage to property.

> 1305. Casualty was not on duty at the time. No damage to property reported.

According to Joan Banger, the pilot of an American fighter accidentally fired his machine guns while flying over Norwich on 23 June 1943: houses between the Earlham and Dereham Roads were damaged but no-one appears to have been hurt.[50]

The last piece of action in the Civil Defence diary also records such a case:

> 27/28 April 1945. 16.55. At 15.20, MG [machine gun] bullets from aircraft north of Burnham Market, penetrated roof and bedroom of house. Several bullets landed in neighbourhood.[51]

Looting

Not everyone behaved well in wartime. One of the most tempting of wartime crimes was that of looting – stealing property from bombed-out houses. This was seen as an especially 'unsporting' crime, taking advantage of one's neighbours' misfortune. Nevertheless, plenty of people resorted to it, mainly on a small-scale level.

There were several cases of looting after the Baedeker raids. The first group were tried in the Norwich Police Court. One involved a soldier, George Broughton. He had been sent to Norwich to help the fire service after the raids. He was accused of stealing items from a bombed-out office, including a watch, a shaving mirror and cigarettes. He pleaded guilty, saying that the items were just lying about the office. The court took a dim view, saying that Broughton was in a position of trust. He was sentenced to three months in prison.

The same court heard the case of John Brown of Oak Street, a pensioner accused of stealing a lady's vest and a curtain. He claimed they were just lying about in the street but was sent to prison for a month.[52]

Other cases of looting came before the court of Quarter Sessions in October 1942. George Moore had gone into 66 Earlham Road, which was damaged by enemy action. He stole a book from the house on 6 August. Asked in court if he had anything to say he replied: 'No – I am fed up walking about hungry.' Moore had well over 20 previous convictions for drunkenness, vagrancy, petty theft and related offences stretching back to 1900. The most recent was for spitting on a public shelter floor and disturbing the persons using the shelter. He had been stopped in the street by a policeman who saw him carrying a number of articles. He pleaded guilty and was sentenced to three months' hard labour. Albert Owen was charged with stealing a soldering iron and a coal shovel from 18, Winter Road: the house had been damaged in the Baedeker raids in April. He was sentenced to four months' hard labour.[53]

The most serious case was heard at the Assize Court, also in October. Walter Nichols, described variously as a rag and bone merchant and as a scissor-grinder, pleaded guilty to looting five houses in Norwich. The total value of the stolen property came to £45 10s. Nichols had been in the Norfolk Regiment but had a very poor record as a soldier, having served terms of imprisonment for larceny, false pretences and wounding: he was discharged from the army in 1941. He was sentenced to seven years for each offence, to run concurrently.[54]

Occasional cases of small-time looting occurred outside Norwich. In July 1942, two girls, June Frary (10) and Monica Hayes (nine) stole some watch straps and silk from bombed-out shops in Comer: they were put on probation for two years. In September 1942, a soldier from Rotherham named Arthur Jackson was also charged with looting in the town: he was sentenced to three months in prison.[55]

Nine

The Kitchen Front – Daily Life in Wartime

Food and Diet

Britain does not grow enough food to supply all its inhabitants: it has to import food from abroad. In a major war, the enemy would try to prevent food reaching the country, in effect to try to starve Britain into surrender. The Government thought about this before the war and decided to introduce food rationing, which had been tried in the last few months of the First World War. It also suggested that households try to maintain a supply of essentials at home. This was not as simple as it would appear today. People did not have fridges or freezers – and in any case electricity could not be guaranteed during a crisis. More fundamentally, many people simply did not have enough money to put anything aside for the future: their weekly wage was fully spent on current needs.

In July 1939, with the prospect of war looming, the Government issued a leaflet entitled 'YOUR FOOD IN WARTIME'. It suggested the following foods as being suitable for storage: meat and fish in cans or glass jars; flour suet; canned or dried milk; sugar; tea; cocoa; plain biscuits. By storing these the better-off householders could help their poorer neighbours: 'By drawing on these reserves instead of making demands on the shops at such a time [when supplies are restricted] they would leave the stocks available for the use of those who have not been able to put anything by.' The advice continued: 'Any such reserves should be bought before an emergency arises. To try to buy extra quantities when an emergency is upon us, would be unfair to others.'

The leaflet also explained the government's plans for rationing:

> Certain foods, soon after the outbreak of a war, would be brought under a rationing scheme similar to that which was introduced during the latter part of the Great War. In the first instance, rationing would be applied to five foodstuffs – butcher's meat, bacon and ham, sugar, butter and margarine, and cooking fats. Later it might be necessary to add other articles.
>
> The object of this scheme is to make sure certain foodstuffs are distributed fairly and equally and that everyone is sure of his or her proper share.
>
> Before rationing begins application forms would be sent through the post to every householder, who would be asked to give details of everyone living in his home. These forms, when filled in, would be returned to the local food office set up by the local Food Control Committee, which would issue the ration books, one for each person.

84 *Carrying on farming within sight of Shipdham air base, 1944. The shortage of labour caused by the war led to increased mechanisation of Norfolk farms.*

You would then register at a retail shop of your own choice for each rationed food. This registration is necessary to enable the local committee to know the quantities of rationed food which each shop would require. There is no need to register with a shop in peace time. It is not advisable to do so.

The Ration Books would have coupons, a certain number for each week. The Ministry would decide how much food each coupon represented, and you would be entitled to buy that amount. In the case of meat, the amount would be expressed in money. Thus, you could choose between buying a larger amount of a cheaper cut, or a smaller amount of a more expensive cut. In the case of other foods, the amount would be by weight.

For children under six years of age, there would be a Child's Ration Book, but the only difference would be that a child would be allowed half the amount of butcher's meat allowed for a grown-up person. On the other hand, the allowance for a heavy worker will give him a larger quantity of meat.[1]

Ration books for food had, in fact, been ready since 1938. In November 1939, each householder was told to register with a retailer. You could choose a different retailer for each product, but most people chose the same store for all

85 *'Grow your own Food'.*

their products except meat for which they would choose a specialist butcher's shop.

Rationing began on 8 January 1940. People were allowed four ounces of bacon or ham, four ounces of butter and 12 ounces of sugar each week. Three weeks later the bacon ration was raised to eight ounces. Meat rationing was introduced on 11 March 1940. This was on a value basis. Each person over six years old was allowed 1s. 10d. worth of meat every week: children under six were allowed 11d. worth. At the peak of rationing, in August 1942, adults were allowed 1s. 2d. worth of meat a week, children under six 7d. worth. The ration covered beef, veal, mutton and pork: because it was based on value, a customer could choose between a small amount of higher quality meat, or a greater amount of lesser quality meat – subject, of course, to what their chosen butcher happened to have at that particular time.

There were extensions to the rationing through the war years as the German blockade began to bite. Preserves – jam, marmalade, syrup and treacle – were rationed from March 1941, cheese in May and tea from July. Milk and eggs were *allocated* rather than rationed: they were given to those who most needed them wherever possible. Many people have a lifelong memory of the taste of powdered eggs in tins: these were introduced in June 1942.

In December 1941, a points system was introduced for many types of food. People had a certain number of points, usually about twenty for a four-week period, to spend on various items, mainly tinned produce – meat, fish, beans etc. A tin of salmon might be 32 points when a tin of pilchards or baked beans was just two points. Thus, there was an element of choice and the possibility of some variety in the diet – always providing your shop had anything in stock, that is.

In July 1942, chocolates and sweets were rationed: the amount of confectionery allowed per person varied between eight and 16 ounces at different periods of the war. Again a personal points system was introduced that covered sweets and chocolates and allowed customers to choose their favourite varieties.

Rationing was organised by the Ministry of Food under Lord Woolton. In 1943, no fewer than 50,000 civil servants were employed by it. Most people had contact with it through their local Food Office, which issued both ration books and identity cards and issued free orange juice and cod-liver oil to boost the diet of children under five.

Sybil Billings remembered:

> We soon noticed a shortage of luxury items and rationing began. Lines would soon form whenever a shop had supplies. We thought ourselves lucky and fortunate if after standing in line for an hour we were able to get a rabbit. Mother would cut it in small pieces, fill a pan with vegetables and bake it, making a meal for eight of us. The Fish Shop was open two days a week, again we stood in line and if we were lucky got some fish and chips. Some times only chips. Fortunately we never seemed to run out of potatoes, cabbage or brussel sprouts.[2]

It is often said that the rationed diet of the war was a far healthier one than the diet of the 21st century. This is probably true, although it does appear that a man working in a physical job might not be receiving as many calories as he needed. This was less true in Norfolk where much of the hard work was in farming. There were usually opportunities for farm workers to increase their calory intake from natural produce.

The two most basic foodstuffs to many Englishmen, beer and bread, were not rationed in the war (although bread was to be rationed after it during the post-war shortages). Beer became both expensive and weak because of enormous increases in excise duties; the duty rose from 24 shillings a barrel to about £7. It was often unavailable. One army lecturer recalled a journey to a base in north-west Norfolk. He was:

> Making his way with some difficulty to a site placed equidistant between the villages of Great Snoring on the one hand and of Little Snoring on the other. Pleasant places enough, no doubt, but, as the names suggest, scarcely teeming with bustle and activity. The inn in the former bore the legend 'Sorry, sold out', that in the latter the less apologetic but more definite announcement 'No beer'. This unfortunate situation meant that no one had bothered to leave the site for some time.[3]

86 'Dig for Victory'. Propaganda played a vital role in mobilising the civilian population.

Bread, too, changed in character in the war. Normally, white bread is obtained by extracting just 70 per cent of the wheat. By March 1942, the extraction rate had risen to 85 per cent, producing a 'National Wholemeal loaf' – which was most unpopular. However, it was healthier than pre-war bread, as a food specialist like Rachel Dhonau in Sheringham was aware: 'One of the good things of this war is the National Wheatmeal loaf.'[4]

To obtain a ration book, you needed an identity card. The National Registration Act of 1 September 1939 made it compulsory to carry an identity card and 46 million were issued. The cards were green for adults, brown for those under sixteen. The Identity Card and the Ration Book were two essential documents for life during the war. Failure to carry an identity card was an offence, and losing either one's card or one's ration book caused an immense amount of red tape, as John Turner was to experience:

> Laura went into Hunstanton to get a new Identity (Registration) Card for [their daughter] Ursula, who has succeeded in losing hers. Endless red tape about this, of course. Clerk in Office seriously put forward proposition that he ought to fill in necessary forms in case it should be question of Fifth Column activity. This about a child of ten!

Worth a Fortune.

YET she looks for no reward beyond the knowledge of duty staunchly done in the midst of danger and distress. For all that, she'd love an occasional box of FORTUNE to cheer her at her post because the best of all Chocolates are specially made by Caley to combine sheer enjoyment with that extra nutrition she needs to keep her going. Such a luscious assortment in every box! So rich in food value—yet so low in cost!

CALEY'S *fortune*

IN BOXES ¼lb. 8d. ½lb. 1/4 FULL POUND 2/8   CHOCOLATES

87   *Wartime advertising for Caley's chocolates.*

6 Sep: Laura left her ration book in the bus (a major disaster, involving taking an oath before a magistrate, in order to get a new one). But luckily Everitt's daughter picked it up.[5]

Five women in Flegg were fined between £1 and £4 after they were questioned on a Norwich-bound bus and found to be carrying borrowed identity cards. Some people were more deliberate in their deception – one Norwich woman had two ration books, one in the name of Ethel Tune, the other in the name of Ethel Adderson. She was fined. In 1942, a man was arrested in Norwich with an identity card in the name of John Walsh. He was found to be Michael Flynn, a deserter from the Royal Artillery: he had paid half a crown for the identity card from a man who had got it from a bombed house.[6]

It became a daily struggle to obtain any interesting extras or treats to add variety to the basic dull diet. Diary entries and letters are full of such comments. Turner lived in Titchwell and shopped in Hunstanton and Brancaster:

13 July 40: there appears to be some needless complication with the butter and margarine, which, although shown on the same coupons, cannot be purchased at the same shop. This, in actual working, means that people who live alone cannot get both. They must take the full ration of one or the other.

29 Dec: yesterday, Mr Kendle (butcher) having, as he said, nothing to sell, locked up his shop and went home. So no Sunday joint today. And I honestly believe that this has never happened to us before, which should make one reflect on one's blessing.

7 Jan 41: at Mrs Sutherland's shop I achieved, to my great astonishment, some 'Chocolate Spread' for Ursula's tea-party with the Reeve boys tomorrow.

25 Feb: achieved a complete rarity (in fact two) by underhand means, a box of Fuller's chocolates for Ursula at Easter, and two bottles of Olive Oil for future salads.[7]

Mr Newstead lived in Gorleston. His letters to his son Peter include thoughts on food during wartime:

We thank you very much for the eggs which I fetched from the Parcels Office this morning. They arrived yesterday I understand, the packing was very good and only 3 were cracked (but contents intact).

Although we have had to register for eggs, it seems to be still a question whether it will be enforced. The general opinion is it will be unworkable. However there is no shortage of eggs at present here.

If the scheme is put into operation, I don't suppose you would be allowed to send any, in any case I should say the distance is too far for safe travel, don't you think so.[8] This was in June 1941: Peter was serving in Northern Ireland!

Rachel Dhonau was in Sheringham in the war. Entries in her diary included several about obtaining food:

7 Jan 42: there is no meat or fish in town – just a few fishes' heads for which the fish shop wanted to charge us 9d, which we didn't pay.

8 Jan: next day: still no meat or fish in the town, but we actually managed to buy an orange for Timothy.[9]

In October 1942, Lord Woolton made it clear that there would be no extras of any kind for Christmas: 'Women will have to make plum puddings with prunes, potatoes and carrots instead of the eggs and dried fruit of other years. Mince-pies may be made with prunes, stale breadcrumbs, chopped apple and spices instead of with suet, peel and dried fruits. Turkeys will be scarce, so Lord Woolton's cooks are writing recipes for spiced beef and stuffed mutton instead. Christmas cakes must not be iced, but women are to be told by the Ministry of Food how to make a mock-almond icing with haricot beans, almond essence and a knob of butter.'[10]

The BBC radio programme *The Kitchen Front* offered homely advice listened to by up to seven million people. Charles Hill, known as the Radio Doctor, gave sensible advice, such as not over-boiling vegetables. Not everyone was impressed. Betty Armitage noted tersely: 'I listened to the Ministry of Food programme this morning. They talk to us as if we were silly.'

The writer of the Women's Diary column in the *Eastern Daily Press* was more tolerant of the Government's efforts:

I was rather intrigued by the game of pot luck, approved by the Ministry of Food for women fighting on the kitchen front. The game, played on a 'paper board', is something like 'snakes and ladders'. The idea is to help

88 *Cod liver oil and orange juice were given free to children.*

home cooks to improvise facts about health meals and 'do's' and 'don'ts' to observe in their economical preparation. A player soars upwards for 'serving a health meal every day'. She crashes for 'wasting bacon rinds and trimmings'. Points are scored for 'eating lots of vegetables' – or lost for 'refusing to eat oatmeal porridge'. There are many ups and many downs before the winner reaches the 'golden wedding' which concludes the game.[11]

People were encouraged to 'dig for victory', to make use of undeveloped land to grow more food. In October 1939, the Norfolk War Executive Committee sent a circular letter to parish councils about allotments. Brundall is a good example of what followed. Applications for allotments were invited and by the end of the month there were fifteen. By January 1940, the council had asked various local landowners for land but received negative replies. They decided on land owned by Mrs McCall who had not replied to their letter, and resolved to ask for compulsory powers to purchase the land. However, it did not come to that. Mrs McCall wrote that she was happy for her meadow opposite Holme Close to be used; the Council decided they wanted it for two years or for the duration of the war. The land was used for other purposes as well: a demonstration of fire fighting was held there and, in March 1941, an allotment was granted to an applicant from nearby Strumpshaw. However, by April 1942 all 26 allotments had been taken up. After the war, Mrs McCall asked when she could have her land back. The council told the allotment holders that they must leave by March 1946, and expressed their thanks. Mrs McCall replied saying how happy she had been to render service to the council and the people living in Brundall. [12]

The War Agricultural Committee had been at work on a larger scale at Feltwell. More than 1,000 acres at Feltwell Fen had been transformed from 'a desolate wilderness of bog and bush' to cultivated land within just 12 months – including 500 acres of cereals as well as potatoes, carrots and mustard for seed: 'Hutments for workers have been erected along with a canteen and a caretaker's house.' In 1942, it was announced that Hempton Green, site of a sheep fair for centuries, was to be ploughed up. Norwich played its part too, several parks being partly turned over to allotments, including Chapelfield, Eaton Park and the municipal golf course.[13]

These efforts to increase food production could lead to local disputes as to what land should be used. Victor Mann and Edith Lambert were charged in September 1942 with digging up five greens on Dereham golf course and planting cabbages! It was an act of peaceful protest. Mann was seething with injustice: the local Agriculture Committee had ploughed up Brisley Green where Mann played cricket and Neatherd Moor where his children played, but refused to plough up the golf course on the grounds that some cows grazed there. To make matters worse, the land had only been a golf course for eight to ten years. Before that, as Mann, a local farmer, was well aware, it had been very fertile arable land. Unfortunately for Mann, the magistrates were the sort of people who used the golf course. They made sarcastic remarks about why Mann was not fighting, and fined him £5 with £4 costs. Edith was in a slightly different position: she was in the Women's Land Army and was praised by the court for 'doing a man's work'. When they said that she should be ashamed of herself for damaging the golf course, she replied that she certainly was not, and that she had the support of many Dereham people who were offering to chip in to help pay her fine. She was fined £2 with £2 10s. costs.[14]

Another possibility was to turn to less usual forms of foodstuffs. In wartime, one British taboo was broken by many, the eating of horsemeat. The Government made sure that it was never eaten by those who did not fancy the experience, by separating the use of horseflesh from that of other meats. In November 1941, it was announced that the sale of horseflesh for human consumption was prohibited at places where other meat was sold, or where horseflesh unfit for human consumption was sold. Horseflesh was not to be sold to a customer who had not specifically asked for it and 'horseflesh must not be used in meat paste, soup, meat roll, or gelatine, ready or prepared meals, sausages, meat pies or other meat products for human consumption'.[15]

Rabbits and hens had always been eaten by many, but now a lot of people were rearing them too, in their backyards or on allotments. The RSPCA offered advice for new rabbit-keepers not sure how to kill the animals: 'The rabbit should be held up by the hind legs and given a sharp blow at the nape of the neck with the edge of a flat piece of wood. The piece of wood should be about 18 inches long, by 3 wide and 1 inch in thickness with the striking edge bluntly tapered. No great force is necessary in delivering the blow and death is instantaneous. After stunning the throat should be severed.' Newstead wrote to Peter: 'Mr Gosling is now a Rabbit Fancier in fact he is getting quite an expert. He keeps them at Caister, there must be thousands of them around here now, every other person seems to keep them.'[16]

Advice was given on looking after poultry as well:

> Now that the nights are getting
> longer and colder there are
> complaints that colds are becoming
> prevalent, particularly amongst
> pullets. A cold doesn't seem to be
> much in itself to worry about, but
> it may lead to an epidemic amongst
> the birds of some serious disease
> and once that happens it may be

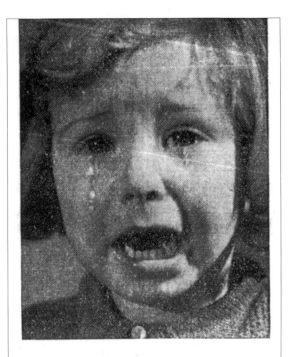

. . . It's her DADDY they're taking away—

When they've seen their mummies and daddies being shot or whipped, thousands of little children have been . . . well, they've had '*their row stopped*.' (A twelve-stone man in jackboots needn't waste much time).

Sooner or later, that sort of thing can happen here, unless we have more weapons with which to drive those 'gentry' into a corner.

There is one way of helping to win the war which is open to all of us—the *hard* way, the way of hard living and not spending.

Spending means trying to use ships and labour and material that must be better used. All too often, it may mean spending *lives* that must be saved for a better purpose. So save where you can on necessities as well as on luxuries.

. . . spend less and save sorrow

89 *War Savings poster. Propaganda often made use of children to pull at the heartstrings of the reader.*

90   *Horlicks advertising stressing the health-giving properties of the product.*

many weeks before they are cured, if ever. Even if one has been lucky and the cold still remains a cold the birds as a result are in poor condition, having lost both weight and stamina: they have received a definite check in both growing and egg production and are not in a fit state to face the winter.

Colds are generally caused by the mistaken kindness on the part of the poultry keeper. Because the nights are chilly the windows and shutters are closed in an effort to keep the birds warm, which means that they are sleeping in a stuffy, badly ventilated house. Provided that the chicken house is dry, light and well-ventilated, there is no need to worry about birds catching cold from fresh air.

There were even ration books for domestic poultry: 'The food allowance is 4 lbs a month for each surrendered shell egg registration, giving a total of 24 lbs for the six months. It is not necessary to buy the exact quantity each month, and on page 4 of the book is given the maximum quantity that may be purchased in any one month. This is to allow meal to be purchased in the standard quantities of 3½, 7, 14 lbs etc.'[17]

Other sources of meat were not neglected. John Vincent of Pettits at Reedham offered advice on wild birds as food. He recommended not just pheasants and partridges but also ducks and other waders. He continued: 'Starlings during winter are not to be despised in a pie or stew. Some people enjoy seagulls, especially the immature. The common house sparrow is very palatable well cooked, though one would require a dozen for a meal. This bird is a pest in many places and those who catch and eat them will perform a dual service to their country.'[18]

Fish were an obvious source of extra protein. Newstead made several references to this in letters to his son in the spring of 1943:

Brother Lee is still dashing about with his rod and bag, I hear the catches in the river have been quite good lately. Mother of course is looking forward to the shrimp season. We shall manage to have a nice 'bit of fish' weekly from Butler's but I miss the lovely herring. Felix too gets plenty, there being a regular supply of his favourite Cheval [horse].

Yes we are feeding well, Mother you know is a good forager, so there's no need whatever for you to worry about this question.

Have had the first gooseberries out of the garden, they were very nice, fruit is such a change … One very strange fact this year is there are no Shrimps which as you will remember is one of our staple Teas. Nobody seems to know why, some say it is owing to large shoals of codling, others to severe tides, but of course the last two seasons were abnormal many big catches day after day, the majority being salted and sent all over the country which was quite a new business.

I am glad to say we are OK and in good spirits, as for St Felix he is far from 'senile', he still enjoys life & 2 lbs of dead horse weekly, also the remains of our Fish dinners bi-weekly (by the way we get good Fish now).[19]

Local newspapers offered tips on the use of wild plants for extra sustenance:

NETTLES AS A VEGETABLE

Fill a big colander with young freshly gathered nettle tops and rinse them thoroughly under the cold water tap. Put just enough water into a pan to prevent burning, bring it to the boil, add salt, and put in the nettles, cover and cook for ten minutes. Strain off the liquid and save for soup; mash the cooked nettles to a pulp, adding a few shreds of margarine if you can spare it, and serve as a second vegetable in place of spinach or any other greenstuff.

NOVEL BREAKFAST DISH

Crush the nettles as above, meanwhile frying any odd and untidy piece of bacon you may have in your ration. Strain the nettles, pour the bacon fat over them and pour a quarter of a breakfastcupful of the nettle liquor into a frying pan. When it boils sprinkle in three tablespoonfuls of medium oatmeals stirring all the time. Season with pepper and a little more salt if necessary and cook until it is of the consistency of very thick porridge stirring all the time to prevent burning (about 5 minutes). Then stir in the well-mashed cooked nettles blending them thoroughly with the oatmeal. Form into individual mounds and serve with the fried bacon.[20]

Food rationing could only work if it was regulated, and if people realised that they faced punishment if they tried to cheat. Many cases of dishonesty came before courts in Norfolk in the war years. These mainly involved over-pricing by shopkeepers. People were also fined for failing to display signs stating what the maximum price was. There were also a good many cases of theft of military supplies and occasional cases of possessing stolen or forged ration books.

Even the smallest breach of food regulations could bring the force of the law upon the shopkeeper. One day in 1941, Mrs McCampling bought a tin of beans in tomato sauce and a tin of vegetable salad in mayonnaise from Mrs Smith, a grocer in Cromer High Street. She was charged 11 pence for the beans and eight pence for the salad. She complained that this seemed very

91 *List of clothes and the number of coupons needed to buy them.*

expensive. Mrs Smith praised the salad: 'There is a lot in the tin. People are spreading it on their bread and butter and it goes a long way.' Unimpressed, Mrs McCampling complained to the local Food Control Officer. The current maximum price of the tin of salad was found to be 6d. Mrs Smith was fined 30 shillings for each of the two offences.[21]

In Norwich in May 1943, Harold Arthurton was accused of 30 offences of fixing false price tags to meat. He was also charged with five offences of selling an amount of meat in excess of the ration, but was acquitted on two of these charges. In the same month, Edward Creasy was charged with 22 offences involving altering price tags on meat. The punishment was harsh – both men were fined £2 *for each offence*, as well as having to pay costs. In Lynn, Cyril Nicholls (trading under the name of W. Nicholls and Son) was accused of selling fish at more than the maximum fixed price. He was charged with 26 such offences, all committed between 27 April and 12 June. He was fined 40 shillings for each offence, and ordered to pay costs as well. Offences on a much smaller scale were committed by Herbert Loads who in December admitted four charges of over-pricing small quantities of fruit: for example, he sold a pound of plums at sixpence rather than for the statutory five pence. He was fined £5 in total and ordered to pay £1 5s. 6d. costs.[22]

Minor thefts of military supplies were fairly frequent. In Norwich in April 1943, Ronald Wilkinson was fined £5 for stealing marmalade and sausage meat from army stores. Hubert Walker, who received the stolen goods, faced a heavier sentence: three months in gaol, with hard labour. In Lynn in June 1942, a soldier – Private Reyner Melsome – was charged with stealing a tin of cocoa, value 4s. 11d., 'the property of the Army Council'. Ivy Payne was charged with receiving the tin of cocoa: they were found guilty and bound over for 12 months. In 1942, James Eden was sentenced to three months' prison with hard labour by Clacklose magistrates for stealing from the RAF a whole variety of goods including 11 tins of metal polish, two tins of canned pork, 10 tins of herrings, nine tins of milk, three pounds of bacon and half a gallon of petrol. He appealed to Quarter Sessions but the sentence was upheld. Charles Kendle, the butcher frequented by John Turner, was also convicted of obtaining rationed food illegally – a seven-pound tin of marmalade and 48 tins of American condensed milk: he was fined a total of £10.

Shopkeepers might not bother too much about coupons with their regular customers. In May 1943, Priscilla Johnson and Alice Banyard were charged in Lynn with 'obtaining rationed food for household consumption without producing to the Retailer a ration document containing a valid appropriate coupon for the rationed food'. Priscilla was fined five shillings. Alice had offended in this way three times and was fined five shillings for each offence. The shopkeepers were also prosecuted: Florence Petch had committed the offence of supplying rationed food without cancelling the appropriate coupon twice, William Lancaster and Eric Bullen once. The shopkeepers received much heavier fines than the shoppers: 40 shillings for each offence.[23]

Many people's lives were changed by the introduction of a hot meal at lunchtime. Communal Feeding Services were originally set up to help feed those who had been bombed-out. Renamed British Restaurants (the name was Churchill's own invention), they were soon established in most towns, self-service restaurants, non profit making, serving plain food at low cost: 'For less than a shilling a hungry customer could have roast beef (or braised tongue perhaps) with two vegetables, treacle tart and custard,

92   *Food ration book, showing the principal foods rationed. In addition, meat was rationed and housewives often handed their whole meat ration cards over to their local butchers' shop.*

bread and butter and a cup of tea.' They changed the eating habits of many people: by March 1942, over 350,000 lunches were being served every day in over 1,320 British Restaurants. [24]

St Faith's District Council wanted to set up a CFC in either Sprowston Central School or Hellesdon Central School, but the Education authorities objected. It was pointed out that there were 240 children at the Sprowston school, 60 of whom came from local villages and had their midday meal at the school. The council decided to open one in Aylsham instead: Mrs Tipple said that such a restaurant would 'solve the problem of woman-power' as it was difficult for a woman to go out to work and look after the home as well. It was in the old Methodist chapel in Mill Road, and was formally opened in November 1942. It ran well for over two years, but by April 1945 it was running at a loss to the council of £8 a week and it was closed down. [25]

There were several British Restaurants in Norwich. One was in Heigham Street School. It opened in January 1942. The menu on the first day included soup, roast beef, potatoes and cabbage, and a choice of trifle or rice pudding. Two main courses cost 9d., soup and tea each being 2d. extra. The restaurant could cope with 300 people a day. Many country people complained that they were being unfairly treated as they

93 *Clothing ration book. The limited number of coupons meant difficult choices had to be made about which items of clothing to replace.*

did not have access to these restaurants. The answer lay in mobility. In Dereham, two vans that were used to provide school meals in surrounding villages were also used to provide hot meals to farm workers in nearby fields. [26]

Clothes and Petrol

It was not just food that had to be rationed: the system was also applied to clothing. This began in June 1941 and involved the first use in this country of a points system. Points or coupons allowed the customer to choose the articles of clothing they wanted or needed most. It was possible for a family to pool its coupons to provide, for example, a new school uniform for a child, or a new suit for a man going to a job interview. Families were continually having to make choices, such as whether to spend points on socks or underwear, or to save up for a larger item such as a new jacket.

The basic rate was 66 coupons a year, but some groups who needed special clothing for work were allowed more. In June 1942, the rate was cut to 60 coupons per 14 months, that is, approximately 51 coupons in a year. Industrial workers and children up to 17 years old were to receive 10 supplementary coupons.[27]

In 1942, Hugh Dalton introduced 'utility' designs for clothing: 'The object of Utility was to ensure, through standardization, that the depleted industry could provide enough clothing at the prices which working-class families could afford.' The *Eastern Daily Press* commented in an editorial that 'changes in fashions forecast as a result are: short skirts, fewer styles, restricted choice of colours, and the end of the turn-up on trousers, sleeve buttons, and double-breasted coats'. The shortness of the skirt was of course only as compared with those of pre-war: fashions of the 1960s were not dreamed of in 1942![28]

The idea of 'utility' – goods of a reasonable standard but with no unnecessary frills – was seen as a sensible one and was soon extended to other items such as furniture and pottery.

Comments about rationed clothing are made in several contemporary letters and diaries. Peter Newstead's Aunt Kit wrote to him from her home in Thorpe Road, Norwich: 'Hope you will find the cardigan warm and useful, when the weather turns really cold. If there is anything else you are wanting that I can knit you if you let me know I shall be pleased to do it – it is useless knitting you a lot of things you have no use for and will find them more trouble than they are worth in the small space for wardrobe allowed to you airmen.' Peter's father was also concerned about his son's clothing: 'I see mother has mentioned about your underwear, but we cannot get them without using our coupons, she did not know that arrangements are being made for men in the services to enable them to buy.'

Rachel Dhonau in Sheringham recorded similar concerns in November 1941: 'Discussion of clothes today. All of us getting short of coupons and everybody is economising on underclothes and night clothes. I shouldn't feel so inclined to if my husband were here, but as he isn't except for brief visits it doesn't matter.' In 1943 her corsets wore out. A new utility pair cost 18s. 5d.: 'They didn't seem very strong but they were all that they had.' They broke after just five days: ' I can't afford to spend 18s. 5d. and three coupons each week on corsets,

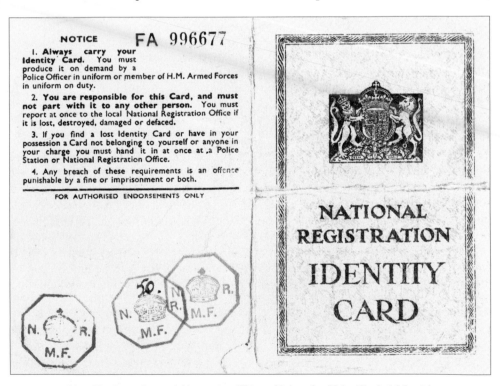

94   *Identity card, essential in wartime. This card belonged to Helen Flood of Norwich.*

and I need to wear them having just had a baby. It nearly made me weep when I discovered this.'[29]

Petrol rationing was introduced in September 1939: private users were limited to a ration of 1,800 miles a year. This was continually cut as the petrol shortage began to bite. In July 1942, the concept of 'pleasure motoring' was abolished and petrol was only available for essential journeys.

In February 1942, soap, which was made from whale-oil, had to be rationed owing to shortage of supplies: the ration was 16 ounces every four weeks. Shaving soap was not rationed but, like razor blades themselves, could be difficult or impossible to find in shops.

As with food, there were several cases in courts of people trying to cheat the system. In Norwich, a man named Partul Chander Malhotra was fined £50 in 1942 for selling utility lighters at 16 shillings each. He was in court again in October 1944: he had been found guilty of selling haberdashery (razor blades, hair grips and snap fasteners) from his shop in St Gregory's Alley at inflated prices. The magistrates had obviously had enough of him and banned him from carrying on in business for a period of two years. On appeal the ban was reduced to a year.[30]

Some offences were on a larger scale. Two Norwich people – Claude Wright of Dereham Road and Dorothy Websdale of Belvoir Street – were tried in 1942 for acquiring stolen cloth. They were apprehended as part of a national CID investigation: the cloth had been stolen in Manchester. They claimed to have no knowledge of this and the court clearly believed them: they were each fined £25. Four young Norwich men – all between 16 and 18 – broke into a railway warehouse and stole 20,000 cigarettes and 49 packets of tobacco. This was on the night of 8/9 May 1945 just one day after the war in Europe had ended. Their leader, 18-year-old Alan Booty, was sentenced to nine months' hard labour, two 16-year-olds were put on probation and the third 16-year-old was sent back to approved school, where he had been for the previous three years after a string of earlier offences committed when he was only thirteen.[31]

News, Entertainment and Daily Inconveniences

How did people know what was going on in wartime? There is one fact I have to stress every time I discuss the war with the younger generation: there was no television in people's homes at the time of the Second World War. The great form of communication was the radio, or, as it was then called, the wireless. Almost nine million radio licences were issued in 1939 and over ten million in 1945, despite the problems of actually obtaining a new wireless set in wartime. Probably 75 per cent of households had a radio at the outbreak of war. Others could crowd around a wireless set in a pub or an air-raid shelter – and a number, by definition unknown, no doubt listened to a wireless without the formality and expense of obtaining a licence.

Regional programmes were suspended in September 1939, and the national programme renamed the Home Service. In February 1940, the Forces Programme came on air, at first only in the evenings but later from 6.30 am to midnight: however, it shared some programmes with the Home Service. Half the population would regularly listen to the news at 6 pm and 9 pm. Sixty per cent of the population might be listening to a speech by Churchill and no less than 80 per cent listened to the 9 pm news on D-Day.[32]

These BBC programmes were the only programmes broadcast from this country, but people could tune into foreign radio stations. By far the most listened-to of these was that broadcast from Germany by William Joyce, nick-named Lord Haw-Haw. During the phoney war of September 1939 to April 1940, up to eight million people listened, many claiming that he gave more hard news about the war than did the BBC. However, after the Germans had conquered France in 1940, he was seen as just a propaganda tool of Goebbels and the show's popularity rapidly declined, though it continued to broadcast until the very end of the war.

As so often, the way in which news was reported was itself a matter for debate. Turner was unsure about the reporting of the Battle Of Britain, writing:

> As regards the BBC recording of the air-battle in the Straits of Dover, there have been many letters protesting at "a life and death struggle being treated as a sporting event". It is certainly a sign of the times in which we live that this should have been possible. There is, on the other hand, another side to

95 *War Bonds poster: a literal representation of the phrase 'The Shadow of the Swastika'.*

the picture. Regrettable or not, our pilots do regard their fights from a sporting angle, and those of them whom I have met, speak of them in sporting language.[33]

Other news was obtained from newspapers, but these were subject to censorship. The general public was also bombarded with leaflets and posters offering advice and suggestions as to how to help in the war effort: we have already seen several examples. The increase in paperwork led to a new word – *bumph* or *bumf*, short for bum-fodder, with its implication that that was the best use for most of the new forms that were being daily invented!

Of course, the radio was a very important form of entertainment as well as a source of news. Sixteen million people regularly tuned in to *ITMA, It's That Man Again*, led by Tommy Handley as the Minister of Aggravation and Mysteries housed in the Office of Twerps. The programme produced a very large number of catchphrases to be heard in all kinds of situations throughout the war, such as 'Don't Forget the Diver', 'It's Being So Cheerful As Keeps Me Going' and 'Can I Do You Now, Sir?' At least one of the catchphrases is still sometimes heard on the lips of the war generation: 'TTFN' ('Ta-Ta For Now').

Another very popular form of entertainment during the war was the cinema. In the 1930s almost 20 million cinema tickets were being sold a year: many young people went several times a week. All the cinemas were closed at the outbreak of the war: they soon re-opened but closed earlier than before to avoid the risk of night time bombing raids. No cinema in Norfolk was bombed while showing a film, but there were disasters in nearby towns. Five people were killed in an air raid that hit a Wisbech cinema, and over fifty died when a cinema in Lowestoft was hit.

Films forever associated with the war include *Gone With the Wind*, which opened in 1940. Popular films with war-related themes included Charlie Chaplin's *The Great Dictator* and *In Which We Serve*. The latter, based on the true story of the torpedoing of HMS *Kelly*, starred Noel Coward and John Mills. Mills was a Norfolk man: he was born at the Watts Naval Training establishment near North Elmham, where his father was teaching.

Sybil Billings recalled life as a teenage girl in Norwich in the war years;

> We tried to carry on as normal as possible, going to the movies and dances. We had to go early as they finished at nine thirty, so everyone could be home before the Air Raid started. Many a night we ran to catch the last bus home. We darned our stockings until they fell apart. We also used brown dye and drew pencil line on the back of our legs. We had one problem. It was water dye and it would wash off in the rain.[34]

Professional football became a totally different game in wartime: all the players volunteered or were called up for military duties. Frank Manders of Norwich City, for example, joined the Military Police and later transferred to the RAF. Sadly he was found drowned in 1942 in the Midlands town where he was serving. He was only 27 years old. Many of the professionals played for Army and RAF sides while they were in the forces. Some might turn up unexpectedly for local teams. The leagues were not played in full. City played only 19 games in the 1940-1 season: 'Norwich City on one occasion met a side purporting to be Brighton and Hove Albion, and in fact consisting of five Brighton men, a couple of Norwich reserves, and soldiers recruited on the ground. Norwich won 18-0; more frequent goals were a pretty general compensation for lower standards of play.' The match was played on Christmas Day (as was then common) and City's record victory was watched by a crowd of just 1,419. In 1941-2, the London clubs formed their own league and the remaining teams of the Third Division South played as and when they could: City played just eight games in the league, but also played a dozen games in the hastily-organised Football League War Cup. For the next three seasons they only played friendly matches. The car park at Norwich City became the site of a machine gun emplacement, manned by the Home Guard: some brick fittings survived well into the 1980s.[35]

The introduction of the blackout had an enormous effect on people's lives. Over 4,000 people were killed on Britain's roads between September and December 1939, not to mention those killed or injured in other blackout accidents. The number of people killed in car accidents increased 100 per cent in September alone, and a poll taken in January 1940 suggested that one person in five had suffered an injury from a fall or walking into something during the blackout. By mid-October the situation had in fact eased as the rules were relaxed: cars were now allowed masked headlights and walkers could use torches provided they were dimmed. Another reason for the decline in the number of accidents was petrol rationing, which cut the number of cars on the roads.

Road fatalities can hardly be classed as war-related deaths, although many of the accidents involved military traffic that would not have been around if it were not for the war. To take just two examples out of many, 17-year-old Rita May Upstone died on 12 February 1943 after being thrown from her bicycle at Hockham by an American army motor lorry. George Whitby and his 72-year-old father Arthur were killed when their car crashed into a Canadian military vehicle at Dunton on 30 July 1943.

The cry of 'put that light out' from neighbours or air-raid wardens is an abiding memory of those who lived through the war. In practice, it was impossible to maintain anything like a complete blackout; a pilot flying at 3,000-4,000 feet over Norwich saw between 200 and 300 window lights caused by badly fitting blinds and curtains.[36]

Nevertheless, breaking the blackout was the most common petty crime in wartime. There were about 350 cases in Norwich alone in 1943, for example. The usual fine was £1. Some cases were fairly petty: a naval reserve officer in Yarmouth was fined for striking a match so that a girl could see the dial in a public telephone box. In Lynn in November 1942 alone, five people were found guilty of breaching the lighting laws, three by showing lights from their houses, one driving a car and another a motor lorry showing too much light. The five were each fined, the sums varying from five shillings to one pound. Again there are many similar entries in the register.[37]

Of course the blackout was a godsend to thieves. The *Gardeners' Arms* in Norwich, like many public houses, had a system whereby the lights went out when the door opened. In March 1942, one thief made sure the door did not shut properly so that

96 *'Carrying on' – Norwich Market Place in 1944. The First World War memorial can be seen between the Market Place and City Hall.*

97   *Norwich Guildhall made ready for war. Sandbags surround the building and the large window has been boarded up.*

her accomplice could take advantage of the darkness to steal the handbag of the lady pianist, which she was in the habit of placing on top of the piano.[38]

Even apart from a lack of petrol, there were many restrictions on travel during the war. In June 1940, a large part of Norfolk, extending 20 miles inland from the coast, was declared a defence area and visitors were banned. The strip was reduced to five miles in December. The whole of the area was defended against possible invasion troops, with tank traps and minefields. The mining of large swathes of the coast as a defence against invasion led to occasional fatalities: it is a question of judgement as to exactly which are to be described as war-related. When L/Cpl J. Skipton and Private J. Higgins died on 20 May 1940 after being blown up by mines on Hunstanton Beach, they were no doubt involved in laying the mines. The case of two anti-aircraft gunners, John Bassett and Eric Pickering, is less clear: they died on 8 February 1942 'from being accidentally blown up by a minefield'. Presumably they had not been informed exactly where the mines had been laid. We may never know if the four people who were killed on Hunstanton North Beach on 22 September 1940 when a mine blew up were ill-informed or foolhardy. They were a 41-year-old farmer, Ernest Bradfield, his sister Phyllis, their mother Margaret, and, Derrick Burns, a 15-year-old schoolboy.

Travel restrictions also led to prosecutions. Newstead, a railway worker, wrote to his son Peter: 'A man from Yorkshire was charged at Norwich today for entering the said city without permission & was ordered to return home at once.' In September 1942, Isobel Turnbull was fined one pound for 'remaining in the Borough of King's Lynn for the purpose of a holiday, recreation or pleasure'.[39]

There were continued efforts in the war to raise money to pay for it, and also to encourage the recycling of products, especially metal which could supposedly be re-used to make guns or planes. Newstead told Peter: 'Things are still very quiet here. You will see by the *Mercury*, which follows late, some of the Landmarks are going for scrap, the Tower & the two sentinels at the Jetty.' The tower he mentions was the Revolving Tower, a prominent feature on the seafront at Yarmouth since it was built in 1897· it was pulled down in 1941 to supply metal for the war effort.

Norwich War Weapons Week in October 1940 raised just over one million pounds, which worked out at over £8 for every member of the city's population, the highest contribution from any of the large towns in England. Lynn's Week in early 1941 raised £240,000 and Yarmouth's in May 1941, £330,000. There were other similar events: in March 1942 Yarmouth Warship Week raised a further £310,000. 'Wings for Victory Week' at Norwich in May 1943 brought in just under £1.5 million. Advertisements for Warship Week in Norwich in January 1942 evoked the spirit of Nelson: 'Nowhere but in Norfolk, in Norwich, is the true Native Spirit of Nelson in the very characteristics and in the emotions of the people who are called upon to rise to the occasion'.[40]

John Heading's mother wrote to him about a fund-raising meeting in Norwich:

I went to a meeting at the Stuart Hall yesterday, the Air Ministry presented Norwich with a plaque for getting their target in 'Wings for Victory' week, it's having a place of honour in the City Hall.

When General Montgomery was here he told the Lord Mayor that if everyone put every ounce of effort into the war effort these next few months, the war need not enter into its 6 year. (The miners & ship wrights are failing to do this.)

One other little thing I remember of all that was said at the meeting & it's this, 'Private Jones joined up & was asked at his interview what his ambition was in the war? "To get out of it as soon as possible" was the reply.' I expect there are a good many with Private Jones' ambition, what do you say?[41]

Rationing and general shortages of food and other items were constant subjects of wartime conversation. In many ways, life in Norfolk, where there were chances of supplementing the basic diet with foodstuffs from the countryside, was a healthy one: more healthy than today in some ways. The war, and the presence of evacuees, opened the eyes of local people to problems in both urban and rural environments, and led to a willingness for change, with such measures as the Education Act of 1944 and the establishment of the National Health Service in the years after the war.

Ten

The Child at War –
Growing up in Wartime Norfolk

We have looked at life for evacuee children, whether coming into Norfolk or leaving the county, but the great majority of Norfolk children remained in their family homes throughout the war. What were their lives like?

Talking to a group of children about life in wartime is a two-stage process. First, it is necessary to remind them of how different life was two generations ago, regardless of war. To imagine a school or family home without mobile phones, computers, television, fridge or freezer, and heated by a coal fire or coke stove, involves a great leap of thought in itself. Only then can we ask what special conditions were caused by the war.

One key factor that is often forgotten is the absence of male figures in the home. Fathers, uncles and elder brothers were all likely to be away, either in the armed forces or doing essential work in factories or mines. Those serving abroad might be away for almost the whole war. We have seen that a large number of Norfolk men were captured when Singapore fell in January 1942: they were away from home for more than 3½ years. Even men serving in England, whether in the armed forces or in essential services, would be away for weeks at a time.

This was a time when it was not unusual for fathers to use physical punishment, whether the slipper or a clip on the ear, for bad behaviour on the part of their children, especially their sons. One might expect it to be more difficult for mothers to maintain control over their older children, and there is anecdotal evidence of teenagers involved in truancy and petty theft. This absence of discipline is reflected in the numbers of young people being sent to Norwich Remand Home: the figure rose from 27 in 1940 to 47 in 1942 and 57 in 1944. (The Home itself had been evacuated from Earlham Road to Bramerton Lodge in December 1940.) Attendance rates at school are only given in the county reports: they fell very slightly from 87.39 per cent in 1942 to 86.5 per cent in March 1945. Obviously it would be easier for children in heavily-bombed areas to slip through the system in the confusion. The very fact that the education authorities in Norwich and Yarmouth did not record attendance rates in their annual reports may be significant.[1]

Some homes would have extra people in the house – evacuee mothers and children. However, as we have seen, evacuees were put in houses with spare rooms. These houses were most commonly ones where children, if there had ever been any in the household, had grown up and moved away. A few families housed refugees from Europe. At the end of 1938, the British Government accepted 10,000 unaccompanied

170

Jewish children from Germany – the *Kindertransporte*. They arrived at a reception camp at Harwich and some came to Norfolk, including one girl who was looked after by the Robbins family at New Catton vicarage and went to the Blyth School. When Robbins died suddenly in December 1939, the girl joined a group of child refugees in Wiltshire and later went to Birmingham University. Her father and mother both died in concentration camps. Another child refugee, Hertha Fischer, also went to the Blyth: it had taken her five months to learn enough English to go to school. She thought that schools in her hometown of Vienna were much harsher, with more homework, a longer school day – starting at 7.45 – and compulsory attendance on Saturday mornings![2]

One little-recorded aspect of the war affecting children was the fate of family pets. They were not allowed in shelters, and were seen as consuming food that would be needed by humans. Juliet Gardiner says that over 400,000 pets were destroyed in the first weeks of war, mainly cats. The Animal Defence League responded by organising an evacuation system for pets. Those who agreed to look after them were compensated financially, the sums varying from about ten shillings a week for a dog down to a penny a day for a budgerigar!

The loss of a beloved pet could have an effect on a child's morale. Maureen Elvin remembered her personal hurt:

> I still had this unreal feeling when we heard the very distressing news that all the pets had to be put to sleep. I simply could not believe that our dearly loved pet dog Chips would no longer be part of the family.
> 'How could this be allowed to happen?' I thought.
> So once again I took the view that this terrible thing would not really happen.
> But to my horror it did.[3]

School logbooks are an excellent source for school life in the wartime period. For this chapter, I have looked at logbooks for four schools in Norfolk for the whole period of the war: Feltwell Anchor Fen, Aswellthorpe, Runhall and Wood Norton. I have also looked at many other examples of logbooks, especially of the larger towns: some have already been discussed in the chapter on evacuees.

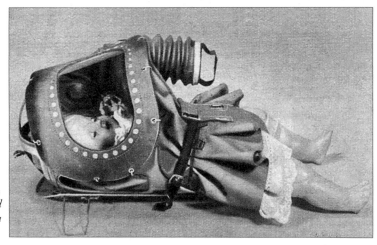

98 *Baby gas mask. Air had to be pumped in for the infant by an adult.*

Anchor Fen in the parish of Feltwell must have been one of the most isolated communities in the whole of Norfolk. A report contained in the logbook says that in 1938 'the school and hamlet were virtually removed from contact with the outside world and although the provision of a road which now links with the nearest village has made transport easier, many of the pupils have little or no knowledge of the world beyond their own homes. Dependence upon broadcasting is increased by the fact that the hamlet receives daily newspapers only three times a week and then twenty-four hours after publication.' The isolation and primitive state of some Norfolk schools was noted by several of the evacuees who came from the crowded urban areas of East London. Leslie Bently recalled: 'I attended Clenchwarton Primary School – a two room school house with gas lights, fireplaces and outside toilets that froze solid every winter.'[4]

A very large number of evacuees could cause havoc to school discipline. The school at Honingham and East Tuddenham normally had about ninety local children. However, as war broke out, Dr Barnardo's children from Essex were evacuated to Honingham Hall and went to the school. In October 1939 there were about 35 of these boys at the school, as well as five girls evacuated from London and three more informal evacuees. Some of these no doubt returned home fairly soon but the boys stayed on for the whole war. According to the school logbook, they had a disruptive effect:

> 6 Nov It was learnt that 9 Dr Barnado [*sic*] boys who were absent, playing truant on Friday last, did considerable damage, the chief being the setting fire to a stack – damage being estimated at £250. This is the third time Dr Barnado boys have played truant, 4 on Oct [blank] and 3 on 31 Oct but no damage has been reported previous to this last occasion. On each of the three occasions the boys were punished on return to school. Very careful watch is being kept from now on upon the eleven boys concerned in the above truancy.

In January 1942, Ernest Simmons, one of the Barnardo boys, was interviewed at the school by a Probation Officer. On 3 May 1943, PC Emms of Honingham made enquiries at the school about a stack fire at Colton. The culprit was Gordon Greenwood, aged nine: it is not said if he was local or an evacuee.[5]

The worst tragedy that could have happened was for a school full of children to have been bombed. This never happened in Norfolk. There were some daylight raids, of course, as shown by the remark of a child in Norwich overheard by Ralph Mottram: 'Oh look Mummie – there's a plane dropping bombs!' Several schools were badly damaged or destroyed by air raids, especially in the large towns of Norwich, Yarmouth and Lynn. Fortunately the raids were all at night time when no children were in class.[6]

Precautions were begun in schools even before the war. All schools in the large towns soon had air-raid shelters: in Norwich, every school had them by December 1940. These were typically underground in the playground, with brick or concrete walls and a roof of reinforced concrete. They were not popular with children or teachers, being damp, unheated and poorly lit, at least at first. If they were badly built, rainwater from the playground might flood them. By the autumn of 1941 they were used far less as children no longer had to troop off to them at the sound of every general alert, but only following a specific alert in that area.[7]

In Great Yarmouth, the re-assembling of local school children was delayed from Monday 4 September until suitable air-raid shelters could be provided. At Church Road School, the Infants did not begin the winter term until Monday 20 November, and then in the mornings only at Stradbroke Infants' School, as no suitable site for shelter was possible at Church Road. At Greenacre Senior, trenches were begun as soon as war broke out. As these could not take all the children, the girls attended from 8.30 to 12.30 in the morning and the boys from 1 to 5 in the afternoon. In the following term the system was changed with boys and girls attending on alternate days.[8]

On 20 November 1939, the buildings of Northgate school were taken over by the authorities and the children moved to Runham Vauxhall School where air-raid shelters had been erected in the garden adjoining the school and were complete apart from seating accommodation and lighting: 'It is intended to hold frequent rehearsals for taking cover therein so as to be in complete readiness for any eventuality.'[9]

Correspondence that survives between the Yarmouth Education Authority and the Governors of the Yarmouth Grammar School (for boys) and High School (for girls) throws light on the early months of the war. In the first month of the war, ARP trenches were dug at the High School in Trafalgar Road and later at their playing field on Barnard Avenue. They were soon occupied by rats: in April 1940 the Borough Rat Catcher had to be called in. Shelters were also built at the Grammar School site in Salisbury Road. The Clerk complained that by August 1940 the latter had become the haunt of 'undesirable characters' who were using them even when there were no air raids: he suggested that they be kept locked, with the keys held at the Warden's post in the school building. In November the inhabitants of 34-37 Rodney Road asked if an opening could be made in the boundary wall so that they could have direct access to the shelters in the High School grounds. The school refused but agreed that the school gates could be kept open at all times.

The question was raised as to whether parents should be allowed to remove their children from a school on an air-raid warning. The Civil Defence Regional Commissioner in Cambridge announced in November 1939 that 'it would be unwise to give official advice against removal, still more to seek to prohibit this, since, if after persuading parents to leave their children at school, a school was hit and casualties resulted, an awkward situation would arise'. He suggested that parents should be encouraged to visit schools and look at the air-raid defences being provided there for their children.[10]

Schools were provided with shelters only when they were thought to be at great risk – in the large towns and in schools near airfields. The Education Committee had advice for the other schools in the county:

> In my circular letter of the 16 July last, I pointed out that every school (except those provided with air raid shelters) should have refuge rooms in which the children would collect in the event of an air raid warning of any kind being received. The windows of these rooms should be protected with wire netting or with shatter resisting varnish. As an air raid might occur without any warning whatever so that children were unable to reach the refuge rooms, it was felt necessary that all windows in every school should receive some kind of protection, and those not specially protected as above should be covered with strips of cloth or stout paper.

99   *Children try out their new air-raid shelter at St Augustine's school in Norwich, 1939.*

It has come to my notice that at several Schools in the County these recommendations have not been carried out. Head Teachers should immediately see that all the windows, glass doors and screens are protected in some way, and I should be glad to hear from any Head Teacher who is unable to carry out this instruction.[11]

Many people in the villages close to Norwich thought that their proximity to the city meant that air-raid shelters should be supplied in their schools. At a St Faith's Rural District Council Meeting in June 1940, Mrs Tipple said: 'All schools should have air raid shelters. If adequate protection is not provided my children will not attend, and many other parents will take a similar line. To put a child under a desk when there is an air raid warning, knowing that he may have to stay there half an hour is a scandalous thing.' She added that a good gust of wind would almost be sufficient to blow down an Aylsham school, let alone a bomb. In September 1940, the parents of the children at St Faith's school got together and built a shelter at the school – but the education authorities would not allow the children to use it, ordering that they continue to sit under their desks in the event of an air raid![12]

No anti-bombing precautions are recorded at either Ashwellthorpe or Runhall schools, even though a bomb did actually fall at Runhall in February 1941, damaging several houses. At Feltwell, ARP wire was fitted to all the school windows in July 1940, and an asbestos fireguard for the blackout arrived in the winter of 1940-41. Wood Norton received two coats of anti-splinter paint in July 1940. As at Runhall, there was also a single air raid at Wood Norton, where several bombs fell on one night in May 1941. This school was the only one of the four to receive air-raid shelters: they were built in the winter of 1941.

After all these precautions, it was the schools in the large towns that suffered most from bomb attacks. Six Norwich schools were destroyed by air raids and a further nine badly damaged.[13]

In at least one case, the Blyth School in Norwich, some of the older children took part in fire-watching. Kathleen Chastney, Joyce Chettleburgh and Julia Byford were there with three teachers when the school was bombed, with a direct hit on the gymnasium: 'Miss Wilson and Kathleen were at the front of the school when the gymnasium was destroyed, and they decided to make a dash through the school to join the others. Everything looked normal in the front hall, but when they entered the quadrangle, to their horror they found themselves falling over glass and doors which were piled up in the corridors: they were amazed when they found that the gymnasium was a heap of rubble, and they immediately called to the others from the tops of the trenches nearby.' The trench was equipped with seats and blankets and the fire-watchers stayed there for the rest of the night: fortunately, none of them had been hurt. The staff and some men cleared up the broken glass and debris: the girls were not allowed to help for fear of tiles falling from the damaged roofs. The girls had a week off school but then returned, having assembly on the tennis courts and most classes being held in the trenches as the rooms were gradually cleared and made safe. Lunch was also had on the tennis courts for the first week, but for two wet days they had to eat lunch in the cold of the trenches. Three weeks after the raid, the school was almost back to normal, despite various missing doors and windows.[14]

It is curious what people remember at moments of great drama. St Augustine's School in Norwich was bombed out on 27 April 1942. When the local newspaper ran an article about the bombing in 1988, several former pupils wrote in. For many, the main memory of that day was seeing a horse lying dead on Waterloo Road after having been machine-gunned. Brenda Amies recalled: 'I remember seeing the bullets in its hind quarters. This memory has always stayed in my mind, because I was so young. It was the first thing I had seen dead.'[15]

100 *St Augustine's school bombed out, 1942. The school was hit by a 500kg bomb during the Baedeker raids.*

101 *Boys look through the rubble of ruined houses in Rupert Street, Norwich, perhaps their own homes.*

St Mark's Church of England Primary and Infants' school in Lakenham was destroyed by bombs on 27 June 1942. Amy Buckley, the head teacher of the school, tells of how she ran through the churchyard before the all-clear, to find a 'blazing inferno' where the school had once stood. The building and its contents were badly damaged. The few items rescued from the fire amounted to a pair of jumping stands, a hat stand, 12 wooden hoops and a few backless forms. A number of desks, which had been stored in the disused Infants' School next door, were also saved. Amy Buckley was desperate to keep her school going: on 29 June, the children were asked to meet in the playground and to bring a story-book and pencil with them. However, it proved impossible to repair the buildings, and bad weather on 17 July revealed leaks in the roof of the Infants' School, caused by shrapnel from the air raid. It was formally closed on 30 July, and the pupils were found alternative schools for the autumn term. The last line of Amy's logbook reads: 'It is a strange end to service of nearly 18 years in the school.'[16]

How the life of a town school might be affected by air raids can be seen in these extracts from the logbook of St Mark's Senior Boys, also in Lakenham:

First air raid warning was at 10.15 am on 17 July 1940: the entire school was in the shelters in two minutes. There was no raid. The sirens were sounded again on 26 July and the trenches occupied until the 'Raiders Passed' signal was given after 15 minutes.

1 August 1940: 3.23 pm. Lone German raider passed by the school. Bombs were dropped almost at once. Boys were first ordered to cover under the desks. Immediately that danger from flying bomb splinters was past seeing that the plane had made off I sounded the gong & all boys were soon in the shelters. I visited Post E3 & asked to be notified when 'White' signal was on & asked for information as to the bombed district. The post sent a messenger to the area, who later reported that no houses had been bombed. Notification of 'White' light was received at 3.26 pm. Work was resumed and the school was dismissed at 4.30 pm.

Children were not dismissed [until] ½ hour after the raid as I thought it advisable to keep them from the vicinity of the bombed area where they would be a nuisance.

One parent (Freeman) withdrew his child.

Half of 2b were on the school garden. These boys took cover by scattering on the asparagus beds & acted promptly & reliably.

There were no fewer than 10 action warnings in the week starting 19 August and so many in September that they were no longer individually recorded in the logbook, the headmaster describing them as 'irritating but not alarming'

28/4/42 Very small attendance after previous night's blitz. Only 3 boys in this school were rendered homeless.
30/4/42. Further blitz. Trafford and Rowington Road areas affected. One more boy rendered homeless.
1/5/42 Mr Grimble was absent for one half-day due to damaged home.
4/5/42 Attendance is better today after three quiet nights. Many boys are sleeping out.
27/6/42 School Gymnasium totally destroyed by enemy action on morning of Saturday 27 June. Most of the windows and frames blown out & incendiary bomb in a room burnt part of the floor and chairs before being put out.
Mr & Mrs Arthur worked wonders on Saturday & Sunday and by 9 o'clock Monday 29 June all class rooms were clear of glass – school carried on without a break.

Emergency work was carried out, but the school had to wait its turn: the bomb damage was not finally repaired until May 1944, after two more years of waiting. However, although far from ideal, working in a half-damaged school was better than having no school at all – although all the children might not agree![17]

In Great Yarmouth, all schools closed in June 1940, but, as children returned, some had to re-open. They faced great risk as the number of air raids increased. The Northgate School in Yarmouth was housed in temporary premises away from the centre of the town, but still suffered occasional attack, as recorded in its logbook:

7 April 41 During the evening of 4 April the School received slight damage as the result of enemy action. Windows were broken and locks on doors smashed. Fortunately all glass in the school has now been protected with muslin.[18]

The logbooks and admission registers survive for Stradbroke School in Gorleston. The school re-opened on 18 November 1940 with over 70 pupils on the books, of whom 59 actually turned up. They must have found the experience terrifying; there was an alert at 9 am and another at 11 am. Each time the children were taken down to the school air-raid shelter. They spent three hours in the shelter on 20 September, and many more hours in the days to come. Not surprisingly it became an extension of the school room: 'Large story books, comic papers and chalks are kept in the shelter for use during long periods.' Some parents would come and take their children away so that the family could be together through the danger. How many children turned up would also depend on the time of the alerts. On 24 February 1941, for example, there was a raid at 9.16 am so most children stayed with their parents, only three early risers reaching the school before the alert. The all-clear or 'Raiders Passed' signal was given at 11.16 and 11 more children soon turned up.

By April 1941, there were 98 children at the school but the alerts were turning into actual air raids. On 8 April, only 32 children turned up because of the previous night's bombing. The school closed at lunchtime and remained closed as there were three successive nights of bombing. Several children left the school, some going back to the Midlands under the Government Evacuation Scheme, others staying in villages not far from Gorleston such as Fleggburgh and Wickhampton. The number of pupils dropped by about twenty, but the others continued to live in Gorleston and attend the school despite the obvious dangers.[19]

There could be difficulties between those schools that remained in Yarmouth and those that had left, with elements of class tension. The Grammar School building in Salisbury Road was occupied by the Home Guard from June 1940. Later it was used by children of North Denes elementary school which had been bombed. In May 1943, Mr Palmer, the headmaster of the Grammar School, wrote a strong letter of complaint to the Yarmouth Education Committee: one of his masters had called in at the school in the Easter holidays and found it in a disgraceful state. The headmaster of North Denes School, Mr Reynolds, was forthright:

> I have read the copy of Mr Palmer's letter with disgust and I am afraid I can hardly reply. That this man and teacher, who has safely 'made his roots' in Retford could be so petty as to attack me here in Yarmouth is past understanding … I can only assure you and the governors of the School Foundation that all is well with the building and the apparatus except the damage done by enemy action.

In July 1944, there were complaints that the school organ had been misused. Reynolds responded:

> I state that no children have ever played on the organ or misused it, as it has been regarded as out of bounds. I welcome the recommendation that a lock should be placed on the organ … but consider it a grave slight on me that this key should not be placed under my care and that the organ should not be properly used for the pleasure of elementary children as well as for the Grammar children.[20]

In King's Lynn, the King Edward Grammar School was shared by its own pupils and evacuee children from Hackney Downs School. It was badly damaged by bombing in 1942; this could have been a disaster as there were boarders sleeping in the school. However, fire-watchers, once again including some of the pupils, were able to save the situation: 'The boys climbed out onto the roof in their pyjamas to tackle the bomb which had lodged beneath the tiles. A third boy named Silk assisted inside the roof. They were joined by policemen who climbed out onto the roof with a stirrup pump, and later had the assistance of the local caretaker. The bomb was finally extinguished by firemen operating a hose from ground level.' There were no casualties.[21]

Schools in the county only suffered an occasional raid. Colney School was demolished by a bomb on 5 May 1943, the only country school in Norfolk to suffer this fate. The children were temporarily dispersed to nearby schools at Bawburgh, Hethersett, Great Melton and Cringleford. The school re-opened in the Church Room on 25 May, with another class in the club room at the *Rose and Crown* public house. In the winter the whole school moved into the pub as the Church Room had no heating. In April 1944 a temporary classroom was erected but this could only take the younger children: the older ones were again dispersed to nearby schools.[22]

Other incidents were much less dramatic. Honingham School log book is laconic:

> 5 May 43   The School was closed today owing to the presence of 2 unexploded bombs in a field approximately 200 yards from the school. The mines were dropped during the raid of last night.
> 6 May   School re-opened at 9 am as the mines have been removed.[23]

Inevitably, some children did die in air raids, usually at night in their homes or in air-raid shelters, often together with their parents. A total of 36 children died in bombing attacks on Norwich. This figure is taken from the civilian casualty returns. Education Committee records, however, say that just 18 schoolchildren died in the raids: the other 18 were presumably children under five, or perhaps youngsters of between 14 and 16 were classed as children in one statistic but not in the other.[24]

The first child victims died on 30 July 1940, all in Victoria Terrace off Horn's Lane. Gwendoline, Jill and Peter Bramble died with their mother Phyllis at number six, 13-year-old Doris Johnson died with her parents at number fourteen. Inevitably, children died during the Baedeker raids at the end of April 1942. Twenty-two children were killed in the first raid, but only two in the second, probably because so many families were moving out of the city for the night. Victims included Doris and Honor King, two teenage sisters killed at Chapelfield, and 13-year-old Sybil Burton who died with her parents and elder brother at their home at 46, Alexandra Road. Three-year-old Valerie Minister was killed in her home at 15, Northumberland Street: her mother Florence was badly hurt and died in the Norfolk and Norwich Hospital five days later. Just four children were killed in later raids on the city.[25]

There were fatalities in Yarmouth too, in some cases of children who had left during the evacuation of June 1940, but had returned later in the year. On 11 April 1941, seven people were killed in a communal Anderson shelter between rows 45 and 47. They included Nora Pitchers aged 27 and her children Jean (seven), Patricia (two), and Margaret (three months): the identification of their bodies was made by the father. The family lived at 59, North Quay: ironically, the house was not damaged in the raid. Twelve-year-old Ethel Merrison died in the same shelter.[26]

Bombing, and the continual threat of air raids, was bound to have a psychological effect upon children. The Norwich Schools Health Inspector noted in 1942: 'There is no doubt that many children have become more nervous with the air raids and that they sleep less well than formerly, more particularly when the mother is nervous and worried with having the sole responsibility for the children in wartime.' In towns, families often slept together in shelters or in their living room, which could be a health risk. In 1942, the Norwich School Medical Officer blamed an increase in head lice on this factor and in the previous year in Yarmouth general poor health amongst the children was blamed on sleeping in unventilated shelters: the situation improved in 1942 because fewer families were spending the night in shelters.[27]

Bombing was only part of the risk faced by Norfolk children in the war. The number of aeroplanes, parts of planes and unexploded bombs that fell on the county during the war can never be known. They presented many dangers; more children died through handling such objects than directly from air raids.

The most dramatic cases were of actual plane crashes. An American Liberator bomber was flying low over Mile Cross on 14 January 1945 when it touched the gable end of a house in Spynke Road and came down in a garden. A group of children were playing there, including five-year-old twins Mary and Richard Kemp and Bryan Jones, aged eleven. Mary and Bryan were killed and Richard was taken to hospital. Two of the crew were also killed. An American airman, Earl Zimmerman, was actually in the house, having tea with his fiancée at her family home: 'All of a sudden we heard a loud noise, a terrific crash. A B-24 from Horsham St Faiths ... crashed into June's house, taking the top off, and landing directly behind the house in a garden ... We pulled two boys out alive; later, on the lawn, one of them died.' The twins' mother and elder sister had both been injured in the 1942 raids on Norwich.[28]

Crashed planes were of course a source of fascination, to boys especially, and souvenirs were prized possessions. Raymond James recalled an incident at Welney, where he grew up:

> On Sunday mornings I used to cycle across the Wash Road to get my milk. On this particular morning to my surprise I suddenly saw an Aeroplane in the Washes. I realised that it was a crashed German Junkers 88. I could see that I was one of the first to get to this plane. I started looking for keepsakes. I got one or two then suddenly I saw a revolver on the pilot seat. I picked up this gun, tucked it in my coat and started for my bicycle. Unfortunately for me I saw Mr Charlie Ray, the local schoolmaster and Home Guard captain. He said, 'What have you got?' Naturally I said, 'Nothing', but he didn't accept that and searched me taking the gun away. I feel sure that he kept it.[29]

Schools might take their children on supervised visits to crash sites. At Great Cressingham, the head teacher recorded in her logbook: 'A brand new aeroplane landed in a nearby field on 25 September 1940: it had run out of fuel. The pupils were allowed to go and look at the plane.'[30]

The last civilian killed as a result of bombing in Norwich was nine-year-old Cyril Cranmer, who died on 19 May 1943 from burns received through the explosion of an incendiary bomb with which he was playing. The family lived at 19, Bowers Avenue. In March 1942, John Craske (eight) and his sister Mary (four) were filling a scuttle with coal in the shed of their family home in Cromer when there was a sudden explosion: John was killed on the spot and Mary severely injured. Looking at fragments of metal, it was concluded that there had been an anti-tank grenade in the coal. How it got there was never resolved: the coalman insisted there was nothing like that in the coal when he had delivered it: 'Naturally if I had seen anything I would have picked it out.' The children were probably the victims of a child's prank.[31]

Norfolk Education Committee sent several circulars to all schools on the dangers of unexploded bombs. A typical example reads:

The Ministry of Information has requested the Committee to draw the attention of children to the danger of unexploded bombs. The Press throughout the country have been asked to give prominence to a warning to the public. This warning is made all the more necessary by the difficulty of providing guards for all such dangerous spots. It may be necessary to erect notices at certain places for which guards are not provided, drawing attention to the presence of unexploded bombs. These notices, in red lettering on white paper, will read;

DANGER. UNEXPLODED BOMBS

Children should be firmly told that they must not approach any place where bombs have fallen, and that if they see any notice such as that mentioned above, they must be particularly careful to follow this instruction.

Some related to specific incidents:

The Chief constable has recently called the attention of the Committee to an incident where two boys of school age, who had picked up the fin of an incendiary bomb, threw this on a fire made of sticks and paper. Both boys received bad burns and cuts as a result of the explosion which occurred.

I am sure that Head Teachers will co-operate by warning scholars of the folly of playing with pieces of incendiary or any other type of bomb.[32]

Runhall School held three talks on touching dangerous objects in 1943 and 1944. Three were also held at Ashwellthorpe, all in 1943, including one specifically on anti-personnel bombs. A talk was also held at Wood Norton in 1943, and in March 1945 a policeman came in to tell the children not to touch anything that had fallen from an aircraft. No talks of this nature are recorded at Anchor Fen.

The fact that the coast of Norfolk was mined was an obvious danger to children, and one of which the Education Committee was well aware:

From time to time we become aware that children meet with fatal accidents through straying on to dangerous and prohibited areas, particularly near the coast. In a recent case two children lost their lives through straying on to a minefield which was properly wired with warning notices on the land side and the beach was closed to the general public.

The Committee would be glad to hear if teachers in all areas, and particularly in those areas near the coast, would call attention to the fact that wire on the ground is evidence of a prohibited area.

The dangers to children of breaking inside a wired enclosure, whether warning notices exist or not, cannot be over-emphasised.

The coastline was protected with barbed wire so it was only those who were prepared to break through the barriers who were at risk. Misadventure was presumably the cause of death of two ten-year-old schoolboys, Ernest Whitwood and Roy Riley, blown up by a mine on Trimingham Cliff on 8 January 1943.[33]

The most striking image of school life during the earlier part of the Second World War is of a child carrying a gas mask. Children had to take their masks to school every day: they were periodically inspected by the teacher to see that they were not broken. The Education Committee laid down rules in various circulars:

Recent gas exercises have revealed defects in the respirators carried by school children. This is to be expected in view of the fact that many children must have grown too big for the respirators issued to them more than two years ago, while all children have carried them about more regularly than adults.

Head Teachers are reminded of the necessity for conducting periodical examinations of gas masks and for reporting any defects to their local ARP Wardens. I should be glad to suggest means by which teachers may obtain assistance in conducting this examination, or in securing replacements or repairs, where necessary. The examinations of gas masks should be recorded in the log book.

Head Teachers have been asked from time to time to conduct a regular monthly examination of children's respirators. It is believed that in most cases this inspection has been carried out regularly and efficiently, and the Committee are grateful for the voluntary work that teachers have done. In some schools, however, it would appear that the inspection has been less thorough than in others, and a recent report from the County ARP Authorities shows that at one centre, out of 350 children's respirators examined, no fewer than 100 were found to be defective or inefficient in one way or another.[34]

By the summer of 1942, the fear of gas attack had passed. Children were told not to bring their gas masks with them to school every day. However, the masks were still to be maintained in sound condition, and children were ordered to bring them to school once each month and at the beginning of each school term for inspection and for testing as to correct fitting. Eventually the duty of checking the masks ceased to be that of the teacher: local ARP wardens did the checking instead.

Our sample schools all held some inspections of gas masks, but the frequency with which they were held varied. Anchor Fen held a gas drill as early as 4 August 1939, the last day of the summer term, and, as it turned out, a month before the war broke out. Inspections of gas masks were held at the school almost every month until nearly the end of the war, the last being in February 1945. The main problem was that, as the children grew, their masks were no longer of the right size. The other three schools were not so conscientious. Ashwellthorpe records no inspections of gas masks before 1942 and none after February 1944. However, they held an anti-gas talk in January 1943 and hosted the Gas Van in March. On this occasion, the masks were inspected and all the children went through the van except one, Tony Chamberlain: the reason for his exemption is not recorded. Wood Norton and Runhall only inspected gas masks about every three months, but Runhall did record any faults in the masks (faulty valves or damage to the mica) in the school logbook.

The appearance of the Gas Van was recorded by several other schools. At Honingham, for example: 'On 11 Dec 1942 the Gas Van was brought to School today by ARP officials. All the children's respirators were inspected and repairs carried out. All children passed through the Gas Van.' The prospect could be stressful. Rachel Dhonau recorded in her diary: 'Timothy was very upset today because his teacher had arranged for them to go into a gas chamber to test their gas masks. He went, and enjoyed it, and was delighted to find that his gas mask really did work.'[35]

Town schools were very aware of the threat of gas attack. The teachers of three schools in Lakenham gathered together for lectures on anti-gas training and first aid at Cavell School. At St Mark's Lakenham, the Mobile Gas Van visited the school in 1941 and all but two of the boys passed through it. There was a gas mask inspection by air-raid wardens in February 1942. Stradbroke School in Gorleston also took the gas threat very seriously: all children had to wear their masks for ten minutes every week during school.[36]

Children going to school of course had to cope with the blackout and there were inevitable traffic accidents. Far fewer people had private cars than do so today, but there was a massive increase in traffic serving the airbases throughout the county: very often the accidents were caused by collisions involving military vehicles and children on foot or on bicycles. There were two such tragedies in the village of Scarning in the spring of 1942. Fourteen-year-old Olga Pratt got off the Dereham school bus near her home in Scarning on a March afternoon in 1942 only to be killed as she was crossing the road to her house at Railway Farm. The army driver was exonerated from all blame. In April 1942, Ellen Tuck of Woodhill Cottages was cycling with her children to their school. In Scarning, one child, six-year-old Brian, fell behind: he was knocked down by an army lorry and killed. Ellen was already suffering as a result of the war: her husband in the Norfolk Regiment had been reported missing in Malaya. There was a similar tragedy in Thetford in the same month. Cecil Allison was a school bus driver in Thetford. One evening he dropped his own son, John, aged six, at their home at Newton, only to see him knocked down as he crossed the road: once again an army lorry was responsible. He took him to hospital in the bus but the boy died.[37]

The special measures taken for children meant that their diet was healthier than that which many had eaten before the war, especially poor children in urban areas. Children received the full meat ration from the age of six – and a full tea ration from the age of five. They also had special privileges – babies between six and 18 months were allowed three eggs a week, children under five were entitled to seven pints of free or subsidised milk a week. By March 1942, 3,500,000 children were receiving milk at school, most in an object never seen today: a small glass bottle containing one third of a pint. These bottles were to be washed and returned for re-use. From 1942, the children also received orange juice and cod-liver oil at school.

Milk was not always readily available. The County Education Committee could sometimes obtain milk – of a sort – to help overcome shortages:

> Sep 42: The Committee have for disposal to Schools and Canteens a large quantity of tinned milk in excellent condition, originally supplied for Rest Centres ... the milk can be used for making cocoa and would provide an excellent addition to normal milk supplies during the winter when milk may be short in some parts of the County.
> One tin contains half-a-pint of condensed milk which should be diluted with water for use. The milk is packed in cases of 48 tins, but any quantity can be supplied. Prices are: for Pet or Carnation (American), 7¾d per tin; for Ideal 5d per tin.[38]

Another wartime development was the increasing provision of school meals. The Norwich authorities already supplied a large number of meals for their schoolchildren and this was expanded in the war years. In Yarmouth, as the number of children returning to the borough increased, so did provision for their welfare. School meals were introduced in September 1942, and a year later over 700 meals were being served every day. Soon, 600,000 children in Britain were having lunch at school. At Greenacre Senior Girls' School, meals began to be served in the first Domestic room on 7 September 1942: 57 children had a meal. Within a fortnight the number had gone up to 78 and the meals had to be served in the Art Room. The School Medical

Officer commented: 'This is a most valuable means of augmenting a school child's daily rations, and should be taken advantage of by as many as possible.' The county schools were obviously in a more difficult situation as they were so widely scattered: even so, the education authority increased the number of schools in which meals were served from 1940 onwards. By 1944, just over one third of county children were receiving a hot meal at school each lunchtime.[39]

Children in schools in the country were encouraged to help in making the most of natural products and all children were asked to help in recycling programmes. Food gathering was especially recommended to schools:

Preservation of fruit

The Ministry of Food is anxious that use should be made of all wild fruits, particularly blackberries, for jam making. They would be grateful if Head Teachers can encourage picking of the fruit by organised parties of school children, for sale to the Women's Institute Preservation Centres or Garden Fruit Committees. The maximum prices payable by these preservation centres are: 3d per pound blackberries; 2d per lb crabapples (which will pass through a 2-in ring); other wild fruits at agreed prices. The Committee hope Head Teachers will do all they can to comply with the wish of the Ministry.

Rose hips were also wanted:

I hope to be in a position in my next circular letter to announce a list of depots set up in the county by the County Herb Committee for the collection of rose hips. Head Teachers will be asked that all hips this year which are not being made into jam or puree by the schools themselves should be sent to the local depot.

Children at three of our four schools helped the war effort by gathering food. At Wood Norton the four oldest boys broke up part of the playground in April 1940, turning it into a potato patch: they supplied their own tools and potato seed. In the summer of 1943 it was recorded that the older girls at the school were employed picking potatoes and fruit. In November 1940, Ashwellthorpe children collected acorns and horse chestnuts, while at Anchor Fen they were collecting dandelion roots: these were sent to a firm in London. No food gathering is recorded at Runhall. Herbs and medicinal plants were also gathered:

The Board of Education, in expressing their appreciation of the work done last year by the schools in the collection of herbs and medicinal plants, draw attention to the continued need for supplies and hope that schools, youth clubs etc will continue to co-operate.
    No steps should be taken for the collection of plants until arrangements have been made for their drying and despatch with the local Herb Committee. The Secretary of the Norfolk Committee is AE Ellis Esq, the Museum, Norwich, to whom all correspondence on this matter should be addressed.[40]

'Ellis' was, of course, Ted Ellis, the well-known Norfolk naturalist, applying his skills to the wartime situation.

Older schoolchildren were strongly encouraged to help in farm work in the holidays, and were even sometimes excused from school to assist. The Minister of Agriculture and Fisheries addressed a leaflet to schools:

102 *Christmas party at Seething airbase. Local children appreciate the generosity of their American hosts of 448th Bomb Group.*

VITAL HARVEST
How the parents of
Public and Secondary
Schoolboys can help

On our harvest this year may well depend the future of our country. We shall need all the extra food that our farmers can grow for man and beast. Every extra load of hay – every extra stack of wheat – will count.

We can rely on our farmers to do their utmost to produce this extra food. But they will need all the help the public can give them – especially at harvest season. **You** can help your country by allowing your boy to do essential work on farms.

Boys from Public and Secondary Schools have done a grand job of work during the past two years. The Government is grateful to them. …

I know that most boys want to fly or do some other thrilling war job when the time comes. Meantime a job of work on the farm, while not so thrilling, is just as vital a form of war service. It is a healthy job, too, that will make them fitter in these difficult times when the usual kind of holiday is out of the question. It will be an invaluable experience for the boys.[41]

Girls were offered opportunities, too. A leaflet issued by the Ministry of Labour and National Service in July 1943 listed 'opportunities of National Service for both girls and boys'. Those for girls included work in research, work in the Women's Land Army, and also traditional roles as nurses and teachers.[42]

103   *Christmas with American servicemen at Attlebridge airbase.*

East Anglian children had one resource denied to those in many other parts of Britain: the Americans. For many people, wartime Norfolk is associated with memories of the generosity of American airmen. The Christmas parties held for children at the airbases were especially memorable, with gifts, ice-cream candy, coca-cola and cakes: it is easy to see how the grand-daughter of a Norfolk publican, who was four when the Americans came, should remember 'Right up to the time when I finally decided there was no Father Christmas, I believed that he chewed gum, spoke with an American accent … and called little girls honey'.

Derek Daniels recalled the Christmas party held at the USAAF hospital near Wymondham:

> They came and collected us from our homes in ambulances and took us back to the Hospital where we had a great time. We saw a film show and were given toys and sweets galore (for in Morley, as elsewhere, we were only allowed two ounces a week, we were rationed). But not here! There was candy, as the Yanks called it, and gum by the yard, the toys were fun – some having been made by the wounded men, when they were convalescing.

Peter Davis and a friend used to crawl under the perimeter fence of one American base in search of souvenirs from the scrap dump. Once they were caught, and after 'a fearful trip to the guardroom' were fed on beefburgers and ice cream and taken for a trip in a Liberator before being 'taken home complete with bikes in a jeep with pockets full of chewing gum and sweets'.[43]

Schools were issued with a circular telling them not to allow their children to beg from these wealthy newcomers:

> Head Teachers might co-operate in putting an end to this somewhat unpleasant practice. It is not suggested that the practice is wide-spread in this area, and in many cases it is known that children ask for no more than chewing-gum or sweets. Some children, however, go beyond this, and there have been reports of their pestering American troops for money. It is suggested that this may create an unfortunate impression, and Head teachers of schools where there are American troops in the vicinity might consider talking informally to the children on the matter, and explaining why the practice is undesirable.[44]

Gifts from schools in America and elsewhere to Norfolk schools were not uncommon, and are sometimes recorded in the school log book as at Church Road School in Yarmouth, for example:

> 12 May 1942: a gift of chocolate from the people of Southern Rhodesia presented to the children.
> 15 Jan 1943: toys from USA distributed to the children by Mrs Sutton at 11.15 am on Thursday 14.[45]

Several such gifts are recorded in the logbook of Greenacre Senior Girls' School. Toys from the American Junior Red Cross and chocolate from the Optimist Clubs of

104   *Children from West Lynn school visit Wendling airbase.*

105 *'Useful Jobs That a Girl Can Do', the cult of 'Make Do and Mend' was strongly promoted during the war.*

America and Canada were given to the children for Christmas in 1942. In January 1943: 'The Chairman, Alderman Greenacre, came and distributed toys to the children. These toys had been sent from America. A photograph of Mr Greenacre with the children was taken.' Gifts from the War Relief Society of America arrived in the following December.[46]

There were shortages of almost everything in schools, including that key classroom commodity, paper. The Education Committee urged economy:

> I would again urge all Head Teachers to exercise the greatest economy in the use of paper. No exercise book should be discarded until it has been completely filled and no paper should be used for school magazines, reports, examination questions etc. The normal written work in English and History should not, and need not, be curtailed, but every care should be taken to reduce note-taking, rough work and mere transcription to the minimum. In writing letters, Head Teachers should use both sides of the paper and the usual requirement that separate sheets of paper should be used for separate items or requests may be regarded as temporarily suspended.
>
> The Committee's contractors have stated that their stocks of paper are almost entirely exhausted for the present.

Children were encouraged to collect waste paper for the war effort: in March 1942, it was reported that the schoolchildren of St Faith's and Aylsham Rural District Council area had collected just under 90,000 lbs of paper during the national scheme in January of that year. Aylsham Senior Girls School had led the way collecting an average of nearly 77 lbs per pupil. However, there were allegations that the school had massaged its figures, taking averages only from the top classes.

Schoolchildren were also encouraged to recycle or, as it was then called 'salvage', all sorts of other items. In March 1941, at Greenacre, Miss Johnson reported: 'We have had an extra salvage drive this week and besides collecting paper, tin-foil, tins, razor blades, cotton reels etc, we have collected 401 jam jars.'[47]

Some schools took a very responsible attitude to the war, making products or financial contributions and encouraging discussions. Of the four schools in our sample, Ashwellthorpe School took its duties of helping fellow men most seriously. They sent a parcel of comforts to the troops in February 1940: 13 pairs of mittens and a balaclava helmet were knitted, mainly by the boys, who also paid for the wool. A second parcel followed four months later of mittens knitted by both boys and girls, accompanied by a pair of socks that someone had donated. In November 1940, a patchwork quilt was made and sent to the billeting officer in Wymondham for the use of evacuees. In the following month, two rugs of knitted squares were sent to the Hospital Supply Depot.

Greenacre Senior Girls' School once again led the way. In 1939, money intended for the school Christmas Party was used to buy wool, with which pullovers, gloves, mittens and balaclava helmets were made: these were sent to the Mariners' Institute in Great Yarmouth. Many such parcels were sent by the school during the war. From 1941, other garments were sent to the WVS for people bombed out of their homes: these included pyjamas and sleeping suits. The school also collected eggs to send to people in Yarmouth Hospital, noting in 1941 that these 'are very difficult to get and cost from 2½d. to 3d. each'.[48]

Ashwellthorpe also looked at the international side of the war. They raised money three years in a row for the Yugoslav Relief Fund, and brought in an American chaplain from Hethel to talk to the top class about America. In 1943, the school received a scrapbook from Fairview School in Dayton, Ohio and spent part of the summer term creating one to send back. Fairview School responded with gifts in December, and one of the American girls was especially keen as she individually sent more gifts the following Christmas.

None of the other three schools record this form of activity, although the oldest boy at Wood Norton, Noel Taylor, did design the 'Indicator' that marked the takings at the local War Weapons week in July 1941. Wood Norton logbook is the only one of the four to notice any military action in the war, recording that Philip Hayhow, a former pupil and now a parachutist, had received the Croix de Guerre for 'much courage and fearless action'. The only other serviceman mentioned in the four logbooks

106   *Blackout poster issued by the local bus company, Eastern Counties Omnibus Ltd.*

107   *Poster to encourage use of 'Shanks's Pony' (one's feet!) in wartime.*

is W.G. Betts, a steward on a minesweeper who wrote to Ashwellthorpe school asking for letters from the children there: the senior children duly responded.

The end of the war in Europe was celebrated with two days' holiday in all County Council schools, and this appears to be recorded in every logbook. However, at a church school like St Mark's Lakenham, part of the first morning was spent at church: 'Two days holiday for Victory in Europe. Boys assembled at 9 am in church

108   *Children at Greenacre School, Yarmouth, with gifts from America; Alderman Greenacre is in the centre of the picture.*

for an Excellent Service of Thanksgiving & were dismissed at 9.35 for two days holiday.'

The sheer length of the war is often forgotten. From September 1939 to August 1945 is just one month short of six years. A child could be ten or eleven in 1945 and scarcely remember a time when there was no war. The disruption caused by evacuees and by bombing meant that education for many children was severely restricted, while other children suffered almost no disruption at all. However, all went through experiences of rationing, the absence of fathers and the presence of so many soldiers and airmen in the country. All in all, school in wartime was an unforgettable experience for Norfolk children. Not everything was bad, as Mr Eckersley, the Headmaster of Fakenham Secondary School, pointed out at his 1942 speech day. The war had brought the children into contact with the outside world in first aid units, salvage work and other enterprises – some were developing qualities of self-reliance and confidence not normally found in schoolboys and girls.[49]

Don Filliston, an evacuee from London who spent the war in Lynn, summed up his war:

> Food rationing did us no harm at all. We weren't overweight, our teeth were sound, and we got used to Spam, dried milk and eggs. Bread was not rationed, but the coarse national offering took getting used to. We all had to 'Make Do and Mend', and salvage drives were regularly held to give scrap metal for ships, tanks and planes. Clothing, too, was rationed from the summer of '41, and 'utility clothes' with men's trousers losing their turnups, and women's skirts were short and straight.[50]

Eleven

The End at Last

The war in Europe ended on 8 May 1945. Norfolk people celebrated in a variety of ways. John Turner captured the moment in his diary:

> 7 May: Everyone on tiptoe at the announcement of the cessation of hostilities in Europe. But nothing happened except that Brancaster apparently got false news of the surrender and immediately put up their flags, while the schoolchildren fled joyously from the school and were seen no more.

> 8 May: The cessation of hostilities was announced by the PM at three o'clock and the King spoke at nine. Laura and I spent a quiet day. A 'Victory' breakfast of eggs and bacon (provided by Mrs Frohawk as a surprise, because there was nothing in the larder!). In the evening we walked over to the *Ship*, thinking to find the place crowded, but there was no-one there except ourselves. We had a glass of sherry, and came home. As a great treat we toasted the Allies in a small dose of inferior brandy and soda.[1]

A friend of Tom Upcher's was in London. He wrote an excited letter to him at a quarter past midnight on 8 May: 'American soldiers were drinking from bottles with girls, Canadians were dead drunk and the non-combatant part of the population were fighting to cross the Circus.' Later, he concluded:

> It is now 10 to 2. The air is cooler, there has been a slight rainfall, flashes of lightning and distant thunder ... So this is Peace Night. One of those nights people will remember for years. Broken taxis, drunken Yanks, singing crowds, kerbside profiteers revelling in their trade selling bunting like hot buns, GI Hats for souvenirs, one smelling sweetly and sickly of lavender. Now all is quiet, except for the thunderclaps faint and far away. The sheer brilliance of the lightning is marvellous. Nature having her fling on this hectic night too.[2]

In Norwich, Agnes Podd's feeling was mainly one of relief: 'Great VE Day, war over in Europe, no more fighting for all the brave men and women who have saved us from untold horror. No more sirens, no more fear and dread, no more bombing.'[3]

War continued against Japan until mid-August. Then there were further celebrations. Mr Newstead in Yarmouth celebrated quietly: 'We passed the 2 VJ Days quietly with a visit to the Pictures, Gary Cooper in "The Plainsman" and Vera Lynn in "An Exciting Night", both quite good and Uncle & I after walking around the Town managed to get one half pint each of flat beer. The Town was crowded all the week & the Pubs did a roaring trade.' Other people in the town, however, were more exuberant

109 *Graves of air-raid victims after the Baedeker raids, Norwich, 1942. Graves were prepared for the victims of future mass bombings. Fortunately they were never needed.*

as he reported in a later letter: 'The Navy what few there were of them played up hell here, pinched all the Flags belonging to the Corporation from the poles on the marine parade about 400 quids worth & generally made themselves seen and heard. Soldiers at the *Granville* lighted a fire in the Courtyard & nearly set fire to the Hotel after stripping some of the interior woodwork.'[4]

Agnes Podd also celebrated:

> 15 Aug. Thank God the war is over in Japan. VJ Day. Went to Jessie's for tea and heard the King's speech, then went out to see bonfires and fireworks. Went through the city and on top of Mousehold where we could see the whole city. Mary and Janet enjoyed it very much, they had never been out so late at night – nor seen such a sight or streets lighted up. It was like fairyland to them and a sight they will never forget.[5]

Constance Beckett and her WAAF friends in Happisburgh were determined to celebrate VJ Day in style: 'We boarded the train to Liverpool Street and took the Underground to Trafalgar Square where we were caught up in the wonderful, crazy, joyful maelstrom of madness. Crowds and crowds of people, intoxicated with the heady wine of freedom. Perfect strangers embracing each other. Dancing in the streets. People jumping, or being pushed, into the fountains splashing, shouting, cheering, singing.'[6]

110   *'On the way home' – Norfolk Regiment prisoners of war leaving Singapore. Changi prison is in the background. Former prisoner Russell Beckett and his brother are marked.*

Dorothy Calvert was in Lancashire on VJ Day:

My pal and I went to Manchester to watch the revels. What a crowd, people were all hugging and kissing each other, and then the lads started to chase the girls, doing the Cave man bit; which made my mate and I a bit wary, as the boys were more than 'Three sheets to the wind', quite tanked up in fact, and becoming too amorous with it with anyone who was willing. We decided to remove ourselves, as we did not want anyone blotting our copybooks at that late stage, so we caught a bus back to our billets, and let the others do as they wished. It was just wonderful to know that the dreadful war was over at long last, and that our men in the Far East could at last find respite and help, and that the Yellow Peril would pay for their crimes in full.[7]

111   *VE party in Fakenham, May 1945.*

At last the war was over. The contribution made by a 'typical' small village can be demonstrated at Syderstone and Barmer where it was decided to give everyone serving in the forces a 'Welcome Home' present at the end of the war. As this was based on length of service, with extra money for service abroad, it was necessary to make detailed records of the military careers of the recipients. There were 57 names on the list, 46 men and 11 women. Of the men, 23 had been in the army, five in the navy and 19 in the air force – the high number of the last group is no doubt explained by the proximity of Sculthorpe airbase. The army men had served on all fronts – France and Belgium, North Africa and Italy, India and the Far East. Five had been prisoners of war, three of the Germans and two of the Japanese.

Of the 11 women, almost all – nine – had gone into the ATS. One woman was in the navy and one woman in the air force. Another woman, Lilian Stanley, was in the Red Cross – the vicar seems to have been unsure whether to include her in his lists or not.

After doing his calculations, the vicar decided that the money raised from jumble sales and similar activities would allow a payment to each person of 29 shillings for each year of overseas service and 14 shillings for each year of service at home. The most that anyone could receive on these figures was just over £8, given to three men, John Powell and Albert and Arthur Smith. They were all privates in the Norfolk Regiment: John and Albert were captured in France in 1940, Arthur went on to serve in Burma where he was

112 *Private grief: the parents of Freddie Viner of the RAF at his grave in Durnbach, Germany in 1951. Viner was killed in action over Germany in 1943: he was 19 years old.*

wounded. The navy men spent less time overseas and so received less money: the largest beneficiary was Philip Havers who had spent 18 months at sea in 1943-4 and a further five months in 1945. Of the RAF men, 13 served at home, but the others saw service in Belgium or in India. Frank Newton was the best rewarded with over £6, having served overseas for one month short of three years.

None of the women served overseas, so their payout was dependent on length of service. Lilian Stanley in fact received the most at over £3, several others receiving a little less than that figure.

The figures underestimate the service put in by the inhabitants of these villages. The vicar mentions in one of the lists his own children – Paul Foudrinier in the army and Barbara and Janet in the ATS, but they do not appear in the final version: presumably he did not want to be seen as benefiting his own family. One other person who is mentioned in one list is Charlie Riches. A corporal in the Coldstream Guards, Riches was killed in action in Belgium in 1940: he is the only fatality recorded in the lists.

The wealth of new experience undergone by the men and women of this village during the war must have made Syderstone and Barmer a very different place in 1945 from what it had been in 1939.[8]

War Graves and Memorials

Memorials in Norfolk take two forms, individual graves and group memorials. Graves include those of German airmen and sailors whose bodies fell on, or were washed up

113 *Dedication of USAAF memorial at Wendling. Over 6,700 American servicemen with the Second Air Division lost their lives during the war.*

in, Norfolk. One of the first of these was on 6 December 1939, when a German aeroplane was washed up on Sheringham beach. One body was recovered, that of Leutnant Emil Rodel. He was buried with full military honours at Great Bircham. Bodies of other Germans found on Norfolk beaches were also buried there. The graveyard also shows how many nations made sacrifices of their young men in the war. There are graves of 37 airmen from the UK, 17 from Canada, four from Australia, six from New Zealand and one from South Africa.

Individual war graves of allied servicemen can be found in many Norfolk graveyards, both in urban cemeteries and in village churchyards. There is one in South Wootton for example, that of Cyril Wagg, a driver in the Royal Army Service Corps: he died on 22 September 1941, aged 21. There are three in Walpole St Peter, including that of a servicewoman, something not found before the Second World War. Her name was Brenda Yeoman and she was in the ATS. She was just 20 years old when she died on 20 November 1946: 18 months after the war in Europe had come to an end, the war was still claiming lives. There are similar graves to servicewomen in several Norfolk churchyards, including that of Joan Burton mentioned in chapter two. Others occur in cemeteries, like that of Eva Gill, also of the ATS, buried with her male colleagues in the Earlham Road cemetery in Norwich, and commemorated with them by the Cross of Sacrifice.

Naturally there are more such graves in churchyards near training camps or air bases. There are 32 war graves in Watton churchyard, for example, and three more in the town's Nonconformist burial ground. Most are of airmen killed in the Second World War, including men of the Canadian and New Zealand air forces as well as men in the RAF. Very often these graves are of a standard form: the plain white headstone designed by the Commonwealth War Graves Commission. These often stand out among the varied forms of headstone found in a Norfolk churchyard or cemetery.

We have looked at some of the graves of bombing victims, which often do not give the cause of death. However, some do: Lily Garrod is recorded as having been killed by enemy action on 29 April 1942. Her grave in the Rosary Cemetery in Norwich also commemorates her husband, who – by tragic coincidence – had been killed in an air raid at Felixstowe in 1917. In Great Yarmouth, the air-raid victims are remembered with a form of headstone giving the coat of arms of the borough, a touching gesture: these, too, are victims of war.

Almost every village and town in Norfolk had put up a memorial to the dead of the First World War. These were very often also used to commemorate the new heroes. The memorials were usually put up by a local committee, often a sub-committee of the parish council. If the memorial is on consecrated ground, there should be a faculty for its erection, often with supporting papers. In many cases, these documents are now in the Norfolk Record Office. Here we can just take a few examples.

At *Kenninghall* in 1947, a War Memorial Committee proposed to place a stone tablet in the parish church. It was unanimously decided that a memorial of simple design bearing just the dates 1939-45 and the names of the fallen would be the most suitable memorial to be placed under the 1914-18 one. Mr Dunn promised to let the Council have a design and the approx cost would be £20. Seven names were to be placed on the tablet, with their ranks and the arm in which they served. At *Holt* in 1951 the same solution was adopted: the cost was to be £61, of which £20 had already been promised. The architect and antiquarian J.B.L. Tolhurst was asked to design the tablet, but the result was disappointing. Another antiquarian, A.G. Thurlow, complained that 'the specimen design of lettering was not considered very good' and that 'a space between the old and new tablets would be an improvement'. Tolhurst replied tartly:

> I must say I am surprised that the lettering is not considered good enough since it is exactly similar to that on the Communion rail I did as a memorial to Canon King. However I will do a revised version and send it on as soon as I can ... I do not see the point of the suggestion that the old and new tablets should have a space between them. The whole idea of the new one was that it should form a base to the old and if there is a space it means that the new one will be still lower down the wall and it is low enough already. Apart from that, any space that could be given would necessarily be very narrow and consequently a dirt trap.'[9]

114 *Wendling Memorial, Remembrance Day, 2005.*

The First World War memorial in *Brundall* church was not a tablet but a stained glass window. It was decided that the new memorial should be a tablet on the wall beside the window. The architect C. Upcher was employed which meant the cost including his fees was £88, of which £30 had been raised. The tablet had six names in alphabetical order, with no ranks given. The tablet had a cross at the top and a biblical text: 'I know that my Redeemer liveth.'[10]

Where the original memorial was a cross rather than a plaque, other solutions had to be adopted. At *Ludham* the architect Edward Boardman was consulted. The First World War memorial consisted of

115 *Walsingham War Memorial: this side commemorates the dead of the Second World War. Those of the First World War are on the other side.*

a granite cross on a stone step. It was decided to dismantle it and re-erect it on three stone steps, on which the names of the dead could be inscribed. At *Thorpe St Andrew* the granite cross is not in the churchyard but on the village green. The names of the Second World War dead have not been added to the cross but placed on two tablets on a granite 'book'. Unusually, there are more names for the Second World War than for the first – 49 rather than forty. They take up much less space as the information given is less. The First World War men are grouped by year of death and their ranks are given. The fallen of the Second World War are in strict alphabetical order, and their ranks are not given. The names fall into four columns of 12 names – the 49th name is added to the bottom of the fourth column, giving an unsymmetrical appearance to the list. There is no Biblical text or any other information beyond a stark heading '1939 1945'.[11]

Walsingham war memorial is also a granite cross on a green at a road junction rather than in a churchyard. The solution here has been to add the names of the dead of the Second World War to the back of the cross.

Every village memorial has a tale to tell. At *Hemsby*, the large granite cross erected to the dead of the First World War stands immediately in front of the churchyard. There are 20 names of the fallen. The memorial to the dead of the Second World War is in the form of a wall behind the cross, with an apposite quotation from the Second Book of Samuel: 'They were a wall to us both night and day.' There are eight names on the memorial, including two people named Gibbs. This name also occurs on the First World War memorial. The names of the dead of both wars are to be found on a memorial on the churchyard wall at *Runton*. Both lists include people with the surnames Abbs. Inside the churchyard there is a Commonwealth war grave for one Abbs from each war, and several graves of family members who died in times of peace. When I was there in November 2005, the air was filled with the sound of children playing and laughing in an adjacent playground. These men did not die in vain.

Memorials in larger towns are not usually in churchyards. That at *Great Yarmouth* is a separate memorial beside the First World War memorial in St George's Park. It specifically states that the names on it include the civilian victims of bombing in the town. The names of the dead at *Norwich* in the First World War were so numerous that they were not inscribed on the city war memorial – which has made it easier to carve an inscription to the fallen of the Second World War on the monument. All that has been done, in fact, is to add the dates '1914-1919' to one wing of the monument and '1939-1945' to the other, so that the dead of both wars are equally included under the main text – a simple and moving solution.

Some more imaginative ideas were also adopted. At *Fakenham* the names of the fallen were inscribed on the south face of the War memorial in the Market Square. They were further honoured in 1948 when quarter-hour chimes were installed to the clock in the church tower. A plaque to this effect was erected in 1950. It did not list the names so cost only £50, and as the faculty petition states 'will be fixed against two other similar tablets in a very inconspicuous position'.[12]

The five men of the Norfolk Regiment to win the Victoria Cross are remembered in street names off the Dereham Road in Norwich, where their stories are told in commemorative plaques. Six memorial cottages beside the Ring Road in Sprowston are another reminder: four are named after the VC winners who lost their lives, and the other two after the principal theatres in which the Norfolk Regiment served – Europe and Asia. The cottages, with their charming Dutch gables, were designed by Cecil Upcher and are now listed buildings.

At *Watton* a plaque containing 17 names has been added to the First World War memorial. As so often, some of the surnames are the same as for the previous war. Here, there are four men named Tennant, adding their place of honour to the two men of that name killed in the previous war. One feature of these memorials is that they will include the names of women who served and made the supreme sacrifice. The Watton list includes Margaret Knott of the WAAF, for example.

Many war memorials include an appropriate text. That for the First World War is often taken to cover the later war as well, but at Watton the 16 men and one woman killed in 1939-45 have their own:

And so they passed over and all the trumpets sounded for them on the other side.

Some small villages were surprisingly tardy in erecting a memorial to their dead. The proposal to put up a memorial to the four men of *Shropham* was organised by the vicar, the Rev. E. Turtle in 1961. It was to consist of a simple plaque listing the men in alphabetical order with their regiments: Turtle thought it would cost about £40. Turtle did a little research, writing to the Infantry Record Office in Exeter and to Dr Barnardo's Homes for information on two of the men. H. Brett of Watton returned an estimate of £20 10s. for the tablet, including erecting it on the church wall. However, R.P. Colman of St Andrew's Hill in Norwich put in a lower estimate of £14 15s., provided the parishioners could collect the plaque and erect it themselves. This estimate was adopted, and the vicar wrote to Colman to say so at the beginning of June. By the end of August he had heard nothing and wrote asking when it would be ready. This stirred the firm into action and he was told he could pick the tablet up on 6 September.[13]

A small number of memorials are specifically for the dead of the Second World War. There is one of these on the village green at *Poringland*. It lists the names of nine men in strict alphabetical order, with no indication of the rank or service arm, or when and where they died. In some ways this is a shame, as the place of death would give an immediate sense of what a world-wide conflict this was, and how the graves of men from a small Norfolk village can be spread across the globe. The names on the Poringland memorial include the following men, amongst others:

> **Charles Brooks**, killed as the Germans advanced through the Low Countries in June 1940, and buried at Coxyde in Belgium;

> **Alfred Pleasants**, who died on board HMS *Harvester* on 11 March 1943 and who is commemorated on the Chatham Naval Memorial;

> **Michael Mitchell**, buried in Taiping War cemetery, who died in 1942 during the Japanese invasion of Malaysia;

> **Bertie Aldridge**, who died in June 1944, commemorated on the Rangoon Memorial in Myamar, which has the names of 27,000 men who died in campaigns in Burma and who have no known grave.[14]

At Winterton, too, the dead of this war are recorded on their own memorial, in this case a clock and two plaques on the Primitive Methodist chapel. Once again, there is no information beyond a simple list of names. This is in sharp contrast to the First World War memorial which is in the churchyard: this gives the service in which the dead served, so that we can see at once how many were in the navy, unsurprising in such a seaside village.

The sacrifices made by thousands of Norfolk men and women in their home county and throughout the world can best be summed up in the words of the memorial at Kohima in India, which itself commemorates so many men of Norfolk who died there:

> When You Go Home
> Tell Them Of Us And Say
> For Their Tomorrow
> We Gave Our Today.

Notes

1. Men at Arms, pp.1-23

1. Norfolk Record Office (hereafter NRO), SO 236/2/1.
2. NRO, HMN 6/2.
3. NRO, MC 2336/1.
4. NRO, BR 270/27.
5. Hart, Peter, *At the Sharp End; from Le Paradis to Kohima* (1998), p.206.
6. NRO, SO 236/2/1.
7. *Eastern Evening News* (hereafter EEN), 5/4/90.
8. NRO, Diary of Russell Beckett.
9. Burton, Reginald, *Railway of Hell* (2002), p.31.
10. NRO, MC 2150/1.
11. NRO, MC 2147/1.
12. NRO, MC 2169/1.
13. NRO, MC 166/184.
14. NRO, MC 166/185.
15. NRO, MC 1984/1.
16. NRO, MC 2150/1.
17. NRO, MC 1984/1.
18. NRO, MC 2336/11.
19. NRO, MC 2153/2.
20. Lincoln, John, *Thank God and the Infantry* (1994), p.180.
21. Turner, David, *The Book of Narborough* (2004), p.149.
22. NRO, FX 312/1.
23. Hart, Peter, *op cit.*, p.206.
24. Younge, John, *Methwold and its People* (undated), p.149; *Eastern Daily Press* (hereafter EDP), 30/1/40.
25. EDP, 31/1/40.
26. Brown, R. Douglas, *East Anglia 1940* (1981), pp.35-41; EDP 31/1/40; *The War Dead of the Commonwealth* (1961).
27. EDP, 22/5/40; *The War Dead of the Commonwealth* (1961).
28. Jefferson, David, *Coastal Forces at War* (1996), *passim*; Johnson, D.E., *East Anglia at War 1939-1945* (1978), pp.130-1.
29. NRO, MC 572/1.
30. NRO, MC 2333.
31. Basey, C. (ed.), *They said it was 'Just a Job that we had to do'* (2005), pp.119-20.
32. Gunn, Peter B., *Bircham Newton, A Norfolk Airfield in War and Peace* (2002), *passim*.
33. NRO, C/UNCAT, War Diary.
34. NRO, MC 2216/2.
35. Hilling, John B., *Strike Hard – a bomber airfield at war* (1995), p.31.
36. NRO, PS 14/1/5,6.
37. NRO, PS 4/1/20.
38. NRO, N/S 1/23.
39. EDP, October 1942.
40. NRO, acc Newstead, 27/11/91 (1940/1 bundle).
41. Berry, Richard, 'Yarmouth Textiles in World War Two', *Yarmouth Archaeology* (2001), pp.25-38.
42. Bridges, E.M. and Baldwin, Jim (eds.), *A Conflict of Memories – Fakenham remembers World War Two* (2005).
43. NRO, acc Newstead 27/11/91 (1944 bundle).
44. NRO, PS 1/1/33; EDP, 14/1/42; 24/2/42; 26/2/42; 23/11/42.

2. Women at War, pp.24-36

1. EDP, 2/9/41.
2. NRO, PS 1/1/33; Brown, R. Douglas, *East Anglia 1942* (1988), p.139; EDP, 22/5/42; EDP, 27/3/42.
3. Calvert, Dorothy, *Bull Battle-Dress Lanyard and Lipstick* (1978), pp.5, 6.
4. http://www.bbc.co.uk/dna/ww2/A3023164.
5. Basey, C. (ed.), *They said it was 'Just a Job that we had to do'* (2005), pp.32, 33.
6. Malcolmson, R. and Searby, P. (eds), *The Diary of Rachel Dhonau,* Norfolk Record Society (2004), pp.42, 68.

7. *Norfolk Chronicle* (hereafter NC), 2/1/42.
8. NRO, Y/TC 89.
9. NRO, MC 2153/1 (I am grateful to Victoria Horth for drawing my attention to this archive); Younge, John, *The Area of Methwold and its People* (undated), p.170.
10. NRO, acc Heading, letters 360, 455.
11. Jefferson, David, *Coastal Forces at War* (1996), p.74.
12. www.bbc.co.uk/dna/ww2/A3429209.
13. Beckett, Constance Mary. *The Sky Sweepers* (1995), pp.20, 113.
14. www.bbc.co.uk/dna/ww2/A2732816.
15. Hilling, John B., *Strike Hard – a Bomber Airfield at War* (1995), p.37.
16. EDP, 24/12/2005.
17. EDP, 1/6/40.
18. EDP, 3/10/41.
19. EDP, 8/9/41.
20. Snelling, Joan, *A Land Girl's War* (2004), pp.14, 15.
21. www.bbc.co.uk/dna/ww2/A2843769.
22. EDP, 4/3/42.
23. NRO, D/ED 23/31.
24. EDP, 28/1/42.

3. Over Here – The Americans in Norfolk, pp.37-51

1. NRO, HMN 6/2.
2. NRO, C/UNCAT War Diary.
3. Gardiner, Juliet, *Wartime* (2004), p.472.
4. NRO, MC 376/153.
5. NRO, MC 376/153.
6. Birsic, Rudolph, *History of the 445th Bombardment Group (H)* (1950).
7. NRO, MC 376/265.
8. NRO, MC 371/882/27.
9. NRO, *ibid.*
10. NRO, MC 371/494.
11. NRO, MC 376/52.
12. Hoare, Adrian, *Standing up to Hitler: the story of Norfolk's Home Guard and 'Secret Army' 1940-1944* (1997), p.163; NRO, MC 371/765; Myler, Patrick, *Ring of Hate* (2005), pp.189-91.
13. Malcolmson, R. and Searby, P. (eds), *The Diary of Rachel Dhonau*, Norfolk Record Society (2004), p.246.
14. Ogilvie, D.B. and Watkins, G.L. (eds), *Hackney Downs Boys in Wartime* (2005), p.64.
15. Calvert, Dorothy, *Bull Battle-Dress Lanyard and Lipstick* (1978), p.37.
16. NRO, MC 371/765.
17. NRO, MC 371/882/9.
18. NRO, MC 371/882/8, 9.
19. NRO, C/ UNCAT War Diary.

20. NRO, MC 376/273.
21. NRO, MC 371/765.
22. NRO, MC 371/813.
23. NRO, MC 371/807.
24. Mackay, Ron and Adams, Steve, *The 44th Bomb Group in World War II* (2003), p.94.
25. NRO, MC 371/882/27.

4. Prisoners of War, pp.52-72

1. NRO, MC, 695.
2. NRO, MC, 371/882/32.
3. NRO, MC, 376/332.
4. NRO, MC 2145/1.
5. Costello, John, *The Pacific War* (1981), p.397.
6. NRO, diary of Russell Beckett.
7. Younge, John, *Methwold and its People* (undated), p.149.
8. EDP, 13/08/05.
9. Basey, C. (ed.), *They said it was 'Just a Job that we had to do'* (2005), p.73.
10. Palmer, Susan (ed.), *Prisoners on the Kwai: Memories of Dr Harold Churchill* (2005).
11. Burton, Reginald, *Railway of Hell* (2002), pp.91-6.
12. NRO, diary of Russell Beckett.
13. Basey, C. (ed.), *op. cit.*, p.68.
14. EDP, 13/08/05.
15. EDP, 21/10/42.
16. NRO, KHC 114; Etherington, William, *A Quiet Woman's War* (2002), *passim*.
17. Ogilvie, D.B. and Watkins, G.L. (eds), *Hackney Downs Boys in Wartime* (2005), pp.66-7.
18. Kochan, Miriam, *Prisoners of England* (1980), *passim*; *The War Dead of the Commonwealth*, 1961; www.455th.ukpc.net/tomfeise/8thusaaf/bases.htm.
19. EDP, 3/1/42.
20. NRO, C/SR 7, circulars 3218, 3283, 3335, 3467.
21. www.bbc.co.uk/dna/ww2/A2843769; Gardiner, Juliet, *Wartime* (2004), p.60, quoting from Sponza, Lucio, *Divided Loyalties* (2000); www.bbc.co.uk/dna/ww2/A3642095.
22. Bridges, E.M. and Baldwin, Jim, *A Conflict of Memories* (2005), pp.22, 35.
23. Ogilvie and Watkins, *op. cit.*, p.117.
24. EDP, 27/12/47.
25. EDP, 11/9/33; 28/9/2005.

5. Evacuees in Norfolk, pp.73-92

1. NRO, Y/D 69/1.
2. NRO, MC 561/164.
3. NRO, MC 631/1.
4. NRO, MC 631/1: NRO, DC 15/3/4.
5. Gardiner, Juliet, *Wartime* (2004), p.22.

6. NRO, Y/ED/S 74, Y/ED 481.
7. Ogilvie, D.B. and Watkins, G.L. (eds), *Hackney Downs Boys in Wartime* (2005), pp.66-7.
8. KLBA, K/TC files, box 8.
9. NRO, ACC 2005/48.
10. NRO, C/ED 60/2; C/ED 1/5.
11. NRO, MC 561/164.
12. KLBA, Town Clerk's files.
13. NRO, MC 2314/1.
14. Brown, R. Douglas, *East Anglia 1940* (1981), p.27.
15. NRO, DC 15/3/4.
16. NRO, MC 661/164.
17. NRO, C/SS 2/3.
18. KLBA, Town Clerk's files.
19. NRO, C/ED 127/1.
20. NRO, C/ED 103/1.
21. NRO, MC 2333/1/4.
22. NRO, HMN 6/2.
23. Ogilvie and Watkins, *op. cit.*, p.61.
24. NRO, MC 561/164.
25. NRO, C/ED 19/15.
26. NRO, N/TC 35/6/5.
27. NRO, N/ED 8/115.
28. NRO, DC 15/3/4.
29. NRO, MC 561/124.
30. NRO, PD 78/152.
31. NRO, DC 17/5/8.
32. *Ibid.*
33. Anderson, Bruce, *John Major* (1992 edn.), p.3.
34. NRO, MC 561/164.
35. NRO, N/EN 1/108.
36. Personal comment.
37. NRO, MC 2092/1.
38. Stagg, F.N., *Salthouse, the Story of a Norfolk Village* (2003), p.202.
39. www.bbc.co.uk/dna/ww2/A2412866; A3129806.
40. Ogilvie and Watkins, *op. cit.*, p.62.
41. www.bbc.co.uk/dna/ww2/A1956738.
42. NRO, N/HE 11/49; www.cwgc.org/cwgcinternet/search.aspx.

6. Evacuees out of Norfolk, pp.93-101

1. Brooks, Peter, *Coastal Towns at War* (1988), p.12; Tooke, Colin, *Great Yarmouth and Gorleston, Front Line Towns* (1999), p.40.
2. NRO, Y/ED 47.
3. NRO, Y/ED 47; Elvin, Maureen, *My Story*, undated, p.5.
4. NRO, Y/ED 47; Y/ED 332; Y/ED S/54, 74.
5. NRO, Y/ED 234-262.
6. Stranack, David, *Schools at War* (2005), p.79.
7. NRO, Y/ED 414.

8. NRO, C/ED 37/97.
9. EDP, 9/7/40.
10. NRO, MC 81/40/3.
11. NRO, MC 2333/1/3.
12. NRO, DC 17/2/7.
13. NRO, C/MH 1/29; D/ED 23/31: EDP, 13/8/45.
14. Perry, Hilda and Edmund, *A Broken Promise: Tottington – a lost village in Norfolk* (1999).

7. The Threat of Invasion, pp.102-18

1. EDP, 24/12/2005; NRO, MC 2333/1/3-5.
2. NRO, HMN 6/2.
3. NRO, COL 12/22.
4. NRO, MC 2333/1/3, 4.
5. NRO, C/UNCAT War Diary.
6. Bird, Christopher, *Silent Sentinels* (1999), *passim*. This has an excellent gazetteer of wartime defences in the county.
7. NRO, Thetford Corporation Archives, uncatalogued.
8. NRO, PC 45/20.
9. NRO, PD 82/44.
10. NRO, MS 10605/58.
11. NRO, HMN 6/2.
12. NRO, Thetford Corporation Archives, uncatalogued.
13. NRO, PD 82/44.
14. NRO, PD 238/115.
15. Hoare, Adrian, *Standing up to Hitler: the story of Norfolk's Home Guard and 'Secret Army'*, 1940-1944 (1997), p.8.
16. NRO, Y/D83 1/4.
17. NRO, MC 2347/1.
18. NRO, PD 238/132; MC 2347/1.
19. Hoare, Adrian, *op. cit.*, p.144; NRO, Acc Heading letter 246.
20. NRO, C/C 10/29.
21. NRO, MC 2333/1/9.
22. Hoare, Adrian, *op. cit.*, p.190.

8. Death from the Air, pp.119-49

1. NRO, C/C 10/24.
2. EDP, 29/7/38.
3. NRO, MC 2019/28.
4. Mottram, Ralph, *Assault upon Norwich* (undated), p.4.
5. NRO, DC 15/3/4.
6. NRO, MS 10605/60.
7. Gardiner, Juliet, *Wartime* (2004), pp.527, 528: Malcolmson, R. and Searby, P. (eds) *The Diary of Rachel Dhonau*, Norfolk Record Society (2004), pp.180, 222.
8. Bowyer, Michael, *Air Raid – the enemy offensive against East Anglia 1939-45* (1986), pp.222-5.
9. NRO, MC 376/273.

10. *Carrow Works Magazine*, Christmas 1941; NRO, N/HE 11/47; www.cwgc.org/cwgcinternet/search.aspx.
11. NRO, N/EN 1/184.
12. NRO, KHC 146.
13. NRO, N/HE 11/49.
14. Swain, George, *Norwich Under Fire* (undated booklet), pp.6, 7.
15. NRO, FX315/1.
16. NRO, N/TC/59/1.
17. Mottram, *op. cit.*, pp.33, 34.
18. NRO, C/UNCAT War Diary.
19. NRO, MC 2299/1.
20. http://www.bbc.co.uk/dna/ww2/A2732816.
21. Malcolmson, R. and Searby, P., *op. cit.*, pp.139-40.
22. N/HE/51,5: MC 2299/1.
23. NC, 1/5/42.
24. EDP, 29/4/42.
25. NRO, MC 695/18; HMN 6/2.
26. NRO, acc Newstead 27/11/91 (1940/1 bundle).
27. Box, C.G., *Great Yarmouth, Front Line Town* (undated), *passim*.
28. NRO, Y/TC 42/10; Box, *op. cit.*
29. NRO, C/C 10/29.
30. Malcolmson, R. and Searby, P., *op. cit.*, pp.96-7.
31. Norfolk Federation of Women's Institutes, *Within Living Memory* (1971), p.147.
32. NRO, C/C 10/29.
33. NRO, C/C 10/24.
34. NRO, C/C 10/29.
35. NRO, C/UNCAT War Diary.
36. *Norfolk Fair*, January 1983; Bowyer, Michael, *op. cit.*, p.176.
37. Calder, Angus, *The People's War* (1992 edn.), p.287; Banger, Joan, *Norwich at War* (1974), p.65.
38. NRO, N/C UNCAT War Diary.
39. *Ibid.*
40. NRO, MC.2333; NRO, acc Heading, letters 343, 344; NRO, MC 2299/1; EEN 9/11/87.
41. NRO, PD 82/44.
42. *Ibid.*
43. NRO, MC 376/273.
44. NRO, HMN 6/2.
45. Arthur, Vivien J., *Colney, the story of a Norfolk Village* (2000), p.77.
46. NRO, C/UNCAT War Diary.
47. EDP, 25/6/87; Parry, Simon, *The Luftwaffe Night Offensive 1940-45* (1987); NRO/C UNCAT; NRO, MC 371/755.
48. NRO, MC 376/169; Clements, Richard, *In Search of Lady Jane* (1998).
49. EDP, 25/6/87; Parry, Simon, *op. cit.*; NRO,
C/UNCAT War Diary.
50. Banger, Joan, *op. cit.*, p.84.
51. NRO, C/UNCAT War Diary.
52. EDP, 9/5/42.
53. NRO, N/S 1/23.
54. EDP, October 1942.
55. NC, 11/9/42; N/RO, PS 24/3/1.

9. The Kitchen Front – Daily Life in Wartime, pp.150-69
1. NRO, Y/D 69/2.
2. NRO, MC 376/273.
3. Calder, Angus, *The People's War* (1992 edn.), p.250.
4. Malcolmson, R. and Searby, P. (eds), *The Diary of Rachel Dhonau*, Norfolk Record Society (2004), p.11.
5. NRO, MC 2333.
6. Thomas, Donald, *An Underworld at War* (2004 edition), pp.36, 203; NRO, PS 1/1/34 (Norwich); NRO, PS 14/1/1 (Methwold); NRO, PS 1/1/33; EDP, 13/3/42.
7. NRO, MC 2333.
8. NRO, acc Newstead 27/11/91.
9. Malcolmson, Searby, *op. cit.*, p.91.
10. NC 23/10/42.
11. Webley, Nicholas (ed.), *Betty's War-time Diary* (2002), p.29; EDP 23/12/41.
12. NRO, PC 20/14.
13. EDP, 20/9/41; 24/1/42; 26/3/42.
14. NC, 11/9/42.
15. EDP, 22/11/41.
16. NC, 23/10/43; NRO acc Newstead 27/11/91 (1944 bundle).
17. EDP, 4/10/41; NC, 2/10/42.
18. EDP, 28/1/42.
19. NRO, acc Newstead 27/11/91.
20. NC, 15/5/42.
21. NC, 2/1/42.
22. NRO, PS 1/1/34; 4/1/20.
23. EDP, 12/1/42; NRO, N/S 4/7.
24. Gardiner, Juliet, *Wartime* (2004), pp.153-4; EDP, 4/3/42.
25. NRO, DC 15/3/4.
26. EDP, 13/1/42, 4/3/42.
27. EDP, 18/3/42.
28. Calder, *op. cit.*, pp.279-83; EDP 4/3/42.
29. NRO, acc Newstead 27/11/91 (1940/1 bundle) Malcolmson, R. and Searby, P., *op. cit.*, pp.70-1.
30. NRO, N/S 3/4.
31. EDP, 12/1/42: NRO, N/S 4/7.
32. O'Sullivan, Tim, 'Listening Through' in Kirkham, Pat and Thomas, David (ed.), *War Culture* (1995), pp.173-86.
33. Gardiner, *op. cit.*, pp.2, 114ff; NRO, MC 2333.

34. NRO, MC 376/273.
35. Gardiner, *op. cit.*, p.119; Lanfranchi, Pierre and Taylor, Matthew, *Professional Football in World War Two Britain, in* Kirkham and Thoms, *op. cit.*; Calder, *op. cit.*, p.375,
36. Calder, *op. cit.*, p.64; EDP 9/10/42.
37. NRO, PS 4/1/20.
38. EDP, 18/3/42.
39. NRO, acc Newstead 27/11/91 (1940/1 bundle); PS 4/1/20.
40. EDP, 28/1/42.
41. NRO, acc Newstead 27/11/91 (1940/1 bundle); acc Heading (letter 182).

10. The Child at War – Growing up in Wartime Norfolk, pp.170-91

1. NRO, N/HE 6; C/MH 29, 30.
2. EEN, 27/7/89, NRO, D/ED 23/31 (The EEN article incorrectly puts Robbins in *Old Catton*).
3. Elvin, Maureen, *My Story*, undated, pp.2-3; Gardiner, Juliet, *Wartime* (2004).
4. NRO, C/ED 2/81-84; Ogilvie, D.B. and Watkins, G.L. (eds), *Hackney Downs Boys in Wartime* (2005), p.68.
5. NRO, C/ED 67/3, 8.
6. Mottram, R.H., *Assault upon Norwich* (undated), p.23.
7. NRO, N/HE 6, 1941.
8. NRO, Y/ED/S/37, 74.
9. NRO, Y/ED 418.
10. NRO, Y/ED 234-262.
11. NRO, C/ED 19/15.
12. NRO, DC 15/3/4.
13. NRO, N/HE 6, 1939-45.
14. NRO, D/ED 23/30.
15. EEN, 3/88.
16. NRO, N/ED 1/86.
17. NRO, N/ED 1/103.
18. NRO, Y/ED 418.
19. NRO, Y/ED S/44.
20. NRO, Y/ED 234-262.
21. Unidentified newspaper report, quoted in Ogilvie and Watkins, *op. cit.*, p.131.
22. Arthur, Vivien J., *Colney, the story of a Norfolk Village* (2000), pp.73ff.
23. NRO, C/ED 67/4.
24. NRO, N/HE 6; MS 11344.
25. NRO, N/HE 11/49; www.cwgc.org/cwgcinternet/search.aspx.
26. NRO, Y/TC 89/1.
27. NRO, Y/HE, N/HE 6.
28. NRO, N/HE 11/52; MC 376/411; EDP, 15/1/45.
29. http://www.bbc.co.uk/dna/ww2/A272169.
30. NRO, C/ED 60/2.
31. NRO, N/HE 11/50; NC 6/3/42.
32. NRO, C/ED 19/15.
33. NRO, N/HE 11/50, NC, 6/3/42.
34. NRO, C/ED 19/15.
35. NRO, C/ED 76; Brown, *East Anglia 1941* (1986), p.42.
36. NRO, Y/ED S/43; N/ED 1/103.
37. EDP, 16/3/42; 25/4/42; 16/4/42.
38. NRO, C/ED 19/15.
39. NRO, Y/HE 130,131; Y/EDS/74.
40. NRO, C/ED 19/15.
41. NRO, Y/ED 234-262.
42. NRO, Y/ED 234-262.
43. South Norfolk Council, *USAAF Airfields in South Norfolk*, undated, p.15; NRO, MC 376/411.
44. NRO, C/ED 19/15.
45. NRO, Y/ED/S/37.
46. NRO, Y/ED/S/74.
47. NRO, DC 15/3/4, Y/ED/S/74.
48. NRO, Y/ED/S/74.
49. EDP, 26/3/42.
50. Ogilvie, D.B. and Watkins, G.L., *op. cit.*, p.101.

11. The End at Last, pp.192-200

1. NRO, MC 2333/1/9.
2. NRO, UPC 146/8.
3. NRO, MC 2299/1.
4. NRO, acc Newstead 27/11/91.
5. NRO, MC 2299/1.
6. Beckett, Constance Mary, *The Sky Sweepers* (1995), p.126.
7. Calvert, Dorothy, *Bull Battle-Dress Lanyard and Lipstick* (1978), p.113.
8. NRO, PD 238/122.
9. NRO, DN/CON 223, Kenninghall; 230, Holt.
10. NRO, DN/CON 230, Brundall.
11. NRO, DN/CON 230, Ludham.
12. NRO, DN/CON 230, Fakenham.
13. NRO, PD 20/19.
14. www.cwgc.org/cwgcinternet/search.aspx.

Further Reading

Local

Banger, Joan, *Norwich at War* (1974)

Bridges, E.M. and Baldwin, Jim (eds), *A Conflict of Memories – Fakenham remembers World War Two* (2005)

Burton, Reginald, *Railway of Hell* (2002)

Calvert, Dorothy, *Bull Battle-Dress Lanyard and Lipstick* (1978)

Etherington, William, *A Quiet Woman's War* (2002)

Gunn, Peter B., *Bircham Newton, A Norfolk airfield in war and peace* (2002)

Hart, Peter, *At the Sharp End; from Le Paradis to Kohima* (1998)

Hoare, Adrian, *Standing up to Hitler: the story of Norfolk's Home Guard and 'Secret Army' 1940-1944* (1997)

Lincoln, John, *Thank God and the Infantry* (1994)

Malcolmson, R. and Searby, P. (eds), *The Diary of Rachel Dhonau*, Norfolk Record Society (2004)

National

Calder, Angus, *The People's War* (1992 edn)

Gardener, Juliet, *Wartime* (2005)

For Children

Diary of Anne Frank (various editions)

Bawden, Nina, *Carrie's War* (1993)

Holm, Anne, *I am David* (1989)

Kerr, Judith, *When Hitler Stole Pink Rabbit* (2002)

Local Video

The Home Front 1939-1945, published by the East Anglian Film Archive

Local Museum

The Norfolk Regimental Museum, Shire Hall, Norwich.

Index

Page references to illustrations are in **bold**.